ISLAM AND ITS CULTURAL DIVERGENCE

Gustave E. von Grunebaum

ISLAM AND ITS CULTURAL DIVERGENCE

Studies in Honor of

GUSTAVE E. VON GRUNEBAUM

EDITED BY

GIRDHARI L. TIKKU

UNIVERSITY OF ILLINOIS PRESS
Urbana, Chicago, London

Manufactured in the United States of America
Library of Congress Catalog No. 75-126522
252 00127 3

ACKNOWLEDGMENTS

I GRATEFULLY ACKNOWLEDGE the financial support of the Office of International Programs and Studies of the University of Illinois which made the publication of this book possible. I hope that this volume will be the first of a series of publications for International Programs and the Center for Asian Studies.

My thanks to the contributors for making this book possible, to my secretary for patience in typing and retyping papers received from the authors, and to Mrs. Gay Menges and the University of Illinois Press for understanding and patience in publishing a book containing difficult scripts. Special thanks also go to my wife for her many helpful suggestions.

CONTENTS

PREFACE

THE COLLECTION OF PAPERS comprising this volume are contributions of the friends, admirers, and students of Professor Gustave Edmund von Grunebaum. They were written to acknowledge appreciation of this great scholar who has contributed in many ways for over a quarter of a century to the understanding of Islam by the West and the East. The occasion chosen is the 60th year of his birth.

The diversity of Professor von Grunebaum's interests is reflected in this volume. Professor Meier's paper, "The Ultimate Origin and the Hereafter in Islam," and Professor Hartman's, "Secrets for Muslims in Parsi Scriptures," deal with the fundamental concepts of religion. The assimilation of influences from Islam by the Greek-Christian tradition is seen in Professor Cantarino's paper, "Averroes on Poetry," and by the Judeo-Persian tradition is seen in Professor Netzer's article, "Dāniyāl-Nāme." Professor Naim's paper, "Arabic Orthography and Some Non-Semitic Languages," discusses cultural influences of a linguistic nature. Professor Banani's paper, "Ferdowsi and the Art of Tragic Epic," interprets a piece of classical Persian literature in terms of Western literary theories. Professor Gabrieli's paper, "The Autobiography of Mikhail Nu^{c}aima," Professor Khouri's paper, "Revolution and Renaissance in al-Bārūdī's Poetry," and the editor's paper, "Some Socio-Religious Themes in Modern Persian Fiction," deal with the problems in contemporary literature resulting from the confrontation of tradition and modernity. The other two papers are those of Professor Yalman, "On Land Disputes in Eastern Turkey," and Professor Dawn's, "Pan-Arabism and the Failure of Israeli-Jordanian Peace

Negotiations, 1950." These deal with two important social and political problems confronting the Middle East.

The papers have been arranged in alphabetical order by author's names. Transliteration systems used by individual contributors have been left without change even though they are different from one another.

Gustave Edmund von Grunebaum, born in Vienna, Austria, September 1, 1909, received his Ph.D. from the University of Vienna, 1931. After teaching at the University of Vienna he came to the United States in 1938 and since has taught at the Asia Institute, New York (1938-43), the University of Chicago (1943-57), and is currently Professor of History and Director of the Near Eastern Center at the University of California, Los Angeles. Under his direction the Center has during the past dozen years become one of the world's finest centers for the study of the Middle East.

Professor von Grunebaum as a historian of culture has helped us in understanding Islamic concepts from within and also in relation to the civilizations and cultures with which Islam came into contact. Historically, these contacts range from the Classical to the Modern Periods, and involve problems of Islamic self-identity over ages under impact from Greek, Byzantine, Judeo-Christian, Persian, Indian, and finally the Western civilizations. It is impossible in so short an introduction to describe the many and varied scholarly contributions of Professor von Grunebaum. The bibliography of his work given in this book shows the immense range of his interests. His panoramic scholarship, understanding of past research, and keen insight have shed light on difficult problems and ambiguities in Islamic studies. His *Medieval Islam* is a classical example. May his scholarship, wit, humor, and warmth continue for many years.

G.L.T.
Urbana, Illinois

ISLAM AND ITS CULTURAL DIVERGENCE

Ferdowsi and the Art of Tragic Epic

AMIN BANANI

FERDOWSI'S MAIN OBJECT is to preserve the "history" of his fatherland, but the sum of *Shah-nama*'s artistic worth outweighs the inherent shortcomings of the poet's conscious scheme. Broadly conceived, it belongs to the epic genre. But it is not a formal epic as the *Aeneid* or the *Lusiad.* Rather, it has the spontaneity of the *Iliad,* and its episodic character reveals its kinship with the *chansons de geste.* More than any of its kindred poems, however, the *Shah-nama* is beset with paradoxes and conflicts, paradoxes that are the protein of its art and the source of its tragic nobility. If there is a unifying theme in the *Shah-nama,* it is no simple wrath of Achilles', but the malevolence of the universe. Yet Ferdowsi is no passive fatalist. He has an abiding faith in a just Creator; he believes in the will of man, the need for his efforts, and the worth of his good deeds.

The pervading paradox of human existence is refracted and made particular in episodes and lives of mortals who, prism-like, reflect the light and shadow of character, the changes of moods and motives, and the many psychic levels of personality. In the strength, variety, and sometimes profundity of its characterization — often achieved with great economy of means — *Shah-nama* is remarkable in the annals of classical literature. Very few of its many protagonists are archetypes. Alas, all too many of its noblest heroes are prey to the basest of human motives. But even the vilest among them have moments of humanity. Although outwardly many a character defies all natural bounds, none is exempt from the inner reality of human nature. The goodness of the best is possible and the evil of the most wretched is not incredible.

Nowhere is this depth of characterization more evident than in the person of Rostam, the foremost of Iranian heroes. He is essentially a man of the arena. Chivalrous, intensely loyal, pious, fearless, steel-willed and obdurate, he is nevertheless subject to occasional moods of disenchantment and indifference accompanied by gargantuan gluttony. He has a mystic reverence for the crown of Iran that inspires him to all his heroic feats. But he is quick to take offense and, at the slightest bruise to his ego or threat to his independent domain, wealth, or power, he reacts with the full fury and resentment of a local dynast. For all his "active" temperament he can be very wordy and didactic. When the occasion demands he is wise, temperate, and resourceful. Of the more than six hundred years of his life, so lovingly recounted by Ferdowsi, only one night is spent in amorous company of a woman. It serves the purpose of siring the ill-fated Sohrab. For the rest, he is infinitely more devoted to his horse. Sometimes he is unable to rein his pride which results in the two monstrous deeds of his life — and shapes the final tragedy of his life.

It is partly this depth of characterization that enhances and ennobles the tragic episodes of the *Shah-nama*. Jamshid the priest-king, world-orderer, and the giver of knowledge and skills, is the victim of his own hybris. The tragedy of Sohrab is not merely in the horror of filicide but in the fear and vanity of Rostam and the repulsed tender premonitions of Sohrab. The tragedies of Iraj and Siyavush evoke the cosmic anguish and the inconsolable pity of the guileless and the pure, ravaged by the wicked. Forud and Bahram are the promise of sweet and valorous youth cut down by the senselessness of war. Esfandiyar is rent by the conflict of his formal loyalties and his piety and good sense. But it is his vanity and ambition that send him to his doom. Nor is this moving sense of the tragic reserved for the Iranians alone. Piran, the hoary Turanian noble, shows compassion to captive Iranians and risks his own life to protect them only, in the end, to lose it for remaining loyal to his sovereign. Even the villainous Afrasiyab — a prisoner of his evil nature — is pitiable and tragic in the helpless moments of self-awareness.

Ferdowsi has no set formulae for tragedy, yet in the early and mythical part of the *Shah-nama* an inexorable divine justice seems to balance most of the scales. Iraj and Siyavush are restored and triumphant in Manuchehr and Key-Khosrow, Rostam is reconciled to his fate as the price for the slaying of Sohrab and Esfandiyar, and Afrasiyab cannot escape his moira. The tragic impact of the *Shah-nama,* however, is not simply the sum of its tragic episodes. It pervades the encompassing conception of the work, and the sources of it are to be found in the conscious and unconscious paradoxes that form the personality, the emotional and the intellectual outlook of Ferdowsi.

The overriding tragic fact of the poet's life is that the glory of which he sings is no more. But this is not to say that the *Shah-nama* is a defiant nostalgic lament. The intellectual horizon of Ferdowsi is that of a rational and devout Muslim. Muhammad and Zoroaster are venerated as if they were of the same root, but Ferdowsi's pride in Iran is his constant muse and his contempt for Arabs is ill-concealed. His concept of history is thoroughly Islamic, but there is no Augustinian righteous indignation in him. The cumulative emotional tensions of his "history" are unresolved. Even in his stark treatment of the final reigns of the Sasanian empire when the succession of evil, tyranny, rapacity, treachery and chaos is unrelieved by any sign of grace, he cannot quite bring himself to a condemnation of the Iranian empire. The only possible catharsis is in the contemplation of the ideal of justice, essential in Islam — yet already far detached from the realities of his time. Nor is the holocaust so distant as the fall of the Sasanians. Ferdowsi was undoubtedly inspired by the renascent Iranism of the Samanid epoch and may have even conceived of his masterwork as an offering to that illustrious house, only to witness its demise at the hands of the Turkic Ghaznavids. The bitterness of the mythical Iranian-Turanian epic struggle that permeates the *Shah-nama* and gives it its dramatic tension is largely the pressing phenomenon of the poet's own time. Thus he has experienced a reenactment of the final tragedy of his poem. The necessity of dedicating the *Shah-nama* to the very Turkic destroyer of the Iranian Samanids must have been a bitter and demeaning fact. Much of the traditional denunciatory epilogue addressed to Mahmud of Ghazna may be accretions of later times, but the tone is true.

The tensions and contradictions in the experience of the poet that are reflected in the tragic paradoxes of the *Shah-nama* and are a source of the validity, profundity, and universality of its art, are not all conscious or external. The interactions of his innate character, his inculcated traits, his social position, his changing environment, and the nature of his creative genius, all fail to achieve a synthesis. Instead, they fashion a personality marred by unresolved intellectual conflicts and spiritual anguish.

He belongs to the class of *dehgans*, or landed gentry, and has an inherited sense of expectation of privilege, which is embittered by gradual impoverishment. He is not yet free of the impulses of generosity and noble detachment that sometimes flourish in the serene and self-assured middle plateaus of wealth and power of a social class; but he is already afflicted with the material obsessions, if not greed and avarice, that characterize the periods of rise and fall of those classes. Thus he seeks, and needs, the patronage and the emoluments of the Ghaznavid court, yet he is too proud, too detached and too dedicated to his "uncommercial" art to secure that patronage in the accepted mode of the day. He is contemptuous of the servility and the parasitic existence of the court poets, of the artificiality of their panegyric verse, of the ignobleness of their self-seeking and mutual enmity, yet he is not without the artist's vanity, envy, and acrimony and, occasionally, he succumbs to the temptation of proving himself in their terms.

Ferdowsi's genuine compassion for the poor and the wronged, his remarkable and persistent sense of social justice, his courageous and vocal condemnation of irresponsibility of rulers, his altruism and idealism — in short, his profound humanity — account for some of the most moving and ennobling passages in the *Shah-nama* and endow it with a consistent integrity. At the same time he has the conservative impulses of the *dehgan*. His yearning for legitimacy, his outrage at disregard of position, his abhorrence of anarchy, his fear of heresy, and his dread of unruly mobs provide the narrative with moments of eerie drama and Jeremiah-like visions and nightmares of the apocalypse.

However much may be said of the formal and philosophical diffuseness of the *Shah-nama,* it is transcendentally successful as a true epic. In that sense only a comparison with the *Iliad* can be meaningful and instructive. In their origin, nature, and function, as well as in form and content, there are arresting similarities between the two poems. This is not to say that the likenesses outnumber the differences. The *Shah-nama* is, of course, the product of a much later and more self-conscious age, and it draws from a vast fund of literary conventions and cliches of Near Eastern cultures. But the *Shah-nama* and the *Iliad* partake of the fundamental mysteries of epic as art. They both represent the instantly and eternally triumphant attempts of conscious art to immortalize the glory and the identity of a people. It does not matter that neither Homer nor Ferdowsi were the very first to attempt such a task in their cultures. It is the supreme elixir of their art which accomplished the miracle. They ennobled the natural epic without losing its spontaneity. Furthermore they did so at a time when the cement of past associations was crumbling and the common identity of their peoples was in danger of effacement. Thus by their creations Homer and Ferdowsi succeeded at once in immortalizing the past and bequeathing the future to the language and life of their nation.

The western reader of the *Shah-nama* will learn much — and may gain in enjoyment — by some comparison of its similarities and differences with the *Iliad*. Although Ferdowsi works with a number of written and even "literate" sources, at least in the first half of the *Shah-nama,* as in the *Iliad,* the roots of oral tradition are close to the surface. Both poems employ a simple, facile meter; and their rhyme schemes are suited to the long narrative and aid in memorizing. The heroes in both epics are affixed with appropriate epithets and are easily recognizable even without mention of their names. Both poems make use of a certain amount of repetition to assist recapitulation. Episodes of battle and heroism are modulated by sequences of chase, ostentatious banquets and idyllic revels, and ceremonious councils and parleys. Semi-independent subepisodes are interspersed to vary the mood and relieve the tedium of the narrative. Of these, several romances in the *Shah-nama,* particularly those of Zal and Rudaba and of Bizhan and Manizha in their exquisite lyricism, poignant intimacy and self-contained perfection have no peers in the *Iliad*. Both poets lavish masterful attention upon the details of the martial life — the description of armors and weapons, the personal and near magical love of the heroes for their mounts and their armor, etc. — that breed and sustain a sense of epic involvement. Both poems abound in little warm human touches that evoke pathos and enhance the evolving drama.

Transcending these more or less formal similarities are the fundamental parallels of human behavior under similar relationships and social conditions and the recognizable range of human types in the *Iliad* and the *Shah-nama*. The affinities of the indispensable hero

Rostam with Achilles; of the capricious, covetous, apprehensive and envious monarch Key-Kavus with Agamemnon; of the stolid and martial Giv with Ajax; of the wily and wise Piran with Odysseus; of the dutiful and sacrificial Gudarz with Hector; of the impetuous and handsome Bizhan with Paris; of the youthful, loyal, and pathetic Bahram with Patroklos; of the impulsive, sensuous and beautiful Sudaba with Helen; of the adoring, meek and resigned Farangis with Andromache; are only a few of the evocative suggestions of artistic kinship between the two epics. In the fragile social order depicted in the *Iliad* and in the first half of the *Shah-nama* tension and strife are never far from the surface. But Ferdowsi has endowed his cosmos with a higher morality and thus the lapses of his heroes are more grave and awful.

In addition to mortal humans both epics are peopled by several supernatural orders of goodly spirits, demons, and magical creatures who intervene in the affairs of men and profoundly affect their fate. But the God of *Shah-nama* is the unknowable God of Zoroastrians, Jews, Christians, and Muslims. Unlike the deities of the *Iliad,* He is not implicated in the struggle of the mortals though He is constantly evoked and beseeched. Only twice does an angel intervene to alter the course of battle. At other times there is only indirect confirmation of the righteous and chastisement of the wayward. On the other hand, prophetic dreams count for more in the *Shah-nama.* Fate is the unconquerable tyrant of both poems, but in the *Shah-nama* it is sometimes unravelled by the stars, robbing the drama of its mystery.

Shah-nama is inordinately longer than the *Iliad*. Essentially it is made up of two segments: the mythical first half and the "historical" second half. The psychological and artistic seam cannot be concealed. The fundamental affinities with the *Iliad* are primarily true of the first half. But even there the unity of theme, the limitation of action and time, the rapid devolution of the "plot," the resolution of the conflict, and the uncanny proportions of the *Iliad* are missing. Ferdowsi's "historical" mission undoubtedly scatters the artistic impact of the *Shah-nama* and diffuses the focus of its aesthetic concept. But the "wrath of Achilles," after all, is not the sole catalyst of Homer's art. The validity and viability of the *Iliad* rests in its general relevance to the human situation. In this sense the artistic "flaw" of the *Shah-nama* is more than made up by, and perhaps makes for, its greater universality. Thus in the *Shah-nama* we come across characters who have no counterparts in the *Iliad,* and one must cull the whole of Greek mythology, mystery, and drama for parallels: Jamshid, the primal priest-king, the divinely inspired creator of civilization, the bringer of world order, whose hybris causes his fall and plunges mankind into evil and darkness; Zahhak, the grotesque tyrant, the personification of irrational and demonic forces who grips the world in a thousand-year reign of terror; Kava, the rebellious *vox populi* triumphant in a just cause; Faridun, the ideal and wise king, compassionate pastor of his people; Siyavush, the tragic guileless youth, maligned, helpless, and martyred; Key-Khosrow, the messiah-king, avenger and restorer. Every one of them is a focal realization of a master figure in the history of man's existence and aspirations.

It is this universality, together with its faithful and unresolved reflection of the human paradox, that is the essence of *Shah-nama*'s art and the cause of its timelessness; for it permits every generation to seek its own resolution.

Averroes on Poetry[1]

VICENTE CANTARINO

The well-known admiration that Averroes felt for the writings of Aristotle, although giving him a well deserved claim to fame as the Stagirite's Commentator 'par excellence,' has often turned against him as far as his personal contributions are concerned. The eighteenth- and nineteenth-century concept and over-evaluation of an author's originality, which still deeply influences modern scholarship, has frequently served more as a deterrent from than an encouragement for an independent search and analysis of the teachings of the Cordovan philosopher. And yet a close scrutiny of almost any part of his prodigious literary production shows that Averroes is not a commentator in our sense of the word. Dressed in Aristotelian colors, Averroes tries in fact to express often a world of ideas different from the Aristotelian ones, ideas that are his own and which will escape us as long as we insist on seeing them only against the original works of the Greek philosopher.[2]

Nowhere are the shortcomings of this attitude seen more clearly than in the attention, or lack of it, that modern scholarship has paid to Averroes's commentary of the Aristotelian treatise on poetics. Previous studies dealing with this one of Averroes's works were based on the premise of its being a commented summary of the Aristotelian inquiry concerning the nature of creative art exclusively. For this reason any misunderstanding or misrepresentation of the teachings of the Stag-

[1] A summary of this study was read at the annual meeting of the American Oriental Society, New York, 1969.

[2] Helmut Gätje, "Averroes als Aristoteleskommentator" *Zeitschrift der Deutschen Morgenländischen Gesellschaft* (114) 1964, 59-65.

irite has been considered an inexcusable error. From this point of view, to the scholar searching for the Greek background of Averroes's work will hardly seem ill deserved the harsh judgment cast by the Czech scholar Tkač some sixty years ago, which has so decisively influenced all subsequent evaluation of Averroes's work: "Der Kommentar des Averroes zur Poetik is nun ein wahres Sammelsurium ungeheuerlicher Missverstandnisse und abenteuerlicher Phantasien des arabischen Philosophen dessen Lieblingschriftsteller Aristoteles war."[3]

Moreover, a common assumption traditionally held is that at the basis of Averroes's poetic theory lies the uncritical acceptance and arbitrary application to Greek poetics of the idea that "all poetry and poetic discourse is either satire or eulogy."[4] Our easy acceptance of the assumption that Averroes uses the terms *madīḥ* and *hijā'*, in their strict sense as the basic premise in his analysis of the Aristotelian text condemns Averroes's analytical dissertation to being entirely irrelevant from its very introductory lines.

It would not be an easy task to attempt to excuse Averroes's errors, who as is known was unable to use, nor even seemed to have felt the need for a recourse to the original text in his study. It would also be of little consolation to state that he is only at the end of and rather the victim of the corruptions, misunderstandings, and unwarranted accretions which accompanied the oriental tradition of the Aristotelian *Poetics*.

Yet it might be time to recognize that this approach to Averroes's treatise on the Aristotelian *Poetics* is undoubtedly and fully justified only if it is to be considered exclusively from the point of view of Aristotle's theory of poetic art and as a link in the chain of the tradition of the Greek text. However, this approach, if considered the only one a scholar can adopt, totally disregards and belittles beyond all reason Averroes's own aim explicitly stated in his opening statement: "The objective in this discourse is to summarize the general rules found in Aristotle's book on Poetry, that are common to all or most people,

[3] Jaroslaus Tkatsch, "Die arabische Übersetzung der Poetik des Aristoteles und die Grundlage der Kritik des griechischen Texten." *Ak. d. Wiss. Phil.-hist Kl.* Vienna, 1928, p. 76.

[4] The formal equivalence between *madīḥ* and *hijā'* with *tragoedia* and *comoedia* was introduced by D. S. Margoliought in his Latin translation of Abu Bishr's text which Averroes follows in this point. See Margoliought's *The Poetics of Aristotle* (London, 1911), p. 231.

since most of what is in it are rules particular to their poetic compositions and customs in regard to them" (p. 1, l. 4).[5]

Averroes therefore is not trying to expound on, or to repeat even in a summarized way, the analysis already offered by Aristotle; nor is he aiming at a practical presentation of the current or ideal Arabic theory of poetics.

He is, on the contrary, considering the primary principles to which in his own opinion poetic art responds. In this respect, we may add, he is fully in the methodological tradition of Aristotelian analysis. The translations of the Aristotelian text he used offered him a guide and an outline of the basic principles on which he based his own observations; and thus he is also here in complete agreement with his usual method of research.

A textual clue to Averroes's intent could have been the use he makes of the so-called *dixit auctoris*. It is not, as is usually assumed, used to introduce formally what he believed to be a literal quotation of the original text.[6] Against such an assumption speaks the fact that *qāla 'dixit'* often introduces a text quotation which has been totally adapted to suit his own context and even at times his own basic statements under discussion, which Averroes could not have intended to have attributed strictly to the Stagirite. It is in fact generally used as a dividing line between paragraphs to help underline the basic statements to be commented upon, whether or not they should formally be attributed to Aristotle.[7]

The basic difference between the Aristotelian and Averroes's approach to the subject matter, leaving aside the point of the author's originality already mentioned, consists in the fact that Aristotle's general principles of poetry can all be applied to Greek poetic art at a lower level of abstraction, since they have been formulated by Aristotle taking Greek art fully into consideration. Averroes, on the contrary, adopts the attitude that Aristotle's general principles must as such have

[5] For this and all subsequent quotations of Averroes's text see the edition by F. Lasinio, *Il Commento medio d'Averroe alla Poetica* (Pisa, 1872). The page number refers to the Arabic text and is followed by the line number.

[6] Marcelino Menendez y Pelayo, *Historia de las Ideas estéticas en España*, 2nd. ed. Madrid, Vol. I, p. 376.

[7] This is especially obvious in the discussion of the parts of the speech where Averroes departs most from the Greek text in his attempt to adapt the Aristotelian divisions to Arabic phonetic and grammar.

a universal validity and, therefore, those among them which cannot be applied "to all or [at least] to most peoples" are not to be considered as having the required universal validity and thus are not to be considered as general principles. The result is logically a dissertation on the creative art that is Aristotelian in outlook and even in approach, but in no way representative of the Stagirite's theory, which in fact was something Averroes did not intend to do.

Yet it would be an unjustified assumption to believe that the Cordovan philosopher was on the whole unable to present a coherent and intelligent presentation reflecting his own observations and opinions on the subject, even on the points in which he most radically departs from the Aristotelian text.

Averroes's conscious or unconscious departure from the Aristotelian approach "to proceed according to the way of Nature herself"[8] is imposed upon him by the translation of the Greek text available to him. Aristotle had chosen for the treatment of the *Poetics* a deductive method, beginning with the first principles to which art "according to Nature" responds. In the analysis of the imitative arts, he had to face the problem of the "nameless art" since he did not know of a Greek name which would fit the literary art using "speech plain" whether in prose or verse.[9] In Aristotle's opinion, at this level of abstraction for a classification dependent on basic principles of artistic imitation, the distinction introduced by the different sound of prosaic or "measured" speech is less important than that existing between an art using only speech and another using speech and rhythm and melody, such as is found in Greek comedy and tragedy.

Averroes instead had to use as a cornerstone of his analysis the technical and highly delimited term of *shiᶜr* which was the accepted rendering of the Greek *poietikes*. Thus while "concerning making" is therefore both a meaningful translation of the Greek *peri poietikes* and one that provides a typically Aristotelian sequence of thought from the most general "making" to the less general "imitation" and to the most specific "literature,"[10] this can only be applied to the Aristotelian treatise. That of Averroes will have to be translated as dealing with

[8] O. B. Hardison, "Poetics, Chapter I 'The Way of Nature' " *Yearbook of Comparative and General Literature* (16) 1967, p. 8.

[9] Hardison, *op. cit.*, p. 10.

[10] Hardison, *op. cit.*, p. 6.

"Poetry," for the ultimate concern of his inquiry is the basic nature of this particular type of literary expression. And since his analysis tends to study those elements which make Arabic poetic compositions (*ash*^{c}*ār*) poetic in the Aristotelian sense, we must conclude that Averroes is following an inductive method, beginning with particulars and moving to larger generalizations.

Moreover, for Aristotle this "nameless art" is only a subspecies of the more general and generic term of artistic mimesis which includes not only the various literary arts but also those consisting in imitation by color, form, rhythm, and harmony, alone or in combination. But Averroes perhaps unconsciously has chosen a method different from the one Aristotle uses here, yet basically Aristotelian in its analytical approach. For the Cordovan philosopher, qualities and mimetic aims of other means of expression are imitative of the poetic art of speech: "And the same is the case with the arts that imitate the art of Poetry (*shi*^{c}*r*), which are the playing of the lute, of the flute and the dance. That is to say, they too are by nature readied to (express) the same aims (as poetic art)" (p. 1, l. 15).

In the preceding lines Averroes has taken from Aristotle those types of artistic imitation which use sound as their natural means of expression, namely rhythm and harmony. It is, therefore, a fair deduction that for Averroes the essential quality of this mimetic art consists in the very capability to express an object through sound, which is naturally found only in speech, man's most natural and elementary way in which an imitation through sound can be created and communicated. For this very reason, as we shall see, some characteristic ways of poetic expression especially important in Averroes's concept of poetic art, such as "embellishment" and "defacement," are found in mimetic speech, as a more general term, but not in the imitation by harmony and rhythm: "These two parts (*taḥsīn, taqbīḥ*) are found only in the comparison and in the mimesis which is through speech, but not in that which is through rhythm nor in that which is through harmony" (p. 4, l. 11).

Mimesis in general is referred to by Averroes with a series of terms, usually understood as being similar in concept and equivalent in their real meaning, which the Cordovan philosopher uses mixing them in what appears at first sight a rather disconcerting carelessness. Such are *tashbīh, tamthīl, muḥāka* and *takhyīl*. A closer study of the use that Averroes makes of them shows that they each have a distinctive function in rendering the general concept of mimesis.

The two first ones, *tashbīh* and *tamthīl,* refer to the act of comparing two objects in the way that is peculiar to speech, whether the comparison is achieved explicitly with such elements as the so-called "particles of comparison" or only implied through a simple substitution of members.[11] Whenever any of the other terms is used in a concrete reference to the imitation achieved through speech, this fact is always explicitly stated: "The imitation which is (achieved) through speech" (p. 4, l. 12).

Thus *muḥāka* and *takhyīl*[12] seem to refer to artistic imitation on a higher degree of abstraction and therefore with a greater general validity be also applicable to the act of creative mimesis in any of its forms, not only by speech or even sound in general: "Men by nature may creatively imitate one another through actions such as the imitation of one another through color, form and sound. And this can be either through art and a property found in those who realize the mimesis or because of a habit existing already in them related to (this act)" (p. 2, l. 20).

[11] It becomes especially clear in Averroes's explanations about the methods of comparison used in Arabic (p. 2) that he considers both *tashbīh* and *tamthīl* more as a linguistic technique than a quality of the speech.

[12] Since the translation of *takhyīl* and its derivatives as a direct reference to the category of 'creativity' is rather our conclusion, it must remain conjectural for the moment.

A diagram of the various categories referred to by Averroes might clarify his exposition:

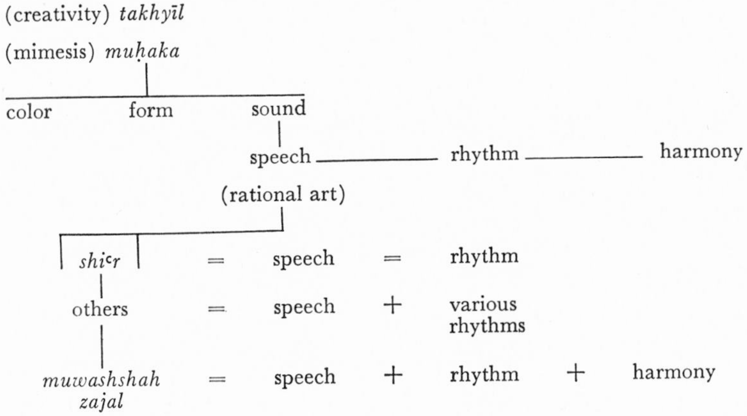

But only *muḥāka* seems to have as its specific object the reproduction in images of forms in a broad sense: "The *muḥāka* is only of forms that sustain the virtues, not of traits of character, since they cannot be represented by images" (p. 8, l. 8). The mimetic art expressed in the term *muḥāka,* when applied to the poetic discourse is not equivalent or equal to the expression of the imitation by speech only: "This *muḥāka* through discourse will be complete when accompanied by harmony and rhythm" (p. 8, l. 9).

The three elements mentioned are constitutive of the *takhyīl* and *muḥāka* in poetic discourses: "The *takhyīl* and the *muḥāka* in the poetic discourses consist of three elements: of the harmonious sound, of the rhythm and of the comparison (*tashbīh*) itself" (p. 2, l. 23). They are not, however, to be considered only as constitutive elements of literary mimesis, but also as arts and creative per se: "Creative arts or those that realize the act of creation (*takhyīl*) are three: the art of harmony, that of rhythm and that of composing mimetic discourses. And this last one is the rational art which we will study in this treatise" (p. 3, l. 9).

Thus, as it seems, while *tashbīh* refers directly to a quality of speech and *muḥāka* to one that while including speech also covers other kinds of mimesis through forms or images, *takhyīl* represents on a more abstract level a different quality which in fact refers to the very essence of artistic mimesis. It is difficult not to think of Ibn Sina's definition that "*takhyīl* is the submission of the soul to astonishment and pleasure"[13] or that quality which makes any mimetic expression in any of its manifestations go beyond a simple, vulgar, unappealing reproduction of an object.

We have chosen "rational art" instead of "logical,"[14] as Averroes's *al-ṣināᶜa al-manṭiqiyya* has often been rendered because of the importance he seems to give speech as the natural means of mimetic expression through sound. This leads to the conclusion that he is underlining the rational character of speech as a means of expression and of artistic mimesis. For speech is not artistic per se, as expression is not neces-

[13] Page 81 (175a) of the Arabic text. Published by D. Margoliouth, *Analecta Orientalia ad poeticam aristoteleam* (London, 1887).

[14] The translation 'logical' has been at times preferred as being suggested by the survival of his 'middle commentary' of the Aristotelian treatise in a manuscript containing his explication of the Organon. v.Tkatsch, *op. cit.,* p. 76.

sarily equivalent to mimesis which is for Averroes, as it is for Aristotle also, the essential characteristic of any artistic manifestation. Artistic is the conscious realization of literary mimesis.[15]

Now for the Stagirite: "Every art or applied science and every systematic investigation and, similarly, every action and choice seem to aim at some good; the good, therefore, has been well defined as that at which all things aim."[16] For Averroes art which is too poetic deals with and aims at voluntary matters, that is to say, those related to good and evil: "Since those who realize the mimetic speech aim indeed with it to incite to the realization of some voluntary acts and to refrain from others, it is absolutely necessary that the themes to which their mimesis aims be virtues and vices" (p. 3, l. 21). This is in fact the causa finalis, the raison d'être, of poetic art, namely to move the audience to good through the proper presentation of good or bad qualities found in actions. In this statement, however, we put special stress on the proper presentation, for not every moralizing discourse is necessarily artistic or poetic. The special characteristic of this presentation is formally underlined by Averroes's statement that it must be realized, "not with a (rationally) convincing discourse, for that is not befitting this art, but with a mimetic discourse. For the art of poetry is not based on argumentation and discussion" (p. 11, l. 2).

Of specially great importance seems the interest that Averroes shows in de-intellectualizing the concept of poetic art. First, he states that poetic art deals with voluntary themes and actions. Secondly, that it must concentrate on the presentation of their qualities; and finally, he makes his point by accepting the very presentations, their mimetic quality, as the only argument. There is no word said about truth which in its relation to man's intellect could not be designated as "voluntary" and persuasion, as the intellectual imposition of an intellectual conviction, is rejected as not being the proper presentation in literary mimesis. In order to achieve its aim, the mimesis must appeal to the human will, not to the intelligence. It is thus only logical that Averroes, more than

15 In contrast with this 'pragmatic' art, there is another 'theoretic' art; it is "the scientific art which teaches from what (elements) poems (*ashᶜār*) can be composed, and how the most perfect and superior quality can be achieved from the composition of the poems" (p. 11, l. 5).

16 Aristotle, *Nicomachean Ethics,* Martin Ostwald, trans. (New York, 1962), Book I, ch. I (1094a).

even Aristotle, underlines the importance of the role played by "delight" (*iltidhādh*) in the origin and development of the mimetic and poetic arts: "For the delight (*iltidhādh*) that the soul experiences by nature with the mimetic representations and with harmonies and rhythms is the cause for the existence of poetic arts, especially for the more lofty characters" (p. 2, l. 10). And it is in relation to this pleasure or delight that Averroes understands the act of mimesis. That is to say, imitation is not "naturally" concerned with the intrinsic moral values of voluntary acts, but only insofar as they are the cause of an aesthetic delight in the soul of the percipient one:

> The (mimetic) exposition is the pillar and foundation of this art, for there is no delight in remembering the object intended to be recalled when there is no mimetic process involved. Rather, there will be delight and acceptance of it only when it is (artistically) imitated. Because of this, man does not find pleasure in the contemplation of the existing objects themselves, but he does in their imitations and reproductions with tints and colors (p. 10, l. 7).

For this very reason poetry, that is, literary mimesis, does not aim at an objective presentation of what is good or bad, of virtuous or vicious actions: "Since every poetic imitation (*tashbīh wa-ḥikāya*) is based on what is good and bad, it is thus obvious that every imitation is aimed at embellishment and defacement" (p. 4, l. 3).

The artistic and creative quality of poetic mimesis lies precisely in the subjectivity of appreciation which must accompany the process cited by Averroes as "embellishment" and "defacement."[17] In the light of these comments we can now try to understand Averroes's statement which is so often quoted to prove his lack of understanding of Arabic, as well as of poetry in general: "All poetry and all poetic discourse is either a praise (*madīḥ*) or a scoffing (*hijā'*)" (p. 1, l. 13). Subsequently, in his direct application of this principle to Arabic poetry, Averroes includes a seemingly different type of approach to poetic ex-

[17] The same idea of the subjectivity in the poet's appreciation of reality is carried to its extreme conclusion in the anecdote reported by Averroes's landsman Abu ᶜOmar Muhammad ibn ᶜAbd rabbih (860-940) in his *Kitāb al-ᶜIqd (al-farīd)*: "A certain expert on the (art of) poetry was asked: Who is the most gifted poet (*ashᶜār*) of all men? He answered: Whoever can present what is false as the truth and what is true as falsehood through the charm of his concept and his delicate perspicacity, in such a way that he deface the most accomplished beauty and beautify (even) utter ugliness" (Cairo, n.y.; vol. III, p. 147).

pression, namely one in which there is not clear praise or scoffing, but a simple equivalence between the object and its literary representation: "As for the type of poetic compositions in which only an equivalence (*muṭābaqa*) is intended, it is frequently found in the compositions (of the Arabs); and it is for this reason that they often describe inanimate things, animals and plants. . . . Thus it seems clear from this discourse that there are three types of comparison" (p. 5, l. 5).

The inclusion of this last term, the *muṭābaqa,* as an objective representation "in which only an equivalence is intended" clearly shows that, contrary to what has been usually assumed, Averroes is not using *madīḥ* and *hijā'* at this point in their technical and concrete meaning of eulogy and satire.[18] He uses them rather to express the poet's subjective attitude in his rendition of the contemplated object, from which only the third type of comparison should be excluded per se since it consists in an objective attitude.

Thus we may conclude that the subject matter or causa materialis of the poetic discourse is the beauty or ugliness inherent in objects and actions alike. But the essential aspect of poetry and poetic mimesis, its causa formalis, is precisely that subjective attitude on the part of the poet that makes the presentation of the reality perceived able to achieve the essential aim of poetic art, namely to move man's spirit to the pursuit of good and flight of evil which the poet achieves through an artistic presentation of both.

Although Averroes insists that "pursuit" and "flight" (*ṭalab* and *harab*) is the essential aim of poetry, it is obvious that his intent is to refer to the emotions ("passiones") that the contemplation of an object arouses in man when it is perceived as good or evil, rather than to the realization of that pursuit or flight.

The third attitude the poet can assume in his contemplation of reality, *muṭābaqa,* which in itself is neither aimed at the defacement of what is evil nor at the embellishment of what is good, should, according to the previous comments, be considered in itself alien to the aims of poetic art. Its frequent use in poetic compositions is explained and, as it seems, accepted in the following lines:

> The third (type) is the comparison with which a mere equivalence between both members in the comparison is intended, without aiming

[18] Edwin J. Webber, "Comedy as Satire in Hispano-Arabic Spain," *Hispanic Review* (XXVI) 1958, p. 1-11.

at embellishment or defacement, just the very equivalence. However, this kind of comparison is like a ready instrument to be transformed into either of the two extremes. I mean that it will be changed some times into embellishment with the addition of some elements and other times into defacement, also with the addition of some other elements (p. 4, l. 13).

There is still another way to express reality which also per se rejects that subjective distortion or interpretation considered by Averroes as the key to poetic creativity and which for this very reason should also be excluded from the poetic methods of realization. It too consists in an objective representation of truth such as we expect to find in logical arguments if they are to possess a scientific quality. The objective equivalence thus established is often referred to by Averroes as "sincerity" and "truthfulness" (*ṣidq* and *taṣdīq*) as the process in which the objective truth is asserted. In this aesthetic morality, objective "sincerity" aims at the presentation of logical relations and therefore is conductive to conviction and persuasion rather than to the stimulation of the emotions of the human soul. It thus belongs to a process of logical thinking and not to poetic and aesthetic ways of expression: "There is another kind of poetry, namely those poems (*ashᶜār*) which belong in the chapter on objective representation (*taṣdīq*) and persuasion (*iqnāᶜ*) rather than to creativity (*takhyīl*) and therefore are closer to being rhetorical examples than poetic mimesis" (p. 23, l. 15). In fact, the objective presentation, the equation between the object as expressed and its reality, its truth (*ḥaqq*), is the basis leading to intellectual persuasion which in Averroes's opinion is the aim of Rhetoric: "Rhetoric is the virtue which embraces the weight of possible persuasion about any external object."[19] The formal difference between the art of Poetry and Rhetoric thus consists, in Averroes's opinion, in their objectives; that of poetry being the presentation of the qualities of the object "as it is," while that of Rhetoric is the examination of its very nature, or "what it is." But there is also an essential difference in their modus operandi, which for Rhetoric is to bring about a conviction and for poetic art to arouse the passions of pursuit and avoidance brought about by a mimetic representation. This distinction is further

[19] "Rhetorica autem est vis amplectens in se onus persuasionis possibilis de qualibet rerum separatarum" L. I ch. 1 *In libros Rhetoricorum Aristotelis Paraphrases,* in Abraham of Balmes' translation, Venice, 1562-1574.

illustrated by Averroes in his discussion of "belief" (*i^{c}tiqād*) as one of the aspects of the poetic method: "To induce belief is that faculty of imitating the way in which something is or is not found. And this is similar to the demonstration with which also Rhetoric is concerned, namely, that something is or is not. Only that Rhetoric deals with this using a persuasive discourse, while poetry with the mimetic discourse" (p. 10, l. 12).

The opposite of literary truthfulness is the literary lie, the fictitious invention which lacks a basis in reality (*ikhtirā^{c}*) and is characteristic of stories and fables. From this point of view it is only logical that Averroes chooses not to follow Aristotle in his comparison between poetry and history but points instead to the famous book of *Kalila and Dimna:*

> And it is also obvious from what has been said about the aim of poetic discourses that the imitation which is based on fictitious themes without basis in reality (*al-'umūr al-mukhara^{c}a al-kādhiba*) is not the work of the poet (strictly speaking). These works are called fables and stories such as those which are found in the book of *Dimna and Kalila* (*sic*). . . . The work of those who compose fables and stories is not that of poets, even if they may compose those fables and fictitious narrations in rhythmic speech. This is because both (fables and narrations) although they share (with poetry) the rhythm, the ones (fables and narrations) achieve their aim through the narrative (itself) even if it is not in rhythmic speech, and this aim is the understanding (*ta^{c}aqqul*) which one can extract from those fictitious narrations (p. 13, l. 15).

The simple fiction such as that in fables and tales is deemed not poetic by Averroes because their invention is determined by a final cause different from that of poetry, namely the useful learning (*ta^{c}aqqul*) derived from comprehension of the fable's moral content. If verse is used in them it is only accidentally and independently from the final cause, the raison d'être of fables and tales, which can be reached equally well with or without employing verse.

The preceding quotations bring to our attention the problem of the relationship between the poetic content and the rhythmic verse form in poetry. Here we must also conclude that more clearly than even Aristotle, though not independently of the Stagirite's theory of poetic art, Averroes claims for the art of poetry its formal independence from versification. Following the Aristotelian statement, Averroes does not consider the simple narration of physical themes as poetry even when in verse form: "There are many discourses which are called poems (*ash*^{c}*ār*) but have of the poetic concept only the rhythm, such as the rhythmic discourses of Socrates and those of Empedocles on physical things. . . . Those are more properly called discourses than poetry. And likewise whoever composes rhythmic discourses on physical themes is more properly called expounder than poet" (p. 3, l. 11). Averroes seems to have a double reason for his judgment. One may be the fact that in the above mentioned cases there is a lack of subjective appreciation on the part of their composer, his aim being exclusively to expound natural themes in order to impart knowledge, not to excite man's emotion; and therefore they must be based on an objectivity which excludes completely the mimetic process of poetry. The second reason being that similarly as he pointed out for the compositions of fictitious tales and fables which have no objective foundation in reality, verse form is also here added to them as an accidental element, while in poetry its rhythmic composition is directly functional of poetry's essential aim: "The aim of the creative representation cannot be achieved by the poet to its perfection (^{c}*alā l-tamam*) except by the use of rhythm" (p. 13, l. 23). It is of interest to point out that Averroes requires rhythm in poetry only to better achieve the poetic aim. In doing this he establishes the formal independence we have indicated between the aim essential to poetic creativity and its rhythmic verse form which is required, one may say, as a necessary concomitant. The omission in the preceding statement of the word "poetry" (*shi*^{c}*r*) is hardly an oversight on the part of Averroes, and although he explicitly speaks of the poet's aim, he mentions only *takhyīl* as the poet's essential aim. On the contrary, since poetry (*shi*^{c}*r*) is taken throughout the book in its concrete and technical application which already includes in its current definition the use of rhythm, Averroes can only state the mentioned distinction at a higher degree of abstraction. Thus in an independent dialectical process similar to that of Aristotle's, Averroes arrives at the same conclusion. In the final analysis of the principles of poetic imitation, speech is not poetic per se, nor is it made poetic only by verse which is an external quality added to speech. It is the mimesis which makes speech creative and poetic: "It is obvious that the poet will be poet through making of plots and rhythm in the same proportion that he is able to achieve the mimetic presentation (*al-tashbīh wa-l-muḥāka*)" (p. 14, l. 21).

The rhythm in the mimetic expression, which must be considered as an integral part in the Arabic concept of *shi*^{c}*r,* still receives the totally accidental requirement of its internal uniformity. This requirement although needed in Arabic is not observed in other languages. "Likewise those creative discourses consisting of mixed rhythmic schemes are not poetic compositions (*ash*^{c}*ār*) although it is said that such can be found among (the Greeks)" (p. 3, l. 16). Here again Averroes does not deny their mimetic or creative quality, nor does he deny their being poetry (*shi*^{c}*r*). They only lack from the Arabic point of view the internal unity that will make them into poems.

In agreement with Aristotle, Averroes observes that the mimetic and creative qualities of poetic speech can also be enhanced by its combined use with the artistic speech of the other forms of mimetic expression through sound, namely rhythm and harmony:

> Creativity and mimesis (*takhyīl, muḥāka*) in poetic discourses can be achieved in three different ways: with melodious sounds, with rhythm and with comparison itself. And these can be found independently from each other as e.g., melody in the flute, rhythm in the dance and mimesis in the phonetic sound of speech. I mean those creative discourses which do not use rhythm. But sometimes all three are found together, as the case is among us in the type called *muwashshahas* and *zajals* which are poetic compositions invented in their language by the people of this Island (*al-Andalus*). Since those are natural compositions which unite the two (rhythm and harmony) with natural (primitive) things, they are only found among natural (primitive) peoples. Arabic poetic compositions indeed do not have harmony; they have either only rhythm or rhythm and mimesis at the same time (p. 2, l. 23).

In the preceding lines, Averroes has offered in a summary Aristotle's concept of the possible relations between the three basic ways with which an imitation through sound can be achieved. But, although he follows the Stagirite in the general lines of his argumentation and accepts the thesis that rhythm and harmony can in fact increase the mimetic effectivity of poetic art, he is consequent to his own particular aim in this treatise and follows an independent trend of thought. The result is disconcerting in a simplicity so pregnant with implication not easy to explain.

In the first place, Averroes does not refer to the elements of the Aristotelian trilogy on the same level. His concern belongs to the creative and mimetic quality in poetic discourses; rhythm and harmony are thus considered only as subservient to the essential qualities of poetry which, as we have already seen, are the mimesis and creativity with which literary art can achieve its essential aim. Secondly, Averroes establishes various categories which, though given in a different order, we may present as follows for the sake of greater clarity:

a) elements used independently:

harmony	= flute
rhythm	= dance
speech plain	= creative speech alone

b) elements used in combination:

of two (speech + rhythm)	= Arabic poetry
of three (speech + rhythm + harmony)	= *muwashshahas, zajals*

The first group (a) is included here, so it seems, not because Averroes considers them to be "poetic discourses" but rather to show their independence from each other at a more abstract level. This is the reason for not including, along with the dance, those cases of Arabic poetic compositions with only rhythm. They also use speech, but it is not creative and thus it does not belong in (a); but neither does it belong in (b), for the elements of mimetic art are used always in combination with mimetic, creative speech. Here Averroes refers to the "poetic discourses"; they are poems in verse form, but not to be considered poetic strictly speaking. In (a) Averroes, a little to our surprise, has also included "those creative discourses which do not use rhythm." Their mimetic quality rests in their creative use of only "the phonetic sound of speech" (*lafẓ*). They are not called "poetic compositions" but "creative discourses" and thus are classified on a higher degree of abstraction and have a more general validity. One might feel inclined, not without reason, to compare the other category of verse compositions often mentioned which lack creativity and mimetic quality with this "nameless art" of Averroes's in which both creativity and mimetic quality rest on the artistic use of speech only. For since they are called "discourses," their artistic quality cannot be attributed to mere speech sound without regard to their rational content. If such were the case, the qualities of those "creative discourses" would be essentially the same as rhythm or harmony and thus make Averroes's distinction lack a logical basis.

The second group, where Averroes categorizes the combined use of rhythm and harmony with mimetic speech, are the "poetic compositions" strictly speaking, which are the object under consideration in the preceding paragraph as a whole. Averroes offers about them some observations that have baffled scholars. The difficulties begin with the use Averroes makes of the word "harmony." He establishes two main categories: one that uses rhythm to enhance the effectivity of poetic speech; the other employs it in a similar way only adding harmony and thus uses all three elements of the mimetic arts of sound. The parallelism with the Aristotelian trilogy that we find here and on so many other occasions in Averroes's work makes it extremely difficult not to understand harmony, in this context also, in the usual way. But then we must face another problem. In the first category Averroes has included Arabic poetry in which, he explicitly affirms, harmony is lacking; in the second, the poetic discourses called *muwashshaha* and *zajal* invented by the people of al-Andalus in which the use of harmony (*laḥn*) is a distinctive characteristic.

F. Gabrieli[20] has tried to solve the problem of "Arabic poetry lacking harmony" by taking refuge in the other possible translation of the Arabic *laḥn,* namely, "incorrect, colloquial, dialectical pronunciation of Arabic"; this, and not harmony, is lacking in Arabic poetry using the classical language. It is, one feels, a desperate solution that creates more problems than it solves. In the first place, it makes the entire logic in Averroes's line of thought collapse by arbitrarily changing the use of the word *laḥn* in only this place. Secondly, it gives Averroes's statement an illogical twist unworthy of a philosopher, since the fact that these compositions were not in classical Arabic is also mentioned, though only *en pasant,* because the language used is not an essential

20 F. Gabrieli, "Estetica e poesia araba nell' interpretazione della poetica aristotelica presso Avicenna e Avèrroe" *Rivista degli Studi Orientali* (XII) 1929, p. 305.

characteristic of poetry, mimesis, or creativity in general.[21] An alternative which we must accept for lack of more evidence is that Averroes considers Arabic poetry or poetic compositions mainly as a literary art to be read and declaimed, but lacking the harmony which would have made them fit to be sung. *Muwashshahas* and *zajals,* the compositions invented in their language by the people of "this Island" were in Averroes's time largely considered an oral art, perhaps more in the line of popular songs orally transmitted than a formal literary art.

In Averroes's reference to "natural" or "primitive" peoples and things one feels inclined to see a reference to the development of artistic achievements he will refer to only some pages later. It is a suggestive thought that, if for Averroes the union of various mimetic elements is due to the "naturalness" of the "primitivism" of certain compositions, perhaps also the opposite could be true, namely that a greater abstraction in the mimetic art would be the result of a greater literary advancement. Thus Arabic poetry would represent still a midway toward the creative stylization only hinted at by Averroes in his nameless art of "creative discourses which do not use rhythm."

In the light of the preceding observations the conclusion seems warranted that while *muḥāka* is a proper rendition of the Greek concept of mimesis, *takhyīl* is for Averroes the very ability to transform an object in order to meet the requirements of creative art. It is in fact closer to the Aristotelian "poiesis" in its higher degree of abstraction and in poetry its ultimate and most essential quality. And although creative art as applied to speech and more concretely to poetry will normally be reduced to a skillful use of images and figures of speech, Averroes's definition of poetic discourse achieves a greatness difficult to overlook: "Poetic discourses are creative discourses" (p. 2, l. 1).

[21] Nevertheless the mention that both of such compositions, *muwashshahas* and *zajals* were invented "in their language by the people of this Island," whether 'this language' should be understood as the colloquial Hispano-Arabic or the current form of Andalusian Romance, offers another problem so far disregarded: namely that the basic distinction between the *muwashshaha* and the *zajal* cannot have been originally, as it is usually claimed, the different Arabic language used in them, classical in the *muwashshaha,* colloquial in the *zajal.* For a complete bibliography, to date, on this topic see Klaus Heger, "Die bisher veröffentlichten Ḫargăs und ihre Deutungen" *Beihefte z. Zeitschrift f. Rom. Phil.* (101) Tübingen, 1960. It was reviewed by E. García Gomez, *Al-Andalus* (XXVI) 1961, p. 453-65.

Pan-Arabism and the Failure of Israeli-Jordanian Peace Negotiations, 1950

C. ERNEST DAWN

Since the formation of the League of Arab States in 1945, Arab governments have unanimously agreed that the Arabism of Palestine is a vital element of the Pan-Arabism which they have bound themselves to bring to fruition. Such unanimity regarding ideals has not prevented sharp differences of opinion about their correct application. Arab governments, like the members of other communities, have been inclined to interpret the advancement of their own special interests as being the pursuit of the community's noblest goals. This tendency has shaped the Arab approach to the Palestine question quite as much as it has the disposition of other Arab national problems. The most widely publicized instance of a particularistic approach to the Palestine problem is the effort made by King ^{c}Abdullāh of Jordan in 1949-50. Israeli and Jordanian negotiators reached agreement on a draft treaty, but the treaty was not submitted to the Jordanian government and was soon abandoned. Jordan then joined the other Arab League states in a denunciation and renunciation of a separate peace with Israel.

Despite the significance of the fruitless Jordanian-Israeli peace talks, the entire episode has been brushed aside with contradictory simplistic explanations. To some, King ^{c}Abdullāh was the only reasonable, or realistic, Arab statesman, and his wise efforts were frustrated by the blind extremism of the Arabs generally. To others, he was a self-seeking traitor to Arab nationalism. The opposing views are in implicit agreement on a vital point. Both assume that ^{c}Abdullāh, in the one case good or wise, in the other evil, received his death-blow from Arab nationalism, in the one case bad, in the other good, in both cases an assumed self-evident entity with a vitality, a goal, and a direction of its own. Both explanations fail to raise some serious questions: why did so astute a politician as ᶜAbdullāh go as far as he did in departing from the Arab consensus, and, then, how was the King compelled to renounce a special interest so obviously dear to him in favor of an opposing national ideal?

As 1950 began, the Arab League governments were one in proclaiming their unshakeable devotion to the Arabism of Palestine. Efforts by agents of the United Nations to lead the Arab states into direct peace negotiations with Israel resulted in Arab reaffirmation of their refusal to enter direct talks. At the same time, the Arab League Permanent Committee on Palestine unanimously agreed to the strengthening of the boycott and other anti-Israeli measures.[1]

Proclamations of unity before the Israeli danger did not prevent each Arab government from following its own course. Each government had its own objectives, and each freely interpreted the public agreement in a way which permitted it to advance its own cause. Jordan and Egypt, which had the greatest immediate interest in Palestine, were the two most active Arab states in the quest for a settlement. Furthermore, they were acting in concert, not alone.

King ᶜAbdullāh of Jordan and his government frankly and outspokenly admitted their special aims in Palestine. King and government, departing from the Arab League agreement, denounced the United Nations General Assembly's resolution in favor of the internationalization of Jerusalem. Jordan's intention of incorporating Jordan-occupied Palestine in the Hashimite Kingdom was manifested in the grant of Jordanian citizenship to the Palestinians and in the assignment to them of half the seats in the new parliament which was to be elected in April.[2] Covertly, the King had gone even further. He had initiated secret peace talks with Israel in November, 1949. ᶜAbdullāh had four demands: (1) a corridor through Beersheba and Gaza to the Mediterranean; (2) return of the Arab quarters of Jerusalem; (3) Jordanian possession of the Jerusalem-Bethlehem road; and (4) free port privileges in Haifa. In return, he offered Israel a free port at

[1] *Al-Ahrām* (Cairo), Jan. 17, 18, 19, 21, 22, 30, 31, Feb. 1, 6, 1950; *Bayrūt* (Beirut), Jan. 31, Feb. 4, 1950.

[2] *Alif-Bā'* (Damascus), Dec. 9, 17, 1949; *Bayrūt,* Jan. 1, 1950; *Oriente Moderno,* XXX (1950), 32.

Aqaba and access to the potash-works on the north shore of the Dead Sea. By December, the negotiations were deadlocked. Israel refused to grant the corridor to Gaza. Then, the United Nations decision in favor of internationalization stimulated the two sides to take a new approach. The negotiations concentrated on a limited solution for Jerusalem. Meanwhile, more general questions continued to be discussed.[3]

Egypt, ostensibly, was a zealous warrior for the Arabism of Palestine. The speech from the throne, delivered on January 16, reaffirmed the "determination of the Arabs . . . and their faith in Arab Palestine and in the necessity to lift the tyranny from it." The general principles were stated more explicitly by the Egyptian representative at the United Nations Conciliation Commission for Palestine, ᶜAbd al-Munᶜim Muṣṭafa, who, in his first interview, said,

> In respect to territorial questions, Egypt continues to hold fast to the necessity of preserving the Arab character of Palestine, which forms a part of the Arab world, provided that all ethnic and religious minorities are guaranteed the legal status which other minorities in the Arab world enjoy.
>
> There is no doubt that the creation of a foreign state in Palestine, in spite of the strong opposition of the majority of the population, the owners of the land, is contrary to the rights of the population to live in peace in their land.

A few days later, the Egyptian foreign minister denied the possibility of direct talks with Israel and reiterated Egypt's intention of working in the Conciliation Commission in order to bring about Israeli withdrawal to the Partition Resolution frontiers and for "the rapid return of the Palestine refugees to their fatherland under the guarantee of life and property."[4]

Despite declamations of undying loyalty to the Arabism of Palestine, the Egyptian government was at work on behalf of a settlement with Israel. In Geneva, Egypt's representative with the Palestine Conciliation Commission, ᶜAbd al-Munᶜim Muṣṭafa, explained his government's policy to a Zionist journalist:

[3] James G. McDonald, *My Mission in Israel, 1948-1951* (New York: Simon and Schuster, 1951), p. 212; *Alif-Bā'*, Nov. 30, Dec. 6, 15, 21, 22, 1949; *Bayrūt*, Jan. 11, 1950; *The New York Times*, Oct. 31, Nov. 1, 6, 16, 27, 29, 30, Dec. 5, 22, 27, 1949, Jan. 1, 5, 6, 1950.

[4] *Al-Ahrām*, Jan. 17, 26, 29, 1950.

> . . . The time was not yet ripe for peace with Israel, with all the trappings of peace. Commerce, the diplomatic niceties, and travel could wait until Arab memories of the war in Palestine had faded and unsettled Arab refugees were a less evident and vivid reminder than at present.
>
> But Israel and Egypt need not fear for their future peace. He considered the first two clauses of the Israel-Egyptian armistice agreement as a *de facto* non-aggression pact between the two countries. Egypt would abide by it.

Muṣṭafa, getting down to specifics, related the Jordanian negotiations to Egypt's objectives. ". . . Egypt's view," he said, ". . . is that Jordan has specific interests in making peace with Israel. That is her affair. Egypt will not intervene, but will pursue her own national interest in the matter."[5]

The juxtaposition of Egypt's national interest and an Israeli-Jordanian peace treaty was calculated. As the Egyptians saw the situation, Jordanian success in the secret negotiations with Israel would be advantageous to Egypt. Unlike the Jordanians, the Egyptians had little desire for Palestinian territory, but the fate of the territorial corridor from Hebron across the Negeb to al-Majdal on the Mediterranean north of Gaza, which Jordan was seeking, was of the utmost concern to Egypt. In the first place, the repatriation of Arab refugees from this region would virtually liquidate Egypt's involvement in the refugee problem. Secondly, and more importantly, the territory in question was crucial in the Egyptian government's approach to its greatest problem and principal concern, the presence of British troops in Egypt. The British had been willing, when the Bevin-Ṣidqi treaty was negotiated in 1946, to evacuate Egypt provided an alternate base were available in southern Palestine. The Wafdist government, like its predecessors in 1949, adopted this plan as a means of persuading the British to withdraw and sign a new treaty. For this purpose, at least a part of the Negeb must be transferred from Israeli to Arab hands, either Egyptian or Jordanian.[6] From the Egyptian point of view, transfer of the region

[5] Jon Kimche in *The Jewish Chronicle* (London), Feb. 3, 1950; cf. Rony E. Gabbay, *A Political Study of the Arab-Jewish Conflict: The Arab Refugee Problem (a Case Study)*, Études d'Histoire Économique, Politique et Sociale, Vol. XXIX (Geneva: E. Proz and Paris: Minard, 1959), p. 319.

[6] *Alif-Bā'*, May 29, 1949; *al-Ahrām*, June 12, 1949, May 7, 1950; Egypt, Ministry of Foreign Affairs, *Records of Conversations, Notes and Papers exchanged*

along with Gaza to Jordan had potential advantages, for then the British base could be located in Jordanian, not Egyptian, territory.

King ᶜAbdullāh, in his secret negotiations with Israel, gave due attention to the Egyptian interest. Jordan won satisfaction of its own interests when Israel offered a compromise concerning Jerusalem and port rights at Haifa, but concern for the Egyptian reaction gave ᶜAbdullāh pause. He rejected a limited agreement and, deferring to Egypt, insisted on the cession of the corridor from Hebron to al-Majdal.[7]

The Wafdist government in Egypt had begun an approach to Israel that relied on an Israeli-Jordanian treaty to provide a means of liquidating Egypt's involvement in Palestine and an escape from the dilemma of the Anglo-Egyptian Treaty. The plan required Israel to make an important territorial cession to Jordan. Egypt did not offer Israel a high price, but the Egyptians did jingle some hard currency. Egypt, rejecting a formal peace treaty, officially reaffirmed the general Arab denial of Israel's legality. On the other hand, the Egyptians made it clear that they would not oppose an Israeli-Jordanian treaty if Egypt's national interest were satisfied. In the total context, an Egyptian-blessed Israeli-Jordanian treaty might have constituted the first stage on the way to a general Arab-Israeli peace settlement. Even if the Egyptian government would not acknowledge the legal existence of Israel, the Egyptian government could strongly influence Arab opinion in such a way as either to intensify or to reduce Arab opposition to Israel. In January-February, 1950, the Egyptian government worked, generally, to restrain Arab activism.

The Egyptian government gave clear notice to the Egyptian and Arab political classes that their expectations regarding Palestine should not be too high. War was excluded. In early January, the press speculated that the alleged approaching expiration of the Mixed Armistice Agreement would permit Egypt to resume military operations. The foreign office issued a statement which said the Agreement "will remain in force until a final peaceful settlement of the Palestine question is reached." Government spokesmen also warned that Egypt must limit its obligations to and expenditures on Palestine. The foreign office's

between the Royal Egyptian Government and the United Kingdom Government (March 1950-November 1950) (Cairo, 1951), pp. 14, 37, 38, 40; cf. Gabbay, p. 318, n. 20.

[7] *The New York Times,* Dec. 4, 22, 1949, June 18, 1950.

statement was accompanied by a commentary, which, it was strongly hinted, came from a high diplomatic official: "It is not possible that the Palestine question remain hanging without end in the face of the intangibles and the unpredictable elements which surround it, and the anxiety and lack of stability which engulf it. There is no doubt that for our welfare and for the welfare of others, we should end at the first opportunity the Palestine difficulty, so that Egypt can then direct its concern and attention to other internal and foreign matters."[8] The same two cardinal points, the renunciation of military means and the primacy of Egyptian interests, were expounded to the public during the conference of Egyptian diplomatic representatives in the Arab states which met in Cairo during the first half of February. The Egyptians were fearful of Israel and slightly bitter at the other Arab countries. Egypt, official opinion ran, was more exposed to the Israeli threat than was any other Arab state. The economic boycott was potentially a most effective weapon, but Egypt bore the burden alone. Egypt, accordingly, could not make peace with Israel, but the truce should continue. Egypt should continue to strengthen its army. But Egypt's Arab policy was not the totality of Egypt's policy. Egypt had other interests and its Arab policy should be one of "sincere Egyptianism."[9]

The Palestine question was treated calmly by the responsible Egyptian press. Throughout January and February, Israeli officials, charging the Arabs and especially Egypt with preparing for a "second round," denounced the British provision of materiel to the Arabs. The campaign was enlarged in the United States by Zionist organizations, members of Congress, and labor and political organizations. The responsible Egyptian press did not devote any excessive attention to the matter. Editorials echoed the official line that although Egypt had no intention of making war on Israel, the Zionist danger and Egypt's general strategic position required a great increase in Egypt's armed forces.[10]

In similar fashion, Jordan's negotiations with Israel were treated kindly by official Egypt. The government was silent. The responsible press ignored them. At the beginning of February, the responsible press

[8] *Al-Ahrām,* Jan. 9, 10, 1950; cf. *The New York Times,* Jan. 10, 1950.

[9] *Al-Ahrām,* Jan. 23, Feb. 7, 14, 17, 18, 1950.

[10] *The New York Times,* Jan. 16, 23, 26, 27, 29, 30, Feb. 3, 4, 11, 14, 19, 21, 1950; *Al-Ahrām,* Jan. 16, 27, 28, 29, 31, Feb. 3, 7, 10, 16, 22, 1950.

published reports that Jordan had concluded an agreement with Israel which contained a Jordanian abandonment of the corridor to Gaza, but the Jordanian denial was also published and there was no hostile comment.[11] The attacks on King ᶜAbdullāh and General Glubb which were made by the recent Jordanian expatriate, Colonel ᶜAbdullāh al-Tall, occasioned only straightforward reporting.[12]

Even though every Arab government was on record as opposing direct negotiations and as denying, or at least as refusing to acknowledge, the legal existence of Israel, Jordan, with Egypt's tacit consent, conducted secret negotiations with Israel. The two states were not alone in their subordination of Pan-Arab ideals to their special interests. Although the world and the Arab presses reported on the secret peace talks, no Arab government took any note of them. Syrian and Iraqi statesmen, to be sure, lived up to their reputations by declaiming often and angrily about Israel,[13] but none made even an oblique reference to Jordan's violation of the Arab consensus. Each, like Jordan and Egypt, was pursuing its own national interest.

The achievement of Jordan's aims was consistent with the general policies of the other Arab states. Lebanon, having no aspirations in Palestine, above all wished a peaceful settlement of the question and the maintenance of the status quo within the Arab League. Iraq, without any direct territorial ambitions in Palestine, was concerned mainly with furthering its ambition to lead the Arabs. The dynastic connection with Jordan precluded any use of King ᶜAbdullāh's activities for propaganda purposes. Saudi Arabia, always the most cautious Arab state in Palestinian matters, and intimately associated with Egypt in Arab policy, was hardly likely to object to an Egyptian policy. The Saudis could have been moved to action only if they had believed it necessary to thwart Hashimite influence in Syria. Saudi-Egyptian cooperation was especially important, for acting together, the two governments exercised a dominant influence in Syria.

In remaining silent, the Syrians were subordinating a special interest as well as the Pan-Arab ideal. Syria, like Jordan, had territorial in-

[11] *Al-Ahrām,* Feb. 3, 6, 7, 1950; although the press services had circulated reports concerning the talks in January, *al-Ahrām* did not publish them.

[12] *Al-Ahrām,* Jan. 24, 28, Feb. 9, 10, 1950.

[13] *Alif-Bā',* Dec. 11, 1949; *al-Ahrām,* Jan. 18, 19, 22, 23, 27, 30, 31, Feb. 7, 9, 10, 11, 15, 22, 23, 1950; *Bayrūt,* Jan. 31, Feb. 1, 8, 9, 10, 12, 22, 24, 1950.

terests in Palestine. Indeed, the Syrian government renewed its demand for the acquisition of Western Galilee.[14] The prospect of Jordanian success while Syria remained empty-handed could not have been contemplated calmly in Damascus, but the Syrian government had more serious concerns. The regime was in dire need of Egypto-Saudi support.

Throughout 1949, Syria had been in the grip of a ferocious struggle for power. In December, Colonel Adīb al-Shīshakli displaced a government which had looked to Iraq for support. The new regime, needing external aid against its Syrian enemies, turned immediately and successfully to Egypt and Saudi Arabia for moral, military, and economic assistance.[15] The Syrian regime, dependent on Egypt and Saudi Arabia for survival, could not object to the Jordanian and Egyptian approaches to the Palestine question. Finally, the pressures on Syria, Egypt, and Saudi Arabia to adopt a militant stance were greatly reduced when, on January 25, an Iraqi cabinet delegation and the Egyptian government signed an agreement which contained a five-year renunciation of Syro-Iraqi union.[16]

The tacit consensus of the Arab League governments, under which they ignored Jordan's peace talks with Israel, was challenged at the beginning of March. King ᶜAbdullāh decided to settle for half a loaf. By late February, Jordan and Israel had initialed a draft five-year nonaggression pact. The armistice lines would remain as they were until a final peace settlement was reached. The frontiers were to be open to trade and travel. Jordan was to have a free zone in Haifa. The draft treaty, or a separate supplementary agreement, included some modifications of the General Armistice Agreement concerning Jerusalem, Bethlehem, and Latroun.[17]

The Israeli-Jordanian peace negotiations, which for two months had been ignored by the Arab governments and slighted by the Arab press, were thrust into the political arena. For some reason, news of the treaty reached the press in Israel. On February 28, the international

[14] *Al-Ahrām,* Feb. 8, 1950.

[15] *Bayrūt,* Jan. 3, 7, 10, 11, 13, 15, 17, 22, 25, Feb. 1, 7, 9, 12, 14, 20, 1950.

[16] *Bayrūt,* Jan. 22, 24, 1950; *al-Ahrām,* Jan. 23, Feb. 4, 10, 1950.

[17] McDonald, pp. 212-213; Jon Kimche, *Seven Fallen Pillars,* rev. ed. (London: Secker and Warburg, 1953), p. 328; Walter Eytan, *The First Ten Years: A Diplomatic History of Israel* (London: Weidenfeld and Nicolson, 1958), p. 41; *al-Ahrām,* Feb. 3, 6, 1950; *The New York Times,* Mar. 1, 2, 1950.

news agencies circulated dispatches from Israel which quoted "a highly placed Israeli source." The revelations may have been counter to the wishes of both governments, which immediately issued clarifications. On March 1, Prime Minister Tawfīq Abu al-Huda stated that Jordan had been negotiating an amendment to the General Armistice Agreement only, not a peace treaty. In Israel, the government gave a similar explanation and denied that the cabinet had held a secret meeting to consider the draft treaty. Nevertheless, press dispatches repeated with more detail the reports of the first day.[18]

Jordanian politics provided an occasion, doubtless unneeded, to keep the peace talks in the world and Arab presses. On March 2, Prime Minister Abu al-Huda resigned with a reiteration of his opposition to a peace treaty. King ᶜAbdullāh charged Samīr al-Rifāᶜi with forming a new cabinet. Despite the continued denials of the Israeli and Jordanian governments, all press agencies in Amman and Tel Aviv, citing informed sources, insisted that a draft peace treaty was under discussion. According to the press, Rifāᶜi, who favored the treaty, would resume the talks after forming a cabinet. When the premier-designate failed and withdrew on March 4, Abu al-Huda's government continued in office.[19]

International press dispatches from Israel reporting a peace treaty between Israel and Jordan could not have been ignored by Arab newspapers under any circumstances. As it happened, when the reports appeared, the Arab political classes had just been given an independent cause for focusing their attention on Israel. On February 27, Washington and London revealed that they were considering Israeli requests for materiel and that the United States had already sold Israel a small quantity of arms. The announcement, coming just when the continuation of the long Zionist campaign against Egypt in the United States had caused some Egyptian popular concern, raised temperatures sharply. *Al-Ahrām*'s headlines shouted that the United States was supplying Israel with weapons. The paper then initiated a series of articles about the Israeli danger.[20]

[18] *The New York Times,* Mar. 1, 2, 1950; *Bayrūt,* Mar. 2, 1950; *al-Ahrām,* Mar. 1, 2, 3, 1950.

[19] *Al-Ahrām,* Mar. 4, 5, 1950; *Bayrūt,* Mar. 3, 4, 6, 1950; *The New York Times,* Mar. 4, 6, 1950; *The Times* (London), Mar. 4, 1950.

[20] *The New York Times,* Feb. 27, 28, 1950; *al-Ahrām,* Feb. 26, 27, 28, Mar. 1, 2, 4, 8, 1950.

Already seized by concern with Israel's quest for arms and the Zionist campaign against Egypt in the United States, the Arab press from the start was eager for details of the Israeli-Jordanian negotiations. Nor was the Arab press to be thrown off the trail by the disclaimers of Israel and Jordan. After Abu al-Huda resumed the premiership, even the responsible Egyptian press kept the subject before the public. *Al-Ahrām* continued to give the leading position to dispatches from Damascus, London, and Ankara well after news agency reports from Amman, Jerusalem, and Tel Aviv had ceased. These reports rehashed the original description of the peace treaty, on occasion improving on the terms for Israel, and insisted that negotiations were still taking place. The French News Agency cited some Turkish students as authority.[21]

The public storm over the Jordan-Israeli peace negotiations soon ran its course. On March 8, the Israeli foreign minister stated that negotiations with Jordan were not complete. On the following day, Jordan delivered identic notes to the Arab governments. Jordan, the note declared, was seeking only to modify the Armistice Agreement and had no intention of concluding a peace treaty. The responsible Egyptian press reluctantly accepted the explanation. *Al-Ahrām* buried the Israeli and Jordanian statements but ceased to publish speculation about Israeli-Jordanian negotiations.[22]

Arab public opinion was outraged by Jordan's negotiations with Israel. Nevertheless, such public unanimity did not destroy the governmental consensus. Most Arab governments, notably the Egyptian, ignored the tumult. Syria, however, did withdraw from the League consensus. In taking this action, the Syrian government was moved by its own particular interest quite as much as by concern with Arab national sentiment. In January-February, the Syrian government followed the Egyptian lead because of the Shīshakli regime's need for Egypto-Saudi support and because of the Iraqi-Egyptian agreement regarding Syria. When the Israeli-Jordanian agreement became public knowledge, the situation had changed.

Iraq rejected the Iraqi-Egyptian agreement of January 25 regarding

[21] *Al-Ahrām,* Mar. 5, 6, 7, 8, 1950 (only one of these is a regular news agency dispatch from Tel Aviv; cf. *Bayrūt,* Mar. 8, 1950, the only report in this newspaper for the period).

[22] Mar. 8, 9, 10, 11, 12, 1950.

Syria. When the Iraqi cabinet delegation returned to Baghdad, the agreement was assailed by all factions. The cabinet resigned on February 1. Then, in late February, the Iraqis mounted a full-scale campaign. The new prime minister, Tawfīq al-Suwaydi, in speeches to Parliament on February 16 and 25, defended the union of Iraq and Syria. On February 24, Nūri al-Saᶜīd, who was returning from London, held a press conference in Cairo. He gave the gist of a statement which he delivered in detail and with fervor in Baghdad on March 6. He urged Syro-Iraqi union, on general principles and with the added ground that only Syria was threatened by Israel. Iraq, he said, would maintain the blockade against Israel. He closed by exhorting the Arabs to arm and unite for the coming campaign against Israel which would then result in an Arab victory.[23]

The resumption of Iraqi expansionism coincided with a great increase in political instability in Syria. By early March, a faction of the People's Party, the major single political group in Syria, had begun to challenge the military regime. On March 12, a Populist minister resigned and the Damascus newspapers began a strike in protest of the government's press policy.[24] Although the dissident Populists did not use the question of federation with Iraq, the party had been identified with the project throughout 1949. Moreover, Populist defection weakened the government and gave others the opportunity to seek power as the agents of union with the Hashimites. A Damascene friend of Jordan was the first to announce, on March 6, that Prime Minister Abu al-Huda had assured him that Jordan was not negotiating a peace treaty with Israel.[25] Some of the major independent deputies from Damascus and Hama had already, on February 12, attacked the Egypto-Saudi orientation as having fastened military dictatorship on Syria. On March 15, in another attack on military rule, they asked questions about the Shīshakli coup which by their very nature raised the issue of federation with Iraq. On March 20, many members of the Constituent Assembly joined in an impassioned denunciation of the past policies and leaders of the Arab League for having lost Palestine.

[23] *Al-Ahrām,* Jan. 27, 29, 30, Feb. 1, 2, 3, 4, 5, 6, 17, 24, 26, Mar. 8, 1950; *Bayrūt,* Jan. 28, 29, Feb. 1, 2, 3, 6, 25, 26, Mar. 8, 1950; *Oriente Moderno,* XXX (1950), 34.

[24] *Al-Ahrām,* Feb. 6, Mar. 4, 14, 1950; *Bayrūt,* Mar. 14, 1950.

[25] *Bayrūt,* Mar. 8, 1950.

The speakers all urged immediate and complete federation of the Arab states.[26] All who heard or read the speeches knew that only Iraq and Jordan were willing to enter a complete federation with any other countries.

The Syrian regime responded in kind. Since the Populist leaders realized that the Army was in control, the cabinet survived the attack.[27] Nevertheless, Prime Minister Khalid al-ᶜAẓm, as he told the Lebanese prime minister and president, was frightened by the strength of the political opposition and deeply worried by the strong undercurrent in favor of Syro-Iraqi federation.[28] Hashimite Iraq and its Syrian allies could be attacked through Hashimite Jordan. On March 6, ᶜAẓm stated that an Israeli-Jordanian peace treaty would endanger all the Arab states, but Syria above all others. He declared that his government was considering closing the Jordanian frontier if Jordan signed the treaty. The Syrian government attacked the whole concept of peace with Israel. A minister denounced the United Nations economic mission (the Clapp Mission), which was investigating ways of resettling the refugees. At the Trusteeship Council in Geneva, the Syrian representative vied with the Iraqi in warning of Israeli aggressiveness.[29]

Neither the public outcry nor the Syrian government's attack had any effect on the Arab League consensus. The furor was entirely a popular one. Most Arab governments ignored it. The Egyptian government maintained a remarkable silence concerning Palestine. When the tumult broke over the Israeli request for arms, the only official statement in Cairo was one by Arab League Secretary-General ᶜAzzām, who railed out at Zionist aggressiveness.[30] Even more surprising was the Egyptian silence during the outcry over the Israeli-Jordanian peace talks. No official comment was expressed until March 11, and that was for American, not Egyptian or Arab, consumption. ᶜAzzām, in an interview with C. L. Sulzberger, said "that Amman denied that such talks were taking place. He added, however, that should such an

[26] *Bayrūt,* Feb. 12, Mar. 16, 22, 1950.

[27] *Al-Ahrām,* Mar. 15, 1950; *Bayrūt,* Mar. 15, 16, 21, 1950.

[28] Bishārah al-Khūri, *Haqā'iq lubnānīyah* [Lebanese realities], III (Beirut: Manshūrāt Awrāq Lubnānīyah, 1961), 288-289.

[29] *Al-Ahrām,* Mar. 7, 1950; *Bayrūt,* Mar. 7, 12, 17, 1950; *The Times* (London), Mar. 6, 1950.

[30] *Al-Ahrām,* Mar. 1, 1950; *Bayrūt,* Mar. 1, 1950.

accord materialize, 'it would violate' the compact among the seven states of the league."[31] The most significant pointer to the Egyptian attitude was the government's treatment of the Ḥusayni Palestinian organization. Despite the presumed popular appeal of Ḥājj Amīn al-Ḥusayni, who was busy denouncing Jordan, the Arab League did not invite the Gaza Government to attend the coming session of the Council. The subsequent protest of the Gaza Government was ignored.[32] The Egyptian government obviously had no quarrel with Jordan in the first two weeks of March, even in the face of the outcry in the press.

The Egyptian government, besides exercising restraint with reference to Israel and Jordan, even gave indications that it was willing to practice moderation in seeking a solution to the great question, the Anglo-Egyptian Treaty of 1936. ᶜAzzām in his interview with Sulzberger had passed quickly over the Israeli-Jordanian peace talks. He showed much greater concern with explaining Egypt's general foreign policy. The Arab states, the Secretary General said, favored the West and supported the democratic camp. He went on to say that, as an individual rather than as Secretary General, ". . . he would favor any regional Mediterranean self-defense pact, including not only Arab lands but peripheral European nations, 'because such would strengthen chances of peace by blocking aggression.' " A few days later, in Cyprus, Sulzberger wrote that he had been assured that Egypt would like to find a way of signing at least a de facto equivalent of peace with Israel and that Egypt was not deadly opposed to the British presence.[33]

ᶜAzzām's views had adherents within the Wafdist government. Although the Wafd, throughout its long exile from office, had promised immediate British withdrawal, some members of the government were advocating a policy of caution and postponement. Others, however, urged immediate negotiations with the British. The advocates of moderation put up a trial balloon. Dr. Ḥāmid Zaki, minister of state, in a statement to the press, said Bevin had expressed his willingness to negotiate "on the basis of realizing the national aspirations," but that the Labour government could not negotiate for some time, perhaps as

[31] *The New York Times,* Mar. 12, 1950; *al-Ahrām,* Mar. 14, 1950.

[32] *Al-Ahrām,* Feb. 26, Mar. 3, 7, 1950.

[33] *The New York Times,* Mar. 12, 17, 1950 (quotations); *al-Ahrām,* Mar. 14, 18, 1950.

long as three months. In the Egyptian minister's view, the British had greater need to negotiate than did Egypt, and a new treaty would be a material victory for Britain and a moral victory for Egypt. Egypt should not settle any outstanding problems, but wait until the British requested negotiations.[34]

A public statement by an Egyptian minister that Egypt could safely delay pressing the national cause on Great Britain was a most unlikely event. Such an occurrence was even more unusual in that it took place when the government was remarkably silent about the Israeli danger and the Jordan-Israeli peace talks which had dominated the Egyptian press for more than a week. The government's interest in the Palestine question to a great degree arose from its belief that Palestine might contribute to the solution of the larger question of the British presence. The government's serenity with respect to negotiations with Britain and the Palestine problem is understandable in the light of the government's belief that Egypt's claims in Palestine were being pressed with some likelihood of success.

The Egyptian leaders were placing their hopes in negotiations with Israel through United Nations intermediaries. The Wafdist government did not attempt to keep its activities a complete secret. Indeed, many at the time, and later, believed that Egypt and Israel were engaged in secret, direct peace talks. On February 9, the Egyptian minister of war and marine, Muṣṭafa Nuṣrat, held a press conference. He was asked what Egypt would do when the Israeli-Egyptian armistice agreement expired on February 26. The minister replied, "The armistice has no term." He added that Egyptian and Israeli delegations would meet in the presence of a United Nations representative about February 26. Nuṣrat continued, "The Jews have complaints and Egypt has complaints. If the dispute continues about them, then Egypt will resort to the United Nations General Assembly to settle them."[35]

There were no direct peace talks. In the flurry of press activity which Nuṣrat's statement excited, both the existence and the intention of such negotiations were denied by Muṣṭafa in Geneva, by Maḥmūd Fawzi at Lake Success, and by Foreign Minister Ṣalāḥ al-Dīn in

[34] *Al-Ahrām,* Mar. 8, 9, 13, 1950.

[35] *Al-Ahrām,* Feb. 10, 1950; *Bayrūt,* Feb. 12, 1950; *The Times,* Feb. 10, 1950; cf. Gabbay, pp. 318-319.

Cairo.[36] There were, however, negotiations. The Egyptian minister of war and marine had been referring to a meeting of the Israeli-Egyptian Mixed Armistice Committee which was to meet on February 24. At the same time, ᶜAbd al-Munᶜim Muṣṭafa was presenting the Egyptian view to the Conciliation Commission in Geneva.[37] Egypt had three proposals: (1) refugees who were inhabitants of the no-man's land north of Gaza were to be allowed to return to cultivate their lands; (2) refugees in Gaza who owned lands in the hinterland were to be allowed to return and cultivate them; and (3) refugees in Gaza from Beersheba were to be allowed, "provisionally and pending a final settlement," to reestablish themselves there.[38]

Egypt's indirect negotiations with Israel seemed promising. On February 22, the Israeli-Egyptian Mixed Armistice Committee agreed to divide the no-man's land of eighty square miles north of Gaza. On the following day, the Conciliation Commission in Geneva took action which was even more promising from the Egyptian point of view. The Commission proposed to Egypt and Israel the formation of a mixed committee to consider the totality of the Egyptian demands that the refugees in the Gaza Strip be provisionally returned to land occupied by Israel. In a reply to the Commission on February 28, Israel rejected the proposal on the ground that the Mixed Armistice Committee's decision of February 22 had settled the question. At the same time, Israel expressed its willingness to meet with the Egyptians to discuss "the conclusion of a peace settlement . . . or any interim measure leading to such a settlement." Whether or not the Egyptians were immediately informed of Israel's reply is unknown. If the Egyptians were informed, their disappointment was dissipated by the Commission's attitude. On March 2, the Commission informed Israel that the agreement of February 22 had settled only a part of the problem. The Commission believed that the mixed committee should be formed to discuss the entire problem.[39] Egypt, seemingly, was receiving support from a United Nations agency.

[36] *Al-Ahrām,* Feb. 11, 14, 16, 1950; *The New York Times,* Feb. 11, 1950.

[37] *Al-Ahrām,* Feb. 14, 1950.

[38] United Nations Conciliation Commission for Palestine, 6th progress report, in General Assembly, *Official Records,* 5th sess., annexes, I, agenda item 20, pp. 13, 15-16.

[39] *The New York Times,* Feb. 25, 1950; Conciliation Commission for Palestine, 6th progress report, loc. cit., pp. 13, 15-16.

As long as the Wafdist government believed that chances were good for realizing Egypt's objectives in Palestine through United Nations agencies, it ignored both popular opinion and the Syrian government's outrage at Jordan's negotiations with Israel. The government's attitude doubtless was effective in dampening the furor in the Egyptian press. The crisis had scarcely passed, however, when it became clear that the Wafdist government had been too optimistic.

By the end of the second week of March, the ground for Egypt's hopes had crumbled. Israel did not reply immediately to the Conciliation Commission's letter of March 2. As the wait continued, an Arab reporter in Geneva wrote that the Commission was "immersed in a deep sleep." His dispatch was published under the lead, "The Palestine problem will not be solved in Geneva."[40] Doubt became certainty. On March 13, Israel finally replied to the Conciliation Commission with a brief letter which did nothing beyond acknowledge receipt of the Commission's letter of March 2.[41] Israel's negative attitude undoubtedly now became known to the Egyptians, for, at about this time, on or before March 13, the Commission began to discuss a new proposal, which would have been unnecessary if Israel had agreed to the Commission's proposal of February 23. The Commission's plan was to form several mixed committees on the model of the proposed Israeli-Egyptian committee. The Commission was considering sending a mission to Israel and the Arab countries in order to obtain approval of the procedure. The Egyptians obviously now knew that Israel was unwilling to discuss the Egyptian proposal regarding Gaza and the Negeb.[42] By March 21, Cairo Arab circles had been informed that the Commission had only complete failure to show for its efforts and that Israel was insisting that the armistice lines were the frontiers of Israel.[43]

[40] *Al-Ahrām,* Mar. 7, 1950.

[41] Conciliation Commission for Palestine, 6th progress report, loc. cit., p. 16.

[42] *The New York Times,* Mar. 14, 1950; *al-Ahrām,* Mar. 15, 18, 22, 1950; for a general exposition of the proposal, see Pablo de Azcárte, *Mission in Palestine, 1948-1952* (Washington, D.C.: The Middle East Institute, 1966), pp. 159-160. The contemporary press reports do not refer to Israel's rejection of the Conciliation Commission's proposal of February 23, which remained confidential, but the Commission may have immediately informed Egypt, since at some time before Mar. 23, the Commission held "numerous preliminary exchanges of views" with the Egyptian delegation about the proposal, presumably including the Israeli response; U.N. Conciliation Commission for Palestine, 6th progress report, loc. cit., p. 13.

[43] *Al-Ahrām,* Mar. 22, 1950.

With the disappointment of Egyptian hopes in the Conciliation Commission and the reappearance of the specter of Syro-Iraqi federation, Egypt could no longer ignore Jordan and Israel. Consequently, in the third week of March, there was a marked change in Egyptian behavior. The responsible press and the government now joined in a campaign against Jordan and Israel.

Al-Ahrām's treatment of Israeli armament and of Israeli-Jordanian peace negotiations in the first week of March had been a bit excited, but it had been occasioned by hard news of important events, including an Israeli-Zionist propaganda campaign against Egypt, and it contained a high percentage of international news agency dispatches. The new campaign was of a different order. Two editorializing reports on Israeli wickedness and evil intentions which were published on March 13-14 possibly were occasioned by nothing more than bonafide press reports of genuine, but hardly momentous, events. The deluge that followed was something else. From March 17 on, hardly a day passed without fulminations about the Israeli danger occupying the feature position of the front page. Most of these essays quoted Arab circles in Cairo or *al-Ahrām*'s own correspondent in London or New York.[44]

Jordan was the victim of a similar attack. A genuine occasion perhaps was provided by news agency dispatches from Amman and Beirut which apparently had been stimulated by a ceremonial visit of the King and Rifāʿi to a British warship at Aqaba. Whether or not these dispatches were, as they could have been, inspired by Egyptian diplomatic officials, the Egyptian press distinguished itself in the amount of emphasis given them.[45] From March 17 on, Jordan was the object of an obvious press campaign. *Al-Ahrām* filled its front pages with reports of the peace treaty, most of them from its own representative in Beirut, some from its representative in Jordan, some quoting Cairo sources, along with an occasional agency dispatch, which, if genuine, had probably been stimulated by the attention given to the subject by the Egyptian press.[46] The campaign climaxed on March 31, when

[44] *Al-Ahrām,* Mar. 13, 14, 17, 18, 19, 20, 21, 22, 24, 25, 26, 27, 1950.

[45] *Al-Ahrām,* Mar. 13, 14, 15, 1950; *Bayrūt,* Mar. 15, 1950; *The New York Times,* Mar. 15, 1950.

[46] *Al-Ahrām,* Mar. 17, 18, 19, 22, 24, 25, 1950. Cf. *The New York Times,* Mar. 25, 1950, and *Bayrūt,* Mar. 22, 23, 1950 (one of which is a Cairo dispatch).

al-Ahrām, summarizing Arab opinion in Cairo, called Jordan "Israel's hope for weakening Arab strength."

The Egyptian government broke its long silence on Palestine. On March 17, Foreign Minister Ṣalāḥ al-Dīn held a press conference. The benevolence toward an Israeli-Jordanian peace which ᶜAbd al-Munᶜim Muṣṭafa had expressed at the end of January was gone. The Foreign Minister said that although Jordan had denied the existence of peace talks, other information indicated that there were such talks whose results would be revealed after the Jordanian elections. He also said, ". . . All Arab states certainly have agreed on the Arabism of Palestine, and any measure contrary to this will be in violation of the Arab League's unanimous belief." After giving assurance that Egypt would never violate the permanent truce with Israel, he denounced Zionist propaganda about Egypt's armament program as a cover for Israel's aggressive intentions. Egypt's foreign minister then rejected any thought of negotiating with Israel. Egypt, he said, would not go beyond working through the Trusteeship Council and the Palestine Conciliation Commission for the sake of the internationalization of Jerusalem and the return of the refugees. He concluded with a reaffirmation of Israel's illegality. The Jerusalem and refugee questions, he said, ". . . do not comprise the whole of the Palestine question. Egypt's policy with reference to Palestine in general is clear. . . . Egypt clings to the Arabism of Palestine."[47]

Egypt commenced to put other weapons in readiness. Arab League officials, so the Cairo press said, began to talk about documents which Colonel ᶜAbdullāh al-Tall was prepared to present to the League Council. These documents proved that King ᶜAbdullāh had maintained secret contact with the Israelis during the Palestine War.[48] On March 20, Ḥājj Amīn al-Ḥusayni, whose claims and protests had hitherto been ignored by the Wafdist government, was received by Prime Minister Naḥḥās, who, it was reported, agreed that Ḥusayni should represent Palestine in the approaching session of the League Council.[49] The Egyptian attack on Jordan and Israel, Egypt's sudden public reaffirmation of a policy of eternal opposition to Israel, grew out of Egypt's bitterness at an Israeli-Jordanian settlement which enabled

[47] *Al-Ahrām,* Mar. 18, 1950.

[48] *Al-Ahrām,* Mar. 19, 1950; *The New York Times,* Mar. 20, 21, 1950.

[49] *Al-Ahrām,* Mar. 21, 1950.

Israel to ignore Egypt's claims. The bitterness was compounded by the concurrent revival of Iraqi prospects in Syria. Egypt's requirements in Palestine and Egypt's rivalry with Iraq were both connected with Egypt's chief problem, the Anglo-Egyptian Treaty. Now that the Egyptian government could no longer view either Palestine or Syria with serenity, it could no longer, as it had in the second week of March, entertain thoughts of leisurely waiting for Great Britain to reopen negotiations.

The Wafdist government undertook an emergency review of its relations with Britain. Prime Minister Naḥḥās was impelled to declare that Zaki's espousal of delay was not the opinion of the cabinet. The question was decided at a meeting of the prime minister, the foreign minister, the chief of the royal cabinet, and the ambassador to London. On March 21, the ambassador flew to London and delivered a note to Foreign Secretary Bevin. The Naḥḥās government was seeking instant satisfaction for the Egyptian political classes. The note declared, "... It would be futile to proceed with negotiations unless based on the immediate withdrawal of British Forces and the safeguarding of the unity of Egypt and the Sudan under the Egyptian Crown. . . ." In return, Egypt was willing to join the Western bloc:

> Should the British hasten to agree to the aforesaid basis, the Egyptian Government would welcome entering into talks with Great Britain with the object of arriving at an understanding over the measures to be taken for confronting the dangers that threaten international security and the independence of nations, and with a view to reaching a practical settlement which would ensure the complete independence of Egypt and The [*sic*] Sudan as one integral whole, and would, at the same time secure wholehearted collaboration in the combined efforts for repelling international communist danger.[50]

The Wafdist government did not receive encouragement in London. British opinion was that a long and difficult period of negotiation lay ahead. As the diplomatic correspondent of the *Times* wrote,

> ... There is no indication that a basis has yet been found for resumed negotiations. Nor is it possible to say yet that the questions at issue have become easier with the passage of time. Had the 1946 protocol

[50] Egypt, Ministry of Foreign Affairs, *Records . . . Mar. 1950-Nov. 1951*, pp. 3-4 (quotations); *al-Ahrām,* Mar. 22, 23, 24, 1950; *The Times* (London), Mar. 23, 1950.

> been confirmed all British troops would have been out of Egypt by September 1 of last year. In the interval the cold war has sharpened, to the extent that countries of the West, including Britain, are not above allowing other countries to station troops in their territories. In 1946 the British Government felt unable to make any commitments limiting the right of self-determination of the Sudanese without consulting them, and since then the Sudanese have made further advances in self-government.
>
> On one thing both Governments are probably agreed. The Middle East is a security vacuum, tempting to Communist aggression. It can be filled to some extent by cooperation between the Arab countries and Egypt, and between them and the United Kingdom, but one of the essentials of that is satisfactory political and military relations between this country and Egypt. The problem is to work out a scheme of collaboration for their mutual interest and defence within which Egypt's strongly felt national aspirations are satisfied and words and forms offensive to Egyptian sentiment disappear from the lexicon of Anglo-Egyptian relations.[51]

In short, the British could not offer the Wafdist government so much as the Bevin-Ṣidqi protocol. The United Kingdom government obviously was concerned chiefly with concluding a defensive arrangement which changed the phraseology of the Anglo-Egyptian Treaty without affecting the British security position.

As the opening day of the Arab League Council's regular session, March 25, drew near, the view from Cairo was bleak indeed. The Iraqis, using the Israeli danger as argument, were active in Syria, with revived prospects of success. The British government had turned a deaf ear to Egypt's plea for immediate modification of the 1936 Treaty. Egypt's best hope of eventually persuading the British, a military base in an Arab southern Palestine, was threatened with extinction by an Israeli-Jordanian treaty which ignored Egypt's interest. King ᶜAbdullāh's bargain with Israel could not be allowed to stand.

The Egyptian government now set about the task of making a unilateral Jordanian settlement of its Palestine problem an act of treason to the Arab nation. As the delegations to the Arab League Council

[51] *The Times* (London), Mar. 23, 1950; cf. Clifton Daniel in *The New York Times,* Mar. 27, 1950. The words of the *Times'* diplomatic correspondent are closely similar to those which British officials were to use later in talks with the Egyptians.

began arriving in Cairo, it was reported that the Council would discuss the future of the Arab parts of Palestine and a resolution which declared a separate peace treaty with Israel to be a violation of the League Pact. It was also reported that the League Council would seat a delegation from the Gaza Government, whose leader, Amīn al-Ḥusayni, had just recently declared that the Palestinians refused to be annexed to Jordan. All this was confirmed in the opening meeting of the Council on March 25, when Prime Minister Naḥḥās moved that the Council elect representatives of the Palestinians to attend its session.[52]

Jordan took up the Egyptian challenge. Before the Council met, Jordan had made a formal protest of the Egyptian press campaign. Instead of sending a delegation to the Council, Jordan was represented in the opening meeting by the minister in Cairo, Bahā' al-Dīn Ṭūqān. On March 26, Ṭūqān delivered a note to the Egyptian government which declared that Jordan would not send a delegation if Jordan's annexations in Palestine were discussed or if the Gaza Government were represented. These terms had already been widely reported in the press, and King ᶜAbdullāh announced them in an interview with the London *Times*. Egypt transmitted the note to the Council at its meeting on March 27. No Jordanian representative was present.[53]

Jordan's persistence may have originated in nothing more than ᶜAbdullāh's stubbornness, but it is more likely that the policy was based on the belief that the situation was not totally hopeless. Whatever the thinking in Amman, Egypt had not yet been able to persuade the other Arab governments to join in the new course. Jordan was not quite isolated. Only Syria, which had initiated the campaign before Egypt's conversion, was identifiably in the Egyptian camp. The other Arab governments, whatever their positions, remained silent. Saudi Arabia may have supported Egypt, but its silence might also indicate that the Saudis still favored a peaceful settlement of the Palestine question and the solidification of relations with the West. Iraq was silent, but appears to have participated in a search for a compromise. Iraq's aspiration to lead the Arabs and Saudi Arabia's desire to

52 *Al-Ahrām,* Mar. 21, 25, 26, 1950; *Bayrūt,* Mar. 21, 25, 26, 1950.

53 *Bayrūt,* Mar. 24, 25, 26, 28, 1950; *The Times* (London), Mar. 27, 1950; *al-Ahrām,* Mar. 27, 28, 1950.

thwart Iraqi ambition precluded open opposition to Egypt's policy, but the silence of either was the same as opposition as long as another League government was willing to take responsibility for resisting the Egyptians. Lebanon, with some hesitation, was willing.

The only Lebanese anxiety, a fear that peace between Jordan and Israel would expose Lebanon to Israeli aggression, had been put to rest by the American and British ministers in a conversation with President Bishārah al-Khūri.[54] The Lebanese government was divided, but the dominant opinion was that the League should ignore Jordan's annexation of Arab Palestine and the negotiations with Israel.[55] In Cairo, the Lebanese delegation refused to take a positive position, but busied itself with efforts to prevent a break between Jordan and the League.[56] Lebanon and Iraq appear to have cooperated in seeking to mediate the clash. When Naḥḥās, in the Council on March 25, moved to take up the question of Palestinian representation, the Jordanian minister in Cairo objected. Although the Egyptian press reported that Lebanon and Iraq supported the Egyptian motion, the Council agreed to postpone discussion of the question for two days.[57] On March 26, the Iraqi and Lebanese prime ministers had a very long discussion of the problem with Secretary-General ᶜAzzām.[58]

The contest was joined in the Council's meeting on March 27. The Egyptians were obviously excited. Prime Minister Naḥḥās himself opened the debate with a vehement call for an invitation to the Gaza Government to represent Palestine. His motion was approved.[59] Then Lebanon entered the debate. "We must speak to the case of Transjordan . . . ," Prime Minister Riyāḍ al-Ṣulḥ said. "We had hoped that a Transjordanian delegation would come to inform us of its view in this matter, but it has delayed its arrival, and we must decide in this matter at once. We must not leave the way open to the government of Jordan to excuse itself from attending the Council sessions because of the representation of the Arabs of Palestine. That is one thing, but the matter we are now dealing with is another thing." Naḥḥās replied to Ṣulḥ's intimation of the need to conciliate Jordan

[54] Khūri, III, 280, 288.
[55] *Bayrūt,* Mar. 23, 25, 1950.
[56] *Al-Ahrām,* Mar. 30, 1950.
[57] *Al-Ahrām,* Mar. 26, 1950.
[58] *Al-Ahrām,* Mar. 27, 1950; *Bayrūt,* Mar. 28, 1950.
[59] *Al-Ahrām,* Mar. 28, 1950; *Bayrūt,* Mar. 28, 1950.

by voicing agreement concerning the desirability of Jordanian attendance, but the Egyptian prime minister refused to compromise. "We must settle this matter definitely and categorically," he declared, "otherwise these meetings will be just as unproductive as those which preceded them. . . . If the Arab states do not wish to deal with matters with complete lack of ambiguity, then [the League] obviously is headed for dissolution. . . ."[60] The advantage lay with the Egyptians. The Council voted that the Political Committee would immediately take up the matter of a League member's making a separate peace with Israel.[61]

The obvious political appeal of the Egyptian campaign did not overawe Jordan. The Council's actions were met by a public statement, issued on March 28, which declared that the Jordanian minister in Cairo would represent Jordan in the session of the Arab League but that he would boycott any meeting which discussed Jordan's annexation of parts of Palestine. Jordan also wished to keep a free hand with reference to Israel, but was unwilling to use so public a means. The prime minister sent a telegram to the Egyptian foreign minister. He said that his government had not communicated, and would not communicate, with the Israelis in order to conclude a settlement of the Palestine case. He asserted that his government was not prepared to ratify a peace with Israel, had not carried out discussions in the matter, and would not participate in such discussions before the elections which were scheduled for April 11.[62] The telegram, of course, left the way open for Jordan to negotiate with Israel after the elections.

Egypt and Syria countered Lebanese caution and Jordanian intransigence by a muted but firm appeal to Pan-Arab sentiment. Although the Arab League's rule concerning the secrecy of its debates was generally respected, the press published the speeches of Naḥḥās and Ṣulḥ. The Egyptian press also informed the Arab public of Lebanon's attitude.[63] While the press was pointing out Lebanese tepidity, the Syrian government was presenting itself as the model of a Pan-Arab champion. Prime Minister Khālid al-ᶜAẓm stated that Syria had been prepared for a year to outlaw separate agreements with Israel. In another statement, on the following day, a member of the Political Committee

60 *Al-Ahrām,* Mar. 28, 1950.

61 *Al-Ahrām,* Mar. 28, 1950; *Bayrūt,* Mar. 28, 1950.

62 *Al-Ahrām,* Mar. 29, 30, 1950; *Bayrūt,* Mar. 29, 30, 1950.

63 *Al-Ahrām,* Mar. 28, 30, 1950; *Bayrūt,* Mar. 31, 1950.

who was implicitly identified as ᶜAẓm asserted that the Political Committee had approved economic and political sanctions against Jordan which would "not be less than the sanctions imposed on Israel."[64]

The Lebanese could not risk doubts about their Arabism. The government issued a statement claiming that Lebanese-Egyptian agreement had insured the Political Committee's passage of the resolution concerning a separate peace in such a way as to give hope that Jordan would return to the League.[65] The Lebanese had won a measure of compromise from Egypt. The proposal to raise the question of Jordan's annexation of Arab Palestine was dropped.[66] When the Political Committee's resolution regarding a separate peace was introduced in the Council on March 29, Naḥḥās moved to postpone the discussion until a Jordanian delegation was present. The Lebanese prime minister was now able to demonstrate his devotion to Arabism. Ṣulḥ seconded Naḥḥās's motion to postpone the discussion, but, he said, "on the condition that Jordan will sign the resolution and be bound by it." The motion carried.[67]

Lebanon's joining with Egypt decided the issue. If the Lebanese government, which had neither territorial ambitions nor hope of leading the Arabs, would not chance being painted as false to Pan-Arabism, no other government could. Iraq, which had remained completely silent, now took action. The government, it was reported, urged the Jordanian cabinet to give way. The Regent, so the press said, warned ᶜAbdullāh that his policy was a threat to the entire Hashimite family.[68]

It may be that Jordan had already accepted the compromise before the Council met on March 29. Before the meeting, Ṭūqān had a talk with the Egyptian prime minister and the foreign minister. The Jordanian minister then attended the Council's session. After the resolution to postpone discussion, Ṭūqān promised to return to Amman in

[64] *Bayrūt,* Mar. 28, 29, 1950.

[65] *Bayrūt,* Mar. 31, 1950. Khūri, III, 289, provides implicit confirmation of the contemporary press reports that Lebanon did not support Egypt at the beginning of the League session and joined with Egypt only in the course of the session: "Just as April drew near, we received news of its [the Lebanese delegation's] activity, and it was good news . . . , because it had stood beside Egypt in the matter of rejecting a separate peace with Israel."

[66] *Bayrūt,* Mar. 30, 1950.

[67] *Al-Ahrām,* Mar. 30, 1950; *Bayrūt,* Mar. 30, 1950.

[68] *Al-Ahrām,* Mar. 31, 1950; *Bayrūt,* Apr. 1, 1950.

order to persuade his government to send a delegation. The delegates were all optimistic that Jordan would give in.[69] But, externally at least, the Jordanian government still had to be convinced. On March 31, the Jordanian cabinet listened to Ṭūqān's review of the situation. Ṭūqān was authorized to represent Jordan in the meetings of the League. The cabinet also approved the resolution to expel any Arab state which concluded a separate peace treaty with Israel. On April 1, the Political Committee, with Ṭūqān present, approved the resolution by a unanimous vote. That night, the Council approved the resolution, also by a unanimous vote which included Jordan.[70]

[69] *Al-Ahrām,* Mar. 30, 1950; *Bayrūt,* Mar. 30, 1950.
[70] *Al-Ahrām,* Apr. 1, 2, 1950; *Bayrūt,* Apr. 2, 1950.

The Autobiography of Mikhail Nu^caima

FRANCESCO GABRIELI

THIS AMPLE AUTOBIOGRAPHY in three volumes, entitled *Sab^cūn,* was published about ten years ago by Mikhail Nu^caima, one of the surviving leaders of the neo-Arabic literary renaissance.[1] To the best of my knowledge it has passed unnoticed in the West. While Taha Husein's *Ayyām* and Salāma Mūsa's *Tarbiya* are translated into European languages and have been reviewed in Europe, the present life by a writer living in solitude in Biskinta does not seem to have aroused the same interest among us; it is not even quoted in the histories of Arabic literature published during the last ten years[2] which deal with Nu^caima's work. Nevertheless this history of a lifetime, called on the title page an autobiographical trilogy, amply repays our attention, thanks to the author's outstanding personality, the wealth of his literary production, and above all his exceptional experiences, both biographical and cultural, comprising three different worlds.

The book has come into our hands long after its publication; having celebrated his seventies the author has now reached the next, rarer,

[1] Mikhail Nu^caima, *Sab^cūn. Ḥikāyat ^cumr.* Beirut, Dār Sādir, 1959-60, 3 vols., 266 + 340 + 244 pages. Bio-bibliographical data on the author in GAL, Suppl. III: 472-77, and earlier in Kratčkovskij, *Die Welt des Islams,* XIII (1931), 104-110, with an autobiographical letter by Nu^caima himself. For later souvenirs of Kratčkovskij's see note 12.

[2] J. Vernet, *Literatura árabe,* Barcelona, 1967, 201-202 and H. A. R. Gibb and J. M. Landau, *Arabische Literaturgeschichte,* Zurich-Stuttgart, 1966, 279-282. Also my *Letteratura araba* (1st ed. 1951, but the 4th ed. 1966, 266-67) was not yet acquainted with *Sab^cūn* (I take advantage now of this information on the base of II: 72-73, to make a correction: the famous poem *Akhī,* which I have translated, was not inspired by post-war disappointments, but rather refers to the tragic famine in Lebanon during the war.).

goal of his eighties — may he abundantly surpass them. Being one of those who, in these last years, have written about Nuᶜaima without being acquainted with this uncommonly valuable book, we wish, however late, to make up for lost time by offering these pages to a dear friend and colleague, who is enthusiastically dedicated to the study of ancient and recent *ᶜurūba,* and is also a particularly acute researcher in the field of acculturation processes.

Nuᶜaima's three-sided life and culture are in point of fact one of the most successful instances of such a phenomenon: as an Arab Christian of Lebanon, not a Maronite but a Greek Orthodox, he had in his youth the good fortune to live for a long time in close contact with the Slav world, spending some years in Poltava, where he became familiar with the Russian language and literature and observed Russian society on the eve of its revolution. From this experience he passed almost without interruption into the Anglo-Saxon world and spent about twenty years in the United States, where he contributed intensively to the literature of Arab emigrants in their own language. Finally, since his return to Lebanon in 1932 Nuᶜaima has been one of its most eminent literary figures, although his solitary life, alien from political passions and ambitions, may have kept him somewhat apart from younger generations. He appears fully aware of the exceptional character of his exterior life, and also of his uncommon nature, tastes, ideals, and loves, and has wished, through this autobiography, to rehearse, for himself and for all readers of *ḍād,* his interior and exterior treasures.

Even apart from its artistic merit (which, as we shall see, is great) this book is interesting, at least for us Westerners, in the first place as the document of an Arab Christian's contact with Western civilization in its contrasting forms, his parallel reaction to the static tradition of his national literature, the need he felt to renew and rejuvenate it; the curve of a life begun at the opening of this century in Lebanon, then an Ottoman province, and arriving through Ukraine, Seattle, New York, and the battlefields of World War I, to the convulsive Middle East of our own times, where he has found a haven, away from the turmoil of humanity, in the peace of his native mountains under the snowy Ṣannīn. One cannot help traveling under Nuᶜaima's guidance through the seventy years of his rich and varied experiences, even if seen only at a distance, as from the air.

Mikhail Nuᶜaima[3] was born at Biskinta, some twenty kilometers Northeast of Beirut, in October 1889,[4] in a family farming a small property. His father, after having tried to better himself by emigration, had come back to eke out a bare living from his forefathers' land, plowing and sowing. His mother brought up many children and young Mikhail learned very early to enjoy a life of freedom, unembittered by decorous poverty, between the tiny houses of his village, a rustic home in nearby Shakhrūb, and his favorite haunts on the slopes of Mount Ṣannīn. As is often the case with childhood memories, the most attractive pages are those evoking his father's house, the family circle, and above all the beloved mountain, rich in cool rivulets, bright with trees in flower and ringing with the twitter of birds (see particularly I: 49-51). The Russian Empire's political and religious interest for the Greek Orthodox communities in the East led the future Misha, at an early age, to the small day-school in Biskinta, where he learned his first words of Russian. Then, under a portrait of Czar Nicholas II, in a choir of Arab children he sang hymns of praise to the good Sultan ᶜAbd ul-Ḥamīd (I: 77-79). Later, still under the patronage of the imperial eagle, he continued to attend the Russian school in Nazaret and, having been picked out as a particularly gifted pupil, he studied between 1906 and 1911 in the seminary of Poltava; its description (I: 171-273) is one of the most original sections in these memoirs. Gorki's stormy petrel was already soaring in the skies of Holy Russia, but the provincial Ukrainian town does not seem to have felt the approach of the last tempest. The young Lebanese student, with his exceptionally prompt talent for assimilation, became acquainted with the great Russian literature and familiar with the majesty of Russian nature; he also tasted Russian feminine charm, embodied by the voluptuous Varja. In November 1910 he read in a street of Poltava the news of Tolstoi's death; two years earlier the Imperial government had sent a special circular to forbid schools and students any celebration of his eightieth birthday.

With 1911 the author's life enters the second of those periods

[3] See in I: 32 the final precise form of the surname and an explanation of fluctuations between the forms Naᶜīma, Naᶜīmi and Nuᶜaima.

[4] See in I: 106-107 the witty incident of a hunt for his birth certificate. The mistaken date, 1894, in Abd-el-Jalil, *Brève histoire de la littérature arabe,* has passed into Wiet, *Introduction à la littérature arabe,* Paris, 1966, p. 286.

(*marāḥil*) to whose threefold rhythm his autobiography unfolds. He returned to Lebanon from Russia, but left almost immediately to join two of his brothers in the small town of Walla Walla near Seattle on the Pacific; he completed his legal and literary studies at Washington State University, obtaining both B.A.'s in 1916. Also in America his assimilation of the language was surprisingly quick; English soon became his third and later his second language, after his mother tongue. He used it with the same ease as Arabic and Russian in composing prose and poetry. But the new world, whose citizen the Lebanese immigrant became at that time,[5] and where he spent, between the Pacific and the Atlantic, more than twenty years, does not seem to have had any beneficent influence on his spirit, inclined as it was to meditation and the inner life. It appeared to the young man mainly in its materialistic and commercial trends, its worship of money and prosperity, the stifling existence of its vast urban masses. Only one delightful interlude of rural peace near New York is described (II: 257-63), and Babbit's world, in all its superficial pretentiousness, is amply exposed in this part of the memoirs; on the other hand, the value of more genuine and positive elements in the American life and society is hardly ever recognized.

On his return from a brief campaign in France, where he landed in time to risk his life under the last German grenades, on the eve of the armistice (II: 112-22), Nu^caima settled in New York and eked out a living by undertaking several practical activities, while in the literary field he rose to the forefront among the representatives of the Arab emigrants' *intelligentsia*. Since the first war he had established relations with the review *al-Funūn* and its chief champion Khalīl Jubrān, the founder, in 1920, of the Writers' League (*Rābiṭa qalamiyya*). For about twenty years the *Rābiṭa,* with its periodical *as-Sā'iḥ,* was the leading organ of young neo-Arabic literature in America. To these American years belong Nu^caima's works of literary criticism, edited in book form in 1923 under the title *al-Ghirbāl* (the sieve), and a large portion of his poetry, essays, and fiction, which in some cases reached their final form and were published much later (the play *al-Ābā wa*

[5] This is never actually stated in the memoirs, but we cannot find any other explanation for the fact that an Ottoman subject, after living only six years in the United States, should be drafted into the American army in 1917 and sent to the front in Europe.

'l-banūn, the collected lyrics *Hams al-jufūn,* the *Mudhakkirāt al-Arqash,* etc.). His intimacy with Jubrān dates from those years; on his friend's early death in 1931 it was Nuᶜaima who closed his eyes; later he wrote a biographical and critical book about him, which raised heated debates with the almost idolizing admirers of that genuine artist and very difficult man, leader of the neo-Arab *Nahḍa.*[6]

This second volume of Nuᶜaima's memoirs contains few traces of fondness for Anglo-Saxon society, but it abounds in portraits and opinions concerning persons and events in the world of Arab emigrants, reflections and heated discussions about its literature. Particularly it sets forth the author's matured vision of life, his literary program and the partial fulfilment of his life in that central twenty-years period.

He often assures us that the purpose of his very long *ghurba* had been to provide from a distance for his paternal family, to help his brothers in their studies and his parents in their old age; for himself he had not succeeded, perhaps he had not cared, to put much money by. When the former emigrant sailed in 1932 on his final homecoming, his whole capital amounted to 500 dollars. He was leaving behind him a world for which he had never actually felt any affection, although a Vila and a Neonia had gladdened the years of his manhood with their love. The bitter humiliation of his struggles for money had been in such contrast with his idealistic and warmhearted nature, that he took leave of America without any regret. On his return he found the faithful subjects of ᶜAbd ul-Ḥamīd transformed into citizens of the Lebanese Republic; small Beirut of the Ottoman period had become an uproarious Arab-French metropolis; his native town, Biskinta, was already touched by a dubious type of "progress." Now began the third *marḥala* of life, described in his third volume and at present continuing in his green old age, beyond seventy. Like Ulysses returning to stony Ithaca, Nuᶜaima arrived just in time to close the eyes of his favorite brother, Nasīb, who died prematurely, and to see the last days of his parents, finding compensation in the affection, old and new, of his surviving brothers and their children. In the new home in Biskinta and in his hermitage at Shakhrūb he has since been busy developing the

[6] The book on Jubrān, written after Nuᶜaima's return to Lebanon, is dated 1934. See in III: 101-122 an echo of the controversies it raised, among them a political exchange of letters with Rīḥānī, and a visit to Jubrān's last resting-place in his native land at Mār Sarkīs.

sum of meditations and experiences gathered in his long wanderings over the world; the books written in this period have given him a permanent place in the forefront of the entire neo-Arabic and Lebanese literature; their echoes, through English translations and elaborations, have penetrated far beyond the Arabic-speaking world. The last of them, to the best of our knowledge, is precisely the present book of memoirs, which brought Nuᶜaima, in 1961, a solemn official recognition in his own country.[7]

We have given a summary outline of this vast autobiography, coincident with most of the gifted and lovable author's life. But such a rapid summary cannot do justice to the rich humanity, the wealth of problems discussed or merely suggested, the vivid style, of its almost 800 pages. Too many, maybe, for an alien and remote reader (but we all know that *the thoughts of youth are long, long thoughts*). As in all autobiographies, not everything that the author finds interesting and loves can move his readers in the same manner.[8] Nevertheless the cases where such a full communication is reached are frequent enough to prove that *Sabᶜūn* is vital both from a human and from a literary point of view, particularly for twentieth century readers of the West who are also not uncritical friends of Arabism.

These 800 pages can be read without labour, written as they are in a clear, simple, and elegant Arabic. Like Taha Husein, Mikhail Nuᶜaima has turned a language which he did not learn at his mother's knee into an instrument of expression admirably natural and flexible, capable of communicating every delicate hue of his fancy, every impulse of his soul and every aspect of reality. The smell of midnight oil — as far as a foreigner may judge — is never present in this crystal-clear modern prose, true to the rules of the best *ᶜarabiyya,* and at the same time untouched, in its vocabulary and syntax, by the archaisms too often associated with those rules. In faultless Arabic form the author has succeeded in representing his world, vast and varied as it appears even in this biographical outline — an adequate idea could be gained only from an anthology of quotations. We see the diminu-

[7] *Anthologie de la littérature arabe contemporaine,* I (Paris, 1964): 66.

[8] The book abounds in extracts from diaries and letters to his family and friends. He dwells on ties of affection and family matters, far beyond the poetic halo of childhood memories; this is one of the points where his art is somewhat too indulgent to his personal feelings.

tive Lebanese fatherland, living the patriarchal life of the late nineteenth century, holding out its arms to the absent children who earn their living all over the world, and gain for their country not only money, but a deep renewal, social and economical, capable of putting an end to feudality.[9] We read about the country of Jesus, known to the author during his school years in Nazaret; his strong attachment to the Christian message will never be rejected, but will be partially blended with alien elements into the "philosophy" of his maturity. Next come Gogol's Ukraine, Whitman's and Mark Twain's America, and France martyred by four years of warfare. Nature is always present, now unclouded now overcast with melancholy, always in harmony with our poet's heart. And in this changing scene is a throng of persons, some famous others obscure, more or less close to the author and dear to him; he is able to look upon all of them with human understanding, charity or affection: his father ploughing ("I close my eyes at this moment and see that pure-hearted man, chaste in soul and speech, urging his oxen on, grasping the plow in his right hand and the goad in his left, while the earth gushes out, as if boiling over, on both sides of the ploughshare . . ." (I: 64), or singing a little love song he had learned overseas. In Russia we meet Kotya, passionate Varja's husband, spineless and downtrodden, against the background of a remote village, Gherasimovka (I: 199 ff.). In Washington, early in 1921, President Wilson, already destroyed physically and politically, mutters his thanks, with tearful eyes, to the Arab patriots who come to pay him homage as the apostle of self-determination for all peoples (II: 183-87). In New York we see the genial, hot-tempered and capricious Jubrān, surrounded by a Pleiad of the *Rābiṭa Qalamiyya* (Ilia Abū Māḍī, Nasīb ᶜArīḍa, ᶜAbd al-Masīḥ Ḥaddād, etc., II: 180-82); today Nuᶜaima is probably their only survivor. And there were other types of women, beside the three heroines of his love life, like Madeleine in Rennes, or Hilda in Boston and New York. The celibate ascetic of Shakhrūb, who in his heyday must have been a very charming "Arab lover," turns such delicate pages of memory's book with a tender touch; a few inevitable traces of vanity are compensated by sensitive and scrupulous moral feeling. His youthful tribute to earthly love

[9] See all the beautiful chapter *Nakba wa hijra* (I: 14-102) where the tragedy and the epic of Lebanese emigration is represented in a manner faithfully true to life.

once paid, Nuᶜaima has been able, like Petrarch, to purify and sublimate it as love celestial.

In the center of this crowded fresco we find throughout — according to the nature of all autobiographies — a single hero, the author. First a child in Biskinta, chasing lizards and birds, then the returning Ulysses, next the aged patriarch writing the memoirs in his "grotto" — a man standing before us with the maximum of sincerity we can be capable of when we observe and represent our own self. The experience of a long life has matured his philosophy, or his religion, or his vision of the world, whatever we choose to call it; he never tires of instilling it in this book and also outlines it in several other books containing poetry and moral reflections. His wisdom is a sort of spiritualistic monism (*waḥdat al-wujūd,* first and last word of his faith).[10] The Godhead is immanent in cosmos, the life totally pervading it is indestructible and transmutable into endless forms; right and wrong are not due to chance, they are always associated with man's responsibility, through the chain of his numberless incarnations. It is a mixture of Christian *charitas generis humani,* with a pinch of Indian wisdom, the transmigration of souls, theosophy, and a Christian faith in Providence. A "secret hand" (*yad khafiyya*) ultimately leading the fates of man toward good, was more than once revealed in the author's life: the hand that, as a child, kept him unharmed when he fell from the roof of his house (I: 57 ff.); which sent the friendless boy, landing all alone in Haifa, a generous stranger, to be his guide, host and adviser (I: 112); that saved him as a man from German shrapnels in France's battlefields, and placed in his way unhoped-for anchors of safety in the throes of babelic New York. What we wish to point out is Nuᶜaima's ethical-political reaction in relation to other men, the various inhabitants of this *aiuola che ci fa tanto feroci.* He rarely mentions politics, but this book leaves an impression of equilibrium, of a rational mind superior to the most burning passions of our times; one is glad to discover it in a contemporary Arab. Naturally opposed to any tyranny and exploitation, from those of the Ottoman Empire to the hypocritical Mandates between two wars, Nuᶜaima seems never to have been a supporter of nationalistic direct action as practiced yesterday and to-

10 ᶜȲsā an-Nāᶜūrī, in his *Adab al-mahjar,* Cairo, 1960, pp. 367-401, deals almost exclusively, in the chapter on Nuᶜaima, with his ideas on this point, and gives a final parallel between him and Jubrān.

day — he may even sometimes have been criticized because of his too Goethian disdain of contingent politics. The chapter entitled Independence (III: 189-94) shows the difference between formal independence, apparently gained by the Arabs, and its true substance, yet to be obtained: ethical and social maturity. This point of view is certainly not in harmony with the extreme currents of present-day Arab nationalism.[11] Similarly his *barā'a* of both blocks now facing one another (*Ab^{c}ad min Moskū wa Washington* is the title of one of his recent works) calls upon each of them to renounce competing for this world's goods and for heaven's abysses, and to seek the highest, most immaterial values of man's ethical perfection. These are words of wisdom which give us food for thought. We take the liberty of commenting that a philosopher should be allowed to make a necessary choice between two evils, by finding out which of the two blocks gives us the greater liberty or oppresses us least, when we try to find and to declare, individually or collectively, those superior values and to preach in their favour. *Allāh a^{c}lam,* but we too are convinced we know something about this.

Mikhail Nu^{c}aima, at least for us, is not so much a philosopher, a theologian, or a prophet, as a literary man and a poet; hence we find it natural to look above all for this aspect in his book, where the many exterior references to the chronology and the fortunes of his various works are less interesting than the author's literary ideas, the consciousness he shows of his production as a whole and of the elements concurring to form it. The point he prefers to dwell upon is the spontaneous compulsion — felt since his first youth — to renew the forms and spirit of Arabic literature, forsaking a mechanical imitation of the past and considering art as a direct expression of our soul. He assures us that this demand for an inner impulse and renewal has inspired the whole of his literary work; though only partly acquainted with it, we are ready to grant this. Less acceptable we find his polemic rejection (II: 182, and in the book on Jubrān 201-202) of the current opinion

[11] The following lines, written in 1960 (III: 194) read rather sadly in 1970: "Would that the Arabs might turn their vast lands into an oasis of health, mutual understanding and brotherhood, within the desert of greeds, hatreds, terrors, from which the present-day world is desperately seeking a way out. Would that among them might arise intelligent and far-sighted chiefs, capable of leading them on that path!" *Laita* . . . , o peaceful sage of Shakhrūb!

that the expansion and rejuvenation of the Syro-American school, culminating in the *Rābiṭa,* springs from contacts with Anglo-Saxon literature, and in general with Anglo-Saxon society. Such a spiritual impregnation may have been more or less important for each single writer, according to talent and temperament, and we may believe that Nuᶜaima already felt a spontaneous need for renewal before he ever came under the influence of American surroundings. But it would not be easy to convince us of this in the case of Jubrān, so deeply rooted and involved, biographically and spiritually, in many aspects of wholly Anglo-Saxon poetry, art, and culture. Anyhow, this is Nuᶜaima's thesis; his understandably subjective vision inclines him to place a higher value on the indigenous character of his spiritual world and to reduce the part of external influences. This does not mean that such influences are not apparent; he partly refers to them in his memoirs and they can partly be recognized directly by an experienced reader; thus Kratčkovskij, even before being fully informed of Nuᶜaima's biography, had detected in him the literary influences of Russia. Nuᶜaima in fact does not reject this debt.[12] He seems less disposed, at least in his memoirs, to admit his debts to American writers and poets, but it is difficult to imagine that his lyrics, essays, and philosophical works were written in ignorance and unawareness of Poe, Whitman, Longfellow, Masters, Emerson, and Melville.

What chiefly strikes us in this autobiography, whose language is so purely Arabic, is the meagre weight of Arabic literary tradition; it can partly be explained by his position as an Arab Christian, but apart from a half-serious hymn to the grammarian Ibn Malik (I: 124) and some occasional quotations from al-Mutanabbi, the classic par excellence of

[12] Kratčkovskij, *Nad arabskimi rukopisiami,* 2nd ed., 1946, pp. 49-55 ("Poltavskij seminarist"). It gives a passage of Nuᶜaima's letter to him in excellent Russian concerning his literary experiences while in Ukraine. It is curious to notice that from the final edition of Kratčkovskij's precious booklet (*Socinenja,* I: 57) a scruple of sovietic cultural orthodoxy has eliminated Nuᶜaima's enthusiastic words on Dostoievski: "The high humanity of the most powerful and profound, of the most complete and penetrating among all Russian writers." Three dots have replaced these words. It is well known that for a long time Dostoievski had been as much appreciated by Soviet Russia as Tolstoi had been by the official Russia of the Czars.

Still another short visit was then paid by Nuᶜaima to that country in 1956 (III: 222-24), but our curiosity to know more about this second experience fifty years after the first one remains unsatisfied: here he is simply referring to his above quoted book *Abᶜad min Moskū wa Washington,* for the time being unavailable to us.

all "speakers with *ḍād*," one may say that the world of classical Arab-Islamic literature is absent from the mental horizon of this extremely elegant writer, who seems to have absorbed and employed in a masterly manner only the exterior clothing of its language. Taha Husein, to approach the West, had to cut off one by one all the threads binding him to the traditional heritage of his country's crystallized culture; he was only later to experience and appraise it anew, by the light of European critical thought. Nuᶜaima never knew this dramatic experience; at first the simple fact of his birth, later the circumstances of his life, placed him from the beginning in a position of entire independence from the cultural tradition of the East and allowed him to receive, uncontradicted, the vital sap of foreign art and thought. Perhaps he has not been entirely fair to the Western sources of his intellectual life, but whatever may be the precise, scrupulous balance between what was inborn and what was acquired, between originality and imitation in the work of this genial contemporary of ours, he remains none the less the lovable Misha portrayed in his book, endowed with three souls like Ennius of old. He is an excellent literary talent and a fraternal Christian spirit.

Secrets for Muslims in Parsi Scriptures

SVEN S. HARTMAN

It has been observed that the Pahlavi writings avoid expressly mentioning Muhammad, the Muslims, or Islam, when they speak about these phenomena. West[1] says the following about Martān Farrux (the author of the *Škand Gumānīk Vičār*[2]) and his description of Islam: "Like all Pahlavi writers, he never mentions that religion by name, but when, in the position of a Zoroastrian in Persia, he states that he did not admire the religion that was then in supremacy, there can be little doubt that he refers to Muhammadanism." And after this West refers to a couple of obvious allusions to passages in the Koran and to the mentioning of the Muᶜtazila sect, and these facts allow us to be absolutely sure that Chapters XI and XII of the *Škand Gumānīk Vičār* (*ŠGV*) really deal with Islam.

It is very remarkable that the writers have acted thus in the case of Islam, because this has not been done in the descriptions of the other religions in *ŠGV*. Judaism is described in Chapters XIII and XIV,[3] and here we find direct references to the Old Testament and to Moses (§§ 1-4). Christianity is treated in Chapter XV[4] and here the terms Christians and Christ are frequently mentioned. From the very first sentence the reader knows that what is dealt with is Christianity. And Chapter XVI[5] about Manichaeism states in the first paragraph that it is "the heresy of Mani" which will now be described.

[1] *SBE* XXIV, p. XXVI.

[2] Ed. by de Menasce. *Collectanea Friburgensia* N.S. XXX. Fribourg, 1945. Translation in *SBE* XXIV: 117-251.

[3] Ed. by de Menasce, pp. 175-203. Transl. by West, pp. 208-229.

[4] Ed. by de Menasce, pp. 205-225. Transl. by West, pp. 229-243.

[5] Ed. by de Menasce, pp. 226-261. Transl. by West, pp. 243-251.

Consequently it is only Islam that one strictly avoids mentioning by name. Nevertheless, there are two entire chapters on Islam and the refutation of its doctrine. Obviously the author has wanted to conceal from some people that what he has written on Islam really concerns Islam. No particular ingenuity is needed to understand that it was precisely from the Muslims themselves that he wanted to keep this secret.

We have the same situation in the Denkart, Book III, where the Muslims are vaguely called *Kēšdārān,* "adherents of a (false) doctrine," whereas the Jews and the Christians are explicitly characterized as "Jews" (*yahūt*) and "Christians" (*tarsāk*).[6]

The tendency to avoid a direct mentioning of Islam and the Muslims has survived in the riwāyat literature of the Parsis, where it has found various expressions. Some of them will here be looked at.

I

(1) In several instances we can find the word *darwand* (دروند) referring to Muslims. This word comes from Pahlavi *druvand,* derived from Avesta *drgvant — drvant,* "one who holds with the Drug, companion of Drug" (of men), "holding with the Drug, wicked, fiendish" (of evil gods, demons).[7] Thus the word originally concerns *daēva*s and those worshiping *daēva*s. It has not become a common word in Modern Persian. It has been preserved only in the language of the Parsis. We may therefore presume that the word *darwand* has been unintelligible to others than the Parsis. Not only Muslims, it is true, may be called *darwand,* but *all* non-Parsis. But the riwāyat texts principally speak about *darwand*s that are Muslims. I shall now first quote some passages where *darwand* obviously refers to Muslims. Thereafter I shall try to show that this word has actually preserved some of its pejorative and demonical ring.

In a riwāyat from Surat about the year 1670 worries are expressed as to the possibilities of maintaining the ritual purification with the bull's urine "now in the age of the *darwand*'s" (الحال در دور دروندان).[8]

[6] de Menasce, *Une encyclopédie mazdéenne. Le Dēnkart.* Bibliothèque de l'école des hautes études. Sciences religieuses. LXIXe volume. Paris, 1958, p. 19.

[7] Bartholomae, *Altiranisches Wörterbuch,* coll. 774 ff. Reichelt, *Avesta Reader,* p. 236. Nyberg, *Hilfsbuch des Pehlevi* II: 60.

[8] *Dârâb Hormazyâr's Rivâyat* (*DHR*) I, p. 192:-17. Dhabhar, *The Persian Rivayats,* p. 206 and n.6.

And a little further on in the same text it is said that "in these days owing to the dread of the *darwand*'s"[9] (در این ایام ازجهت خوف دروندان) one can no longer perform the purification just mentioned.

In Surat, as in great parts of India there was Muslim rule at this time. The Great Mogul Awrangzīb ruled with a Muhammadan fanatism typical of him, harassing subjects of other confessions. Under the circumstances it was surely advisable to have one or two secret words to use about the Muslims, if one wanted to express critical views on them.

According to the riwāyat's all *darwands* are dangerous and so is also all that has been in contact with them. A Parsi becomes unclean and sinful through direct or indirect contact with them.[10] This may be illustrated by the following examples:

a) The question when one may use water from a pool or a pond is answered thus:

"If a *darwand* has taken possession of it, the Behdīns (i.e. the Zoroastrians) should in no case use it."[11]

(که دروند دخل کرده باشد به هیچ بابت بهدینان کار نفرمایند)

b) To the question whether one may eat the food of a *darwand*, while on journey, the answer is:

"The food of a *darwand* should, in no case, be eaten."[12]

(خوردنی دروند به هیچ جا نشاید خوردن)

From this follows, of course, that one cannot either buy eggs,[13] honey,[14] or clarified butter[15] from the *darwands*. In the case of the article last mentioned, it is said that not even the *Bareshnūm* purification can cleanse a person who has eaten of it (وبیرشنوم نیز پاك نشود).[16]

c) We said above that the mere touching of things coming from the *darwands* is sinful. Hence, it is stated:

9 *DHR* I, p. 192:18 f. The word از is written twice in the text.

10 See Dhabhar, *The Persian Rivayats,* pp. XL f where many such taboos are enumerated.

11 *DHR* I, p. 92:13 f.; Dhabhar, p. 95.

12 *DHR* I, p. 350:15; Dhabhar, p. 312.

13 *DHR* I, p. 264:8; Dhabhar, p. 265. Here it is the question of eggs to be consecrated.

14 *DHR* I, p. 268:10; Dhabhar, p. 266.

15 *DHR* I, p. 271:6-7; Dhabhar, p. 267.

16 *Ibid.*

> "If a person writes Avesta and Zand with the ink of the *darwands*, then he obtains a farman sin at every (stroke of the) pen."[17]

(اکر کسی به سیاهی دروندان اوستا وزند بنویسد اورا به هرقلم فرمانی گناه بود)

Another example, illustrating the same thing: It is asked whether the Niyāyiš ceremony may be performed on a carpet that has been in contact with a *darwand*. The answer is:

> "If a *darwand* comes in contact with that carpet, (the ceremony) is not valid"[18]

(چون دروند در آن بساط پیوست ثابت نباشد)

When reading these and similar passages, one gets the impression that the greatest obstacle to the Islamic mission among the Parsis must have been the taboo conceptions of the latter and not any particular dogmatics or theology. Through the centuries the question of cleanness and uncleanness thus seems to have been the essential one in the religion that has had the *Avesta* as its Sacred Scripture.[19]

(2) The word *jud-dīn* may be interpreted as "a person who is without or separates from the true religion." It is a Parsi word, not found in ordinary Modern Persian. Its direct linguistic equivalent in the Pahlavi scriptures is *yut-dēn,* as one might expect. In any case the word must have been enough private and obscure to make a suitable secret designation for Muslims and certain non-Zoroastrians.

The term *jud-dīn* stands for the same people as the term *darwand,* hence we find the same kinds of taboos combined with them both. A few examples:

a) In Narīmān Hōšang's riwāyat, there are the following questions and answers:

> "Is eating of fruits of every kind brought by Muslims with their hands allowed or not? And is sitting with *jud-dīns* and unworthy people and eating with them allowed or not?"[20]

[17] Dhabhar, p. 346 and n.6. This passage is missing in *DHR*.

[18] *DHR* I, p. 325:13 f.; Dhabhar, p. 304.

[19] See my article "Aspects de l'histoire religieuse selon la conception de l'Avesta non-gāthique." *Orientalia Suecana* XIII (1964): 93-104.

[20] *DHR* II, p. 386:1-2 (=I, p. 271:15-16); Dhabhar, p. 267.

(میوه هر بابت که مسلمانان می آرند بدست ایشان خوردن ونخوردن وبا
جددینان ونااارزانیان وبا ایشان خوردن یا نی)

To the first question the answer is that certain such fruits are allowed to [be] eat[en] when washed, but eating others is against the religion. The answer to the second question is:

> "Sitting and eating food with them is not in any way and at all proper."[21]

(با ایشان نشستن وطعام خوردن به هیچ نوع وبه هیچ چیز نمی شاید)

b) Another text says:

> "If a man gives a Niyāyiš on the clothing of *jud-dīns*, it is not accepted."[22]

(اگرچه مرد بر جامه جددینان نیایش بدهد پذیرفته نباشد)

There are many other similar taboos,[23] and they all show the same thing: the impossibility of contact between Parsis and non-Parsis.

(3) A third way of writing about Muslims without their discovering it was to write the word "Muslim" in an alphabet unknown to them, that is in Avesta characters. In the following quotation the word "Muslim" and derivatives of it are mentioned no less than 5 times, always written in Avesta characters.

"Question: A certain *Behdīn* whom Muslims by force make a Muslim, [who] has not got Islam in his heart (what is the decision)? — Answer: Whenever he is made Muslim by force and he has not Islam in his heart and his mind, then the fault does not belong to him."[24]

(پرسش که شخصی بهدین را که *muslmąną* بزوراورا *muslmą* کنند واورادردل
muslmąnī نیست پاسخ اینکه هر گاه بزور *muslmą* کرده باشد و اورا دل ومنش
ba muslmąnī' نیست اورا تقصیر نیست)

This quotation is a reflection from the time of Awrangzīb,[25] both

[21] *DHR* II, p. 386:3-4 (=I, p. 271:16-18); Dhabhar, p. 267.

[22] *DHR* I, p. 326:11-12; Dhabhar, p. 305.

[23] See Dhabhar, pp. XL f.

[24] *DHR* II, p. 476:5-7; Dhabhar, p. 275. The text is also found in *DHR* I, p. 282:7-9, but there are only two words written in Avesta characters.

[25] For this riwāyat see Dhabhar, pp. XLII f. and pp. 624 f. (It concerns that which Dhabhar calls Maktub-i Suratya Adhyarus.)

as to the compulsion mentioned and the way of concealing the criticism against Islam. But the device of using Avesta characters for the word "Muslim" is probably much older, because it is found both in the Riwāyat of Kāma Bohra (A.Y. 896)[26] and the Riwāyat of Šāpūr Barūčī (about A.Y. 940).[27] In both cases the question is what will become of a wife of a man who has turned Muslim.[28]

Many other secrets have also, of course, been written in Avesta characters and later we shall see examples of this. The general rule for this is formulated in the following way in the Riwāyat of Kāmdīn Šāpūr:[29]

> "If one can write a secret in Avesta characters or Sawād characters, i.e. Uzwariš, one should write (it thus)."[30]

(سرّی بتوان نبشت بخط اوستا باخط سواد اوابد نبشت که اوزوارش بید)

This text immediately looks as if it were a transcription from *pāzand,* and I have succeeded in finding at least most of it in a pāzand version in a quotation in Spiegel:[31]

ba. Xata. awstā. yā. Xata. səvāṯ. awāiṯ. nawəšt. kə. uzvarš. bəṯ.

Thus we know with certainty that several passages written in Avesta characters in the riwāyats of the Parsis, have been regarded as secrets, in particular to the Muslims.

(4) Still another way of secretly writing about Muslims has been to identify them with "the seed of Hēšm," which is mentioned in certain apocalyptic texts among the bad omens for the impending end of the world. Hēšm is a word meaning "Wrath." Already in the Avesta

[26] Dhabhar, p. LVI.

[27] Dhabhar, p. LXIV.

[28] The passage from Kama Bohra has Avesta characters only in the H.F. manuscript. (See Dhabhar, p. 197 n. 8), not in *DHR* I, p. 183:14 — the passage from Šāpūr Barūčī has Avesta characters in *DHR* II, p. 466:16 but not in *DHR* I, p. 183:16. In the Riwāyat of Šāpūr Barūčī we also meet the problem what will happen to a daughter after the death of her father who has had a son who has become a Muslim. Then the word "Muslim" is also written in Avesta characters. See *DHR* I, p. 184:13; Dhabhar, p. 198.

[29] See Dhabhar, p. LIX.

[30] *DHR* I, p. 575:18-19; Dhabhar, p. 347. The text, though, has بنوان نبشت instead of نتوان نبشت.

[31] *Grammatik der Huzvâreschsprache,* Wien, 1856, p. 22. Spiegel quotes the passage from "Msc. fonds d'Anq. nr. VI, p. 94."

(where the word is *Aēšma*) it is a personification of the anti-Zoroastrian and the devilish, both in cult and moral.[32] And in the apocalyptic speculations Hēšm, as pointed out, represents one of the heaviest visitations of the ultimate times.

The identification between "the seed of Hēšm" and the Muhammadans is confirmed by Ayātkār i Žāmāspīk (= A. i Ž.) XV,28 (according to Messina's [33] division into chapters), where the pāzand-text[34] runs as follows:

> pas. biāinda. tāzīgąni. uǰārat̰. varaš.
> aža. tuXmaē. hāēšəm.

In Pahlavi this should be restored to:[35]

> pas bē āyēnd tāčīkān i vičārt vars i hač
> tōhm i hēšm

"Then will come the Arabs with dishevelled hair of the seed of Hēšm."

The expression "the Arabs with dishevelled hair of the seed of Hēšm" is obviously depending on and inspired by the expression "the demon with dishevelled hair of the seed of Hēšm" (dēv i vičārt-vars i hēšm-tōhmak), which is so common in Bahman Yašt.[36] There is also the expression "the demons (i.e. plural) with dishevelled hair."[37] I cannot imagine it otherwise than that the Zoroastrians have interpreted their own time in the light of their traditional apocalyptic speculations and have thus arrived at the conclusion that the Arabs must correspond to the demons with dishevelled hair and be of the seed of Hēšm. There is probably not only hatred of the Arabs but also a certain religious belief, a certain interpretation of history, behind this thought.

What we have said has given the prerequisites for something that Dhabhar has declared, viz. that in the Modern Persian versions of

[32] See Wikander, *Der arische Männerbund,* pp. 58 ff. Widengren, *Hochgottblaube im alten Iran,* pp. 312 ff.

[33] Messina, *Libro apocalittico persiana Ayātkār i Ẓāmāspīk* (Roma, 1939), p. 65.

[34] The Pāzand text is taken from Modi, Jâmâspi, Pahlavi, Pâzend, and Persian Texts. Bombay, 1903 (*Pahlavi Translations,* Part III.) at foot of p. 72.

[35] Messina, p. 65.

[36] E.g. I, 5; II, 24; 36; III, 1; 13. *SBE* V, pp. 193, 201, 205, 215, 220.

[37] In *Bahman Yast* II, 28 (K 43, fol. 265 v:12) is written *dēvān i vičârtvars* but not followed by *ī hēšm-tōhmak.*

Bahman Yašt and A. i. Ž. the word Hēšm sometimes means both Hēšm and Hāšim, and again, the word Hāšim sometimes means both Hāšim and Hēšm.[38] One may, indeed, ask oneself whether the word has not got this double meaning also in the pāzand version quoted above, where the word is written *hāēšm*. Modi has interpreted this word as only meaning Hāšim.[39] Messina has interpreted it only as Hēšm.[40] Perhaps one should think both of Hēšm and Hāšim, exactly as in the Modern Persian versions mentioned.

Hāšim is an ancestor of Muhammad as well as of the Abbasids and the descendants of Ali. The Umayyad Caliphs, though, were not descended from this Hāšim. Therefore the Alids and the Abbasids emphasized the importance of being descended just from Hāšim. The situation immediately before the first Abbasid Caliph is described by Hitti in the following way: "The Abbasids . . . began to press their claim to the throne. Cleverly they made common cause with the Alids by emphasizing the rights of the house of Hāshim. The Shīᶜah regarded this family as consisting primarily of the descendants of Ali, but the Abbāsids included themselves as members of the Hāshimite branch of the Quraysh and therefore closer to the Prophet than the banu-Umayyah."[41]

Hāšim's place, genealogically, is seen from the following table:[42]

Hāšim
|
ᶜAbd al-Muṭṭalib
|
ᶜAbd-Allāh	Abu-Tālib	Al-ᶜAbbās
Muḥammad	ᶜAli	

Thus, it is possible that sometimes one has intentionally written

[38] Dhabhar, p. 460 n. 17; p. 484 n. 9; p. 587 n. 5.

[39] Modi, p. 117 n. 11.

[40] Messina, p. 111.

[41] Hitti, *History of the Arabs.* 1.ed. 1937. Pp. 282 f. For the Hāšimites as a class of nobility see von Grunebaum, *Der Islam in seiner klassischen Epoche,* p. 105, and *Der Islam im Mittelalter,* pp. 256, 272. See also Spuler, Iran in früh-islamischer Zeit, p. 46. As to the real origin of the term *Hašimiyya,* see B. Lewis, HĀSHIMIYYA in the new edition of *The Encycl. of Islam* III: 265.

[42] Hitti, p. 283.

Hāšim (هاشم) instead of Hēšm (هيشم), as this writing actually appears a couple of times.[43]

II

We have just seen examples of how the Parsis have tried to conceal from Muslims when they have written about them in the riwāyats. Oddly enough, one has not even dared to write about one's own religion, but out of fear of the Muslims, one has hidden certain things thereof, the technique then being to use Avesta characters, which were secret to the Muslims.

(1) I take the first example from Modi's description of the Persian version of *Mēnōk i Xrat,* according to the S.H. manuscript:[44] "Here, in the Chapter (f. 72 b 1. 9) on the praise of Zoroaster and his miracles, the author gives a few verses in which he places Zoroaster over all prophets. These may offend Mahomedans if they could read them. So, they are written in the Avesta characters."

There is a similar passage in this manuscript, where a version of Sad-dar is rendered. Suddenly there appears a line written in Avesta characters:

bīhīn. az. hamah. dīnhā. ast. īn.

i.e. بهين ازهمه دينها است اين

"This (religion) is the best of all religions." Modi comments upon this passage in the following way: "It appears that it is with a view to avoid being read in Persian by the Mahomedans, that it is written in Avesta characters. The Mahomedans would not tolerate a Zoroastrian saying in their country that his religion was better than the Mahomedan religion."[45]

(2) Of quite another kind is the mystery-making concerning certain details in the religion of the Parsis. It appears, for instance, that one has been very anxious not to let any outsider read about the Zoroastrian purifications with the bull's urine. So, the most common word

43 The Persian version of Bahman Yašt, *DHR* II, p. 88:13. The Persian version of Ayātkār i Žamāspīk, *DHR* II, p. 102:18.

44 *DHR* I, Introduction, p. 27.

45 *DHR* I, Introduction, p. 22. See also Dhabhar, p. 630, where the following words are written in Avesta characters: *mihīn. az. hamh. dīnhā. ast. īn.*

for this fluid, *gōmēz,* is very often written in Avesta characters in Persian texts. (*DHR* I, p. 118:5; 208 (6 times); 209:6 f.; 315:14.) The alleged origin of this kind of purification is described in a poem in the following way. Ǧamšed had become leprous in one hand after having touched Ahriman. When he lay asleep in a field a bull passed by and urinated on the sick hand. The result was that the hand was healed. And thus the blessed qualities of this means of purification had been discovered. In this poem the word *gōmēz* is not used for the bull's urine, but the word شاش *šāš,* "urine," this word however being written in Avesta characters.[46]

We have seen above,[47] that the Parsis have complained, that "owing to the dread of the *darwand*'s," i.e. the Muslims, they have not been able to perform their purification with the bull's urine. Therefore it is easily understood that in the riwāyats the name of this means of purification has been kept secret or has been camouflaged.

(3) Still another Zoroastrian custom that has been kept secret through the use of Avesta characters is *sagdīd,* "the gaze of the dog." This custom consists of having a special dog ceremonially behold the corpse of a human being or an animal, before the corpse is removed. In many places, we then find the word *sagdīd,* written in Avesta characters (*DHR* II, pp. 452:15 f.; 454:3, 472:19; 478:14. Dhabhar, p. 159 n. 7.). That it is from the Muslims one has wanted to conceal this practice, is seen in the following passage from the Riwāyat of Narīmān Hōšang:

> "There are several other cases of *nasā* (i.e. dead matter) and several degrees of showing a dog and of not showing a dog (to the corpse) of a Behdīn and of an Akdīn, and there are several cases of dog species. We can write about all, but let it be known that this will be sent through Moslems."

(ود يگر چند بابت نساست چند پاى سكديد ونديد بهدين واگدين سگ سررگان چند
بابت همه توان نوشت كه بدست مسلمانان فرسته خواهد شد تا معلوم باشد)

What we have seen here may partly be called a sort of *taqiyya,* i.e., dissimulation or concealment of one's real religion or real belief. The

[46] See Spiegel, *Die traditionelle Literatur der Parsen,* p. 325. Christensen, *Les types du premier homme et du premier roi* I, p. 188, *DHR* I, p. 314. Dhabhar, pp. 295 ff. *DHR* I, Introduction, p. 28.

[47] See above, p. 65.

principle of dissimulation was especially adopted by the Shīᶜites as a fundamental tenet. But it was also practiced by other suppressed minorities such as the Mandaeans, the Manichaeans, and the Zoroastrians.[48] It seems as if this *taqiyya* was not always and not only a defense, but sometimes also an obligation dictated by the Muslims. The conditions of the *dhimmī*'s were at times such that they were obliged to conceal their religion. Thus in Islamic towns they were not allowed to exhibit the cross, manifest their polytheism, build churches or other houses for prayer, etc.[49]

[48] von Grunebaum, *Der Islam im Mittelalter,* pp. 245 f. and 524-526. Spuler, *Iran in früh-islamischer Zeit,* p. 181.

[49] Fattal, *Le statut légal des non-musulmans en pays d'Islam.* (Beyrouth, 1958) P. 79. (The author quotes Šāfiᶜī)

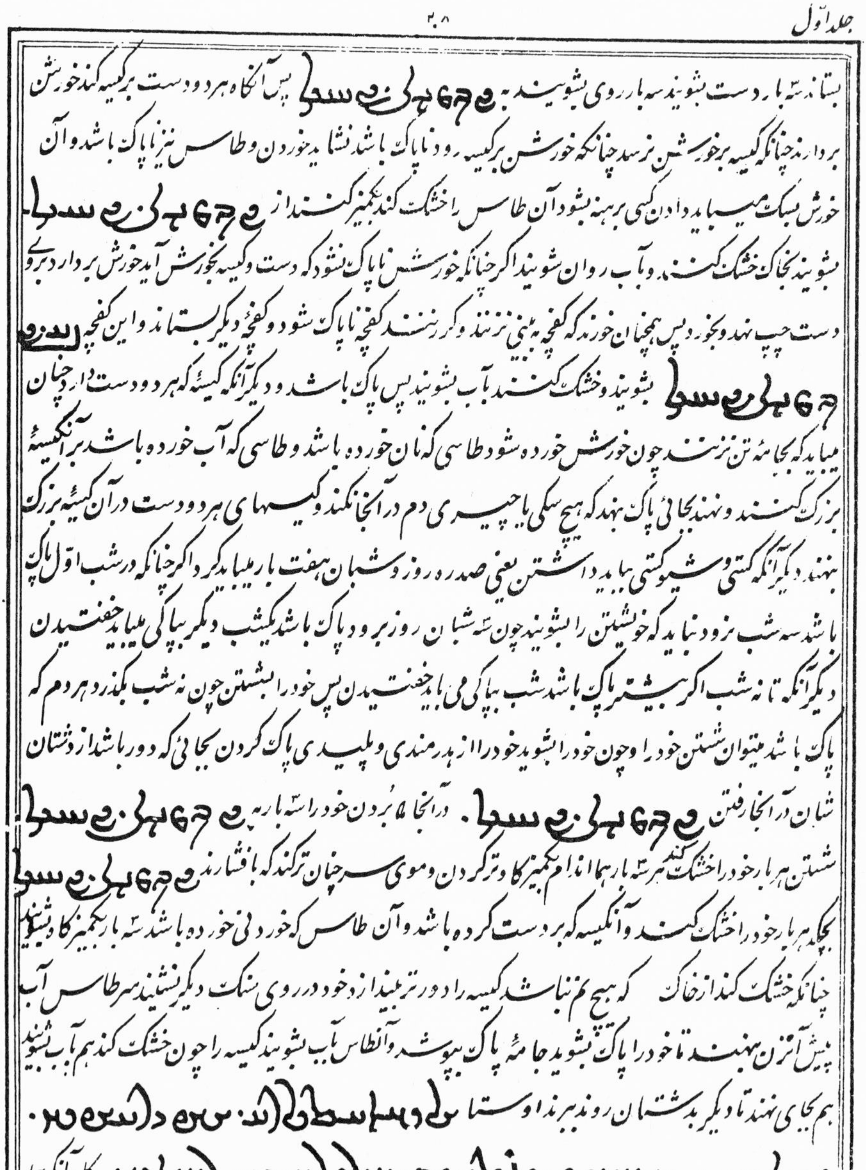
جلد اول

بستانند سه بار دست بشویند سه بار روی بشویند ... پس آنگاه هر دو دست بر کیسه کند خورش
بردارند چنانکه کیسه بر خورش نرسد چنانکه خورش بر کیسه رود ناپاک باشد نشاید خوردن و طاس نیز پاک باشد و آن
خورش بسنگ می باید دادن کسی برهنه بشود و آن طاس را خشک کند بگمیز کنند از ...
بشویند بخاک خشک کنند و آب روان بشویند اگر چنانکه خورش ناپاک نشود که دست و کیسه بخورش آید خورش بردارد در بروی
دست چپ نهد و بخورد پس همچنان خورد که کفچه به بینی نزنند و گر بزنند کفچه ناپاک شود و کفچه دیگر بستانند و این کفچه ...
بشویند و خشک کنند آب بشویند پس پاک باشد و دیگر آنکه کیسه که هر دو دست دارد چنان
میباید که بجامه تن نزنند چون خورش خورده شود طاسی که نان خورده باشد و طاسی که آب خورده باشد بر آنکیسه
بزرگ کنند و نهند بجائی پاک نهد که هیچ سگی با چیری دم در آنجا نکند و کیسهای هر دو دست در آن کیسه بزرگ
بنهند دیگر آنکه کستی و شیو کستی بباید داشتن یعنی صدره و کستی روز و شبان هفت بار میباید کرد اگر چنانکه در شب اول پاک
باشد سه شب نرود نباید که خویشتن را بشویند چون سه شبان روز برود پاک باشد یکشب دیگر بپاکی میباید خفتن
دیگر آنکه تا نه شب اگر بیشتر پاک باشد شب بپاکی می باید خفتن پس خود را بشستن چون نه شب بگذرد هر دم که
پاک باشد میتوان شستن خود را و چون خود را بشوید خود را از هر مندی و پلیدی پاک کردن بجائی که دور باشد از دشتان
شبان در آنجا رفتن ... در آنجا ... بردن خود را سه بار ...
شستن هر بار خود را خشک کنند هر سه بار همه اندام بگمیز کا و تر کردن و موی سر چنان تر کنند که بافشارند ...
بجای هر بار خود را خشک کنند و آنکیسه که بر دست کرده باشد و آن طاس که خوردنی خورده باشد سه بار بگمیز کا و بشویند
چنانکه خشک کند از خاک که هیچ نم نباشد کیسه را دور تر بنهد از خود در روی سنگ دیگر نشیند سر طاس آب
پیش آتش نزن بنهند تا خود را پاک بشوید جامه پاک بپوشد و آنطاس آب بشویند کیسه را چون خشک کند هم آب بشویند
هم بجای نهند تا دیگر بدشتان روند برند و ستا ...
... کاه آنکه بید

Škand Gumānīk Vičar

پاسخ اینکه در دین گوید دال من و سارگر و مرغ که مردار خوار اند نسا است و مرغ که شبپرک خوانند سگ سرده است نسا
هست و خرگوش گوسفند سرده است نسا نیست و کورموش و موش پران درینجانب نیست خر و ستر است و موش دو پا
درینجانب است نسا است و موش چهار پا خراستر است در باب پرسش که شخصی را شیطان در خواب بازی
داد و فراموش کرد و زند اوستا خواند و چیزی خورد و بعد از آن معلوم شد و غسل کرد پاسخ اینکه چون نادانسته است
ریمن نیست هرگاه دانسته باشند نشاید و در باب پرسش که شخصی بهدین را که [illegible] . بزور
اورا [illegible] . کنند و اورا در دل [illegible] . نیست پاسخ اینکه هرگاه بزور [illegible]
[illegible] کرده باشند و اورا دل و منشن [illegible] نیست اورا تقصیر نیست در باب پرسش
دختر که پیش از دشتان بشوهر دهند و پسر چهارده ساله کدخدا نمایند و دختر بعد از دشتان بنکاح دهند در باب
پرسش که شهوت و آب منی که از تن جدا میشود در هر ما دام که واقع شود غسل واجب آید یا نه پاسخ اینکه همه وقت
که واقع شود غسل واجب است و در باب پرسش مرطبان یا آوند چینی که ایران و جددینان طعام در او
میخورند ابهد پاک نمودن و شستن روا باشد که بهدینان در وطعام بخورند پاسخ اینکه آنچه از سنگ است یا که با آتش
گداخته میشود شاید و آنچه از خاکست که پخته میشود نشاید و در باب پرسش بعضی زند اوستا را فنام میکنند
و میخوانند و بعضی را بی فنام نمیتوان خواند سبب تفاوت چیست پاسخ اینکه پوریودکیشان در قدیم داد
نهاده اند عمل باید کرد و آنچه آتش در برابر است و برسم و یراق یزشن پیش نهاده است فنام بباید و در باب
پرسش مردم برابر نسا یعنی جنازهٔ مردگان میروند و چون بخانه رفتند همه غسل باید کرد پاسخ اینکه هرکس
نسا را بچشم دید غسل باید کرد و هرکس که نسا را ندید غسل نباید در باب پرسش کی از بهدین گناه گران کرد و میخواهد
که از آن گناه توبه کند و فرموده اند که توبه پیش دستور باید کرد و آمرزد مجرم تحقیق میداند که دستور فاسق است
درین مسئله پیش آن دستور برود یا نرود پاسخ اینکه چند تن دستور انجمن باید نمود که بمشورت دستوران جمع
آنچه فرمایند عمل باید کرد و بجز راه احوال و خواسته توجش کنند در باب پرسش پارچه جامه را که درمیان احتلام

کرده

Škand Gumānīk Vičar

Revolution and Renaissance in al-Bārūdī's Poetry

MOUNAH A. KHOURI

AMONG THE ARABIC SOURCES for the study of the patterns of Egyptian political and literary history, al-Bārūdī's poetry constitutes a historical document of major importance. As a leading participant in the ᶜUrābī Revolution and a pioneer of the contemporary literary renaissance, the poet-statesman played a unique role in the making of modern Egypt.[1]

Al-Bārūdī was born in a small town called Itāy al-Bārūd in a province of lower Egypt. At the age of seven he lost his father who was a prominent government official of Circassian extraction. The family had been long established in the country and had traditionally participated in its life as members of the ruling class. After his primary studies he attended the Cairo Military Training School for four years and graduated in 1855 at the beginning of Saᶜīd's reign. He was for a time secretary for Egyptian Affairs in Istanbul where Ismāᶜīl, then viceroy, became acquainted with him during his visit to the Ottoman capital. Impressed by al-Bārūdī's talents, Ismāᶜīl made it possible for al-Bārūdī to join his military establishment and begin a brilliant military and diplomatic career. In 1863 al-Bārūdī was in charge of the Viceregal Guard's command, and after visiting France and England as a member of an Egyptian military mission and taking part in

[1] For full references see Maḥmūd Sāmī al-Bārūdī, *Dīwān,* ed. ᶜĀlī al-Jārim and Muḥammad Maᶜrūf, 2 vols. (Cairo, 1942); *Mukhtārāt al-Bārūdī,* 4 vols. (Cairo, 1909-11); ᶜUmar al-Dasūqī, *Fī al-Adab al-Ḥadīth,* 2nd ed. (Cairo, 1954), I: 126-176; ᶜAbbās M. al-ᶜAqqād, *Shuᶜarā Miṣr wa Bī ātuhum fī al-Qarn al-Māḍi* (Cairo, 1927); Ḥasan Ḥasanayn, *Shuᶜarā al-ᶜAṣr al-Ḥāḍir* (Cairo, n.d.); Muṣṭafā Ṣ. al-Rāfiᶜī in *al-Risāla,* No. 597, 598 (1944); Yusūf Asᶜād Dagher, *Maṣādir al-Dirāsa al-Adabiyya* (Beirut, 1956), I: 159-62; *Encyc. of Islam,* New Ed., I: 1069-70.

the war of 1865 in Crete, Ismāᶜīl put him at the head of the Khedival Guard. Later he made him his private secretary and sent him to Constantinople on various diplomatic missions. In 1877 his brilliant performance as an Egyptian officer in the Turco-Russian war won him the title of Brigadier General. When Ismāᶜīl was succeeded by his son Tawfīq, al-Bārūdī became Minister of Awqāf and later Minister of War. It was at this time that he became involved in the rising nationalist movement led by Aḥmad ᶜUrābī. In February, 1882, he was at the head of the nationalist government (including ᶜUrābī as Minister of War) which had been imposed upon the Khedive and his supporters. When the Revolt collapsed and the British occupied Egypt, al-Bārūdī, together with ᶜAbduh, ᶜUrābī, and other leaders was exiled. He found himself in Ceylon where he remained for seventeen years. On his return to Egypt in 1900, he was an old man, greatly weakened and blind. He died in Cairo in 1904. It was during these long years of exile that he was able to devote himself to his abiding interest — Arabic poetry. He composed a major part of his *Dīwān* and prepared his voluminous *Mukhtārāt,* the most representative anthology of Abbasid poetry. Neither work appeared until after his death.

Even from the brief sketch outlined above, it is clear that al-Bārūdī was a man deeply involved at the highest level in the political events of his day. At the same time he was justly considered as one of the most effective pioneers of contemporary Arabic poetry.

As described by several of his contemporaries, al-Bārūdī was undoubtedly one of the most distinguished intellectuals of his generation. One of these contemporaries was Wilfrid S. Blunt, the English historian and poet. In 1880 Blunt had settled for a time in Egypt and was able to follow closely the historical events of 1881-82. Indeed he himself played a part in trying to maintain a link between Gladstone and ᶜUrābī's government. In one of his important works[2] he recorded his opinion of al-Bārūdī: "Intellectually he was far superior to Arabi, and was indeed one of the most cultivated intelligences in Egypt with a good knowledge of literature, both Arabic and Turkish, and especially of Egyptian history, besides being an elegant and distinguished poet."[3]

[2] Wilfrid S. Blunt, *Secret History of the English Occupation of Egypt* (New York: Knopf, 1922).

[3] *Ibid.,* p. 180.

This view is confirmed by A. M. Broadley, who was in charge of defending ^{c}Urābī and his fellow rebels at the trial following the collapse of the Revolt. He wrote: "Mahmud Sami had profited more by the 'European contact' than Arabi, he was better versed in modern politics and diplomacy, and he was perhaps more able and intellectually powerful than his former War Minister [^{c}Urābī]."[4]

However, in proceeding to describe al-Bārūdī's attitude toward the national and constitutional movements in this period, the two English authors do not seem to share the same view. Blunt wrote:

> I have found that we formed an erroneous idea of Mahmud Sami. I have had many conversations with him and have got information about him from his opponents. I find he is one of those who first planned the national movement as long ago as in Ismail's time. He suffered a great deal for his liberalism, yet stuck to his principles. Several of the leaders of the party, Nadim, Abdu and even Arabi, confess that they owe their power to his help and constancy. He was tempted by Ismail to give up the party, but he refused all money. He spends all his income in doing good to the party, and his house is like a caravanserai. . . . If he is hated by the Turks, it is a proof of his patriotism.[5]

In another part of his book, Blunt summed up his opinion of al-Bārūdī's part in the Revolt by saying that it was a perfectly loyal one both to the Constitution and to the national cause.[6]

Broadley, on the other hand, presented a less favorable view:

> He [al-Bārūdī] lacked the intense feeling, the wholly unselfish patriotism, and the heart-born qualities of Arabi which begot a magnetic influence of character it was difficult to resist. Arabi thought only of Egypt, Mahmud Sami also thought of Egypt, it is true, but he thought a little of himself and his ambition as well. But then it must be remembered that the race of Egyptian Ministers which preceded them thought exclusively of their own personal interest and aggrandizement, and nothing at all of the country they pretended to assist in governing.[7]

[4] Alexander M. Broadley, *How We Defended Arabi and His Friends* (London: Chapman and Hall, 1884), p. 283.

[5] Blunt, p. 249.

[6] Broadley, p. 283.

[7] *Ibid.*, p. 180.

A similar view of al-Bārūdī was apparently shared by other contemporary English observers and reflected in the "Blue Books."[8]

Among the modern Arab critics, the same type of disagreement concerning al-Bārūdī's allegiance to the national and constitutional movements exists. Muḥammad Ḥusayn Haykal, for instance, the author of the introduction to al-Bārūdī's *Dīwān,* considered him to be intellectually far superior to ᶜUrābī but certainly less sincere in his devotion to the cause of the Revolt.[9]

In order to make a proper assessment of al-Bārūdī's role as nationalist and constitutionalist, it is necessary to give a brief account of his activities, especially as they are reflected in his poetry.

In his memoirs, Aḥmad ᶜUrābī describes his first impression of al-Bārūdī when, as a Commissioner of Police, al-Bārūdī called him to his office in order to investigate his role in the first officers' riot of 1879. This was the riot that forced the dismissal of Nubar's ministry and actually precipitated the deposition of Ismāᶜīl. ᶜUrābī said at that time: "I sensed his opposition to oppression and his inclination toward justice and [the establishment of] the Constitution."[10]

Bankruptcy, despotism, foreign control and strife, characterized the life of the country at the end of Ismāᶜīl's reign. When Tawfīq became Khedive, the influence of the liberal and nationalist ideas that were becoming more articulate through al-Afghānī's teachings still weighed upon him. He inaugurated his reign by promising to carry out the needed political reforms, foremost among them the establishment of the Constitution. Al-Bārūdī, moved by these promises, could not fail to echo them in a eulogy which he composed on that occasion and addressed to the new ruler: "You have freed every chained-one, solved every difficulty, and united every scattered [opinion or group]. The subjects that were the prey of every tyrant enjoyed your justice."[11] In the same poem al-Bārūdī declared, "He established [the role of] Consultation, the most noble of guiding principles, for every rightly guided leader to follow."[12]

The leader of the Constitutionalists at this time was Sharīf Pasha,

[8] Blunt, p. 180.

[9] Al-Bārūdī, I: 27.

[10] Aḥmad ᶜUrābī, *Muthakkirāt ᶜUrābī* I (Cairo, 1953): 42.

[11] Al-Bārūdī, I: 136-137.

[12] *Ibid.,* p. 134.

who headed the first Ministry under Tawfīq. Al-Bārūdī was a friend of Sharīf and in some respects belonged to the same school of thought. Thus he participated in his cabinet as Minister of Awqāf. When Tawfīq failed to fulfill his promise of establishing the Constitution, Sharīf's Ministry had to resign in protest. Riāḍ Pasha, a strong conservative, and one of the most powerful political enemies of Sharīf and later of ᶜUrābī, accepted the premiership of the new cabinet. Al-Bārūdī was promised a free hand in his own department and probably for this reason he retained his office in Riāḍ's cabinet as Minister of Awqāf. Sharīf, obviously, felt betrayed by his friend and never forgave him for his act.[13]

Meanwhile, already favorably disposed toward each other, al-Bārūdī and ᶜUrābī strengthened their relationship through a mutual friend called ᶜAlī Rūbī.[14] When al-Bārūdī became Minister of War (February, 1881) it is almost certain that he warned ᶜUrābī and the officers of their intended arrest. After the demonstration of Qaṣr al-Nīl (February, 1881) he was openly supporting the ᶜUrābists. That was the main reason for his dismissal from Riāḍ's ministry. In the spring of 1881 al-Bārūdī was undoubtedly opposing Riāḍ. But so also was his former friend Sharīf who, in the summer of the same year, found himself in close connection with ᶜUrābī. In this way both of them were cooperating with the resistance movement in an obvious effort to restore their constitutional party to power. This they did in 1882. Under these circumstances, their political activities can hardly be called intrigues. The two men were political competitors seeking office within the framework of the same party. The test of their sincerity is best determined in terms of their allegiance to the cause of the Revolt they were supposedly committed to support.

The idea of a Constitution as conceived by Sharīf and most members of his school of thought was one in which the supreme power, though taken from the Khedive, was to remain in the hands of the only class capable of ruling the country — the Turco-Circassian oligarchy. Despite their professed liberalism, they were essentially as much opposed to the basic demands of the Egyptian nationalists as was Riāḍ and his reactionary group. They all shared the same con-

[13] ᶜUrābī, I: 81-82. See also Blunt, p. 370.

[14] Blunt, p. 102.

tempt for the Egyptian masses and the same resistance to the rising Egyptian officers.

Al-Bārūdī, despite his Circassian origin, was largely divorced from the way of thinking of this whole ruling class. This is evidenced not only by his cooperation with ᶜUrābī and his military associates, but also with al-Afghānī's disciples of the Azhar group — ᶜAbduh, Nadīm, and other civilian leaders.

When the Khedive Tawfīq exiled al-Afgh̲ānī in 1879, ᶜAbduh had to leave Cairo for his village, vacating his position in Cairo at both Dār al-ᶜUlūm and the School of Languages. In 1880 he was back in Cairo looking for a job. He went to see one of his friends, ᶜAlī-Mubārak, who was then Minister of Public Works in Riāḍ's cabinet. But Mubārak received him badly, suspecting that he came in connection with a secret society that had been recently formed by Shahīn Pasha and ᶜUmar Luṭfī. He went then to see another friend, Maḥmūd Sāmī al-Bārūdī, who was then Minister of Awqāf. At that time Riāḍ Pasha was finding it difficult to locate anyone who could write good Arabic in the Official Gazette (*al-Waqā'i al-Miṣrīyya*) and he consulted Maḥmūd Sāmī al-Bārūdī, who told him that if there were three more like him (ᶜAbduh) Egypt could be saved.[15] ᶜAbduh, at the recommendation of his friend al-Bārūdī, was appointed (October, 1880) third editor, and then Chief editor and Director of the Press. During the following two years and until the collapse of the ᶜUrābī Revolt, he published a series of articles on the social and political order and on national education that were very influential in forming public opinion.[16]

Later, Blunt, after an interview with ᶜUrābī, drew up with ᶜAbduh, Nadīm, and other civilian leaders, a statement embodying their national aspirations and sent it to Gladstone and to the *Times*. Al-Bārūdī was then Minister of War for the second time and gave his adherence to that program.[17]

In his description of a nationalist dinner party which was followed by a political discussion, Blunt reports that the nationalists, and in particular al-Bārūdī, preferred the republican form of government.

> Arabi, Mahmud Sami, Ahmad Pasha, Abdu, Nadim, and I were

[15] *Ibid.*, p. 378.

[16] See Albert Hourani, *Arabic Thought in the Liberal Age, 1798-1939* (Oxford: Oxford University Press, 1962), p. 133.

[17] Blunt, p. 132.

in the principal sitting room, where we recited poetry, making or composing elegies and satires and amusing ourselves at Ragheb's expense.[18] Arabi composed a satire, Abdu two, Nadim made four, and Sami two. After dinner we talked freely about politics and about different plans and forms of government. The republican form was preferred and Mahmud Sami, who displayed great knowledge and ingenuity endeavored to show the advantage of a republican government for Egypt. He said:

"From the beginning of our movement we aimed at turning Egypt into a small republic like Switzerland . . . and then Syria would have joined . . . and then Hejaz would have followed us. But we found some of the Ulema were not quite prepared for it and were behind our time. Nevertheless we shall endeavour to make Egypt a republic before we die."[19]

One may be inclined to think that Blunt, a romantic poet and a passionate lover of great ideas, is probably projecting here his own vision of an ideal Egyptian republic rather than that of al-Bārūdī and his friends. But whatever the case may be, it is a fact that al-Bārūdī had more affinity with this circle of Egyptian leaders than he had with his own Turco-Circassian class. Beyond religion and language, the strongest bond that held all the members of the National Party together (and counterbalanced their differences) was their strong patriotic feeling. It is precisely this patriotic sentiment so brilliantly expressed in al-Bārūdī's poetry together with his other liberal ideas that linked him with men like ᶜAbduh, Nadīm, ᶜUrābī, and other nationalists, and made him one of the best known and best loved men in Egypt.

That he was possessed by the love of Egypt is evidenced in his *waṭanīyyāt* or patriotic poems which he composed before and after his exile. In those poems vivid images of the Egyptian *rīf,* farms, the Nile, and other natural scenes are elegantly rendered. Deeply rooted in the traditions of his country and proudly conscious of its glorious past, the great pyramids stirred his imagination and inspired one of his most famous poems:

Ask the spacious Giza about the two pyramids of Egypt, so that you may know the secret of that unknown to you before.

[18] Prime Minister after the fall of al-Bārūdī's Ministry in 1882.
[19] Blunt, pp. 260-261.

Two structures repelling the assault of ages. What a wonder is their overcoming of this assault!

They stood despite the calamities of ages to prove the glory of their builders in the world.

How many nations have perished and ages lapsed while they remain the wonder of the eye and the mind.[20]

Such a poem, reminiscent of al-Buḥturī's[21] "'Iwān Kisrā," was the starting point in modern Arabic verse of a long series of compositions written later by Shawqī and his fellow poets. They became an important factor in the development of Egyptian national consciousness.

However, the most authentic expression of al-Bārūdī's nationalist feeling is found in the great number of poems which he wrote during his lonely years of exile. The following selection may best illustrate his concept of the word *waṭan* with all the memories it evokes in his heart and mind.

Oh Egypt, may your shadow be extended [power increased] and your soil be drenched with the pure water of the Nile.

You are the sanctuary of my people and the branching place of my family, the playground of my age-mates and the racing course of my horses.

A country in which youth took off the amulet of my childhood and hung the scabbard of my sword on my shoulder.

I left behind in it noble kinsmen and neighbors whose image comes back to me every morning.

I left the sweetness of life after their departure and said farewell to the soft flower of youth.[22]

What is this *ḥimā* or *waṭan* to which al-Bārūdī refers again and again in his *Dīwān?* It is definitely the land of Egypt and not any other Arab land. His saying in one of his poems: "It is enough for you to know [that we have] an Arab character . . . like wine — unless enraged,"[23] and, "I long for Najd and its people, but how far is Najd from me now!"[24] is merely a reproduction of some love verses from the classical period and does not reflect any articulate Arab consciousness

[20] Al-Bārūdī, I: 47.

[21] Al-Buḥturī was an Arab poet and anthologist of the third (206-284) and ninth (821-897) centuries.

[22] Al-Bārūdī, II: 361-363. See also pp. 321-328.

[23] Al-Bārūdī, I: 165.

[24] Al-Bārūdī, I: 215.

in his mind. As it was for Tahṭāwī before him, and for his teacher Ḥusayn al-Marṣafī,[25] as well as for his friends ᶜAbduh[26] and Nadīm, the term *waṭan* has for him more or less the same meaning as the French *patrie*. It is the mother country which binds together all those who live in it and share the same feeling.

Al-Bārūdī was conscious, as al-Afghānī and ᶜAbduh had been, of the intolerable conditions of Egyptian society when depressions, foreign intervention, and disturbances reached their height before the outbreak of the ᶜUrābī Revolt. Describing the state of agitation, fear, and ruin which prevailed at that time, and anticipating a revolt which, he hoped, would bring about a brighter future for Egypt and its people, he says:

> Egypt's good fortune has changed beyond recognition, and the foundations of the kingdom have been violently shaken so that the very birds were frightened.
>
> The cultivator, as a result of tyranny, has neglected his land; and the merchant, from fear of poverty, has withdrawn his money.
>
> Such dread has become so dominant that none can sleep in the dark of night, but remain vigilant.
>
> Woe to such a land! Were it not for the great heritage buried therein we would not have lived in its vicinity.
>
> I tolerate it though it gives me no blessing. My hopes would be elsewhere were it not for my people.
>
> My soul, do not despair, for good is expected and the will of a man of patience does not weaken.
>
> Perhaps a gleam of light will illuminate the way, after a night in which darkness has prevailed.
>
> I see souls no longer able to bear their burdens; I see sword bearers about to unsheath their swords.[27]

Again, like al-Afghānī and ᶜAbduh, al-Bārūdī was conscious of the need for reform. This he conceived in terms of his main preoccupation with politics and the problem of power. Thus, turning his attention from the broad ideological questions to the more immediate aspects of political reform, his program stresses two major demands: a constitu-

[25] See Hourani, pp. 78-79 and 194-197.

[26] See Muḥammad Rashīd Riḍā, *Ta'rīkh al-Ustādh al-Imām al-Shaykh Muḥammad Abduh,* Vols. II & III (Cairo: 1324/1906-1907), pp. 200-203.

[27] Al-Bārūdī, II: 128-129.

tional government and a strong army: "There are two things which have never existed together under the leader of a nation without yielding to him the fruits of glory: An assembly working through consultation and an army watchful for the enemy."[28]

The army will defend the nation against its enemies, and the constitution will guarantee its rights. In ᶜAbduh's words, "The inclination of some people to demand a *shūra* ("parliamentary assembly") and to reject absolutism does not come simply from a desire to imitate the foreigner, but is in accordance with what the Sharīᶜa requires."[29] This is rendered faithfully by al-Bārūdī when he says:

> He established [the role of] Consultation, the most noble of guiding principles, for every rightly guided leader to follow.
> Consultation is the protector of the religion revealed to the Prophet Muḥammad by the Lord of Creation.
> He who seeks its support makes firm his rule, and he who disdains it will be led astray.[30]

When ᶜUrābī and his associates assumed the leadership of the movement of national opposition, al-Bārūdī's two aims — a strong army and a constitution — became focal points of their program. Unlike ᶜAbduh, who disapproved of the ideas and methods of the military leaders[31] and was extremely critical of ᶜUrābī,[32] al-Bārūdī was one of their most influential supporters. ᶜUrābī himself undoubtedly had full confidence in al-Bārūdī and never tired of referring to him in his memoirs as the only civilian trusted by the army and as a lover of freedom, justice, and equality.

But while taking a leading part in the resistance movement, al-Bārūdī acted in general with caution and moderation. In fact, at times he seemed to belong to the "quietist" group of Muslim thinkers who believe that they should protest against injustice but submit to it, leaving the ruler's judgment to God. Here is an example of the poet's quietism: "Oh tyrant in your kingdom, are you deceived by the power

[28] Al-Bārūdī, I: 135.

[29] Quoted in Nadav Safran, *Egypt in Search of Political Community* (Cambridge: Harvard University Press, 1961), p. 47. Cf. Afaf Lutfi al-Sayyid, *Egypt and Cromer* (London, 1968), p. 13.

[30] Al-Bārūdī, I: 134-135.

[31] *Al-Manār,* VIII: 412.

[32] Riḍā, III: 528.

which vanishes? Do what you will to us in cruelty. God is just; Judgement Day is tomorrow.[33]

It is mainly this moderate attitude which led some critics to claim that al-Bārūdī was less patriotic than ᶜUrābī or even to explain his conduct during the whole crisis in terms of his selfish interests. They may be only partly true. Of course he was less involved in the movement than ᶜUrābī and disapproved of the solution of problems by resorting to violence. He also encouraged the desire of some people which developed at the time of confusion following the resignation of his Ministry (May 26, 1882), to dethrone the Khedive and install him in his place. Thus he makes allusions to his personal ambitions in a poem which must have been written during this period:[34] "So make haste before it's too late, and throw off the shackles of slowness, for the world goes to the fleet. And entrust your affairs to someone noble and trustworthy who will be your supporter in great events."[35]

Even if it can be agreed that this poem was not written at the end of Ismāᶜīl's reign (as the *Dīwān* shows) and that the allusion made here is not to the young Tawfīq but rather to himself, this is not enough reason to conclude that al-Bārūdī was only motivated in his connection with the ᶜUrābists by selfish interests. His loyalty was further evidenced by the fact of his joining the revolt (though after much thought), when the British attack began on Egypt. At that time, he and the much more moderate ᶜAbduh found themselves by the side of ᶜUrābī, fighting or organizing a national resistance. After the collapse of the Revolt, their fate was the same — "defeat, psychological depression born of shipwrecked hopes and the agony of despair,"[36] trial and return to their country after long or short periods of exile.

Summing up ᶜAbduh's defense at the trial, Broadley quotes ᶜAbduh as saying: "Can anybody doubt that our struggle was a national one when men of all races and creeds . . . rushed to join it with enthusiasm, rendering all the assistance in their power, believing it to be a war between the Egyptians and England. I never heard it said that the Khedive was fighting against his own army." Then ᶜAbduh, as re-

[33] Al-Bārūdī, I: 253.

[34] See M. Ḥ. Raykal's introduction to al-Bārūdī's *Dīwān,* I: 26-27.

[35] *Ibid.,* p. 27. Cf. Abd al-Raḥmān al-Rāfiᶜī, *Shuᶜarā' al-Waṭaniyya* (Cairo: 1954), p. 26.

[36] Broadley, pp. 227-228.

ported by Broadley, continues to justify his participation in the Revolt by saying:

> About this time [the fight between the Egyptian and British forces] the ulema began reading Bokhary at the university of El-Azhar and at Sidy Hussein, and public prayers were offered up for the success of Arabi's troops and the defeat of the English. The Khedive's Imam (Chaplain), the pious and learned Sheikh El-Abiary, was prominent in the vivacity of his patriotic zeal. This man published the soul-stirring poem written by Ibrahim Doraid when the Tartars took Baghdad, in the time of Molasem [Mustaᶜṣim in 1258] the Abbasid Khalifa, which is a prayer to God Almighty. The Sheikh added to it some stanzas of his own composition, and requested the people to read it and recite it publicly, after the reading of Bokhary. He also asked me to insert it in the paper, so that the army might read it too. This was perfectly justifiable, as the war was believed by all to be a Moslem war against infidels; and the same Sheikh I have mentioned was the man who preached the sermon on the return of the Khedive to Cairo after the war exhorting all men to obey him.[37]

If the views expounded in Broadley's report are those of ᶜAbduh, and there is ample evidence that they can be taken as such,[38] then according to him (ᶜAbduh) ᶜUrābī's Revolt was a war between Egyptian nationalists and foreign invaders as well as a Muslim war against infidels. Thus by 1882 Egyptian national consciousness, though more articulate than before, was still fused with Muslim consciousness. The idea of the political unity of the nation and that of the Umma were inextricably linked. The same ambivalence in ᶜAbduh's thought between these two ideas existed in that of his master al-Afghānī and was the prevalent attitude of other Egyptian leaders.[39] It is clearly reflected in al-Bārūdī's defense of himself when he says: "I committed no offense which should condemn me to this, my state. Why [must I suffer] this distress and grief? Was that, my defense of religion and country, a crime for which I should be unjustly condemned and exiled?"[40]

[37] Broadley, p. 232.

[38] See Riḍa, III: 524-530.

[39] See Hourani, p. 155. See also Maḥmūd al Khafīf, *Aḥmad Urābī, Al-Zaᶜīm al-Muftarā ᶜalayh* (Cairo, 1947), p. 427.

[40] Al-Bārūdī, I: 65.

Elsewhere al-Bārūdī's Islamic feelings are more fully expressed. After denying that it was his intention to overthrow the Khedive, he asserts that his revolutionary acts were guided by his convictions as a true Muslim reformer. He wanted to secure for the Egyptian people their constitutional rights enjoined by the Sharīᶜa along with their liberty. When the ruler denied these rights his revolt against him became legitimate since it had no other purpose except to serve God and the Egyptian community:

> Some people say that I revolted to dethrone [the Khedive]. Such defects (disloyalty) are far from my character.
>
> Nay, I called for justice, seeking to please God, and I awakened the people of truth.
>
> I commanded good and forbade evil, and that is but the obligation of all people.
>
> If my action was a rebellion, then I intended through my rebellion to please my Lord.
>
> Is the call for consultation a disgrace to me when in it lies the guidance (that which makes a distinction between truth and falsity) for the seeker of the right way?
>
> Nay, truly it is an obligatory observance imposed by God on every living soul, ruling or ruled.
>
> How could anyone be free and cultured while approving of that which every sinner commits?
>
> Though others have been treacherously hypocritical in their religion, praise be to God that I am not of their number.
>
> Verily I did my utmost to advise those whose treachery prevented them from accepting sincere advice.
>
> They decided to rule the people by force, and so they hastened to violate their established agreements.
>
> When oppression continued a military group raised their banners in revolt.
>
> The people of the country supported them and rushed to join from all sides.
>
> They wanted the ruler of the country to carry out the sincere promise he had sworn to his people.
>
> This is the evident truth, so do not ask others, for verily I am the knower of truths.[41]

While in exile, al-Bārūdī recollected in tranquility his experiences

[41] Al-Bārūdī, II: 359-361.

with the ᶜUrābī movement and embodied them in a series of moving poems that reflect his self-image as he says: "Look at my poetry and you will find my soul mirrored in it, for my poetry is the reflection of my self."[42]

They also reveal certain aspects of the general state of confusion which prevailed among the exiles after the collapse of their movement, namely, suspicion, accusation, despair, guilt, self-defense, revolt, and other currents of turbulent and mixed feelings born of crushing defeat.[43] However, in these poems Egypt[44] and Islam[45] remained his favorite themes and the object of his affection and pride.

In his elegy to al-Bārūdī written shortly after his death a fellow poet, Khalīl Muṭrān, summed up the activities and achievement of the poet-statesman by saying: "O you conquerer of miraculous [heroism], O you poet of [art] sublime. Both the glory of the pen and the honor of the sword have chosen you for their crowns. The former you secured, the latter you missed, though it should have been yours.[46]

Of the two crowns al-Bārūdī sought to obtain, he lost that of political leadership but was able to secure the crown of poetry, which he retained until his death in 1904. His preeminent position passed then to Shawqī, Ḥāfiẓ, and Muṭrān. The first was "officially" crowned as the Prince of Poets.

What was al-Bārūdī's literary contribution? And in what sense can he be considered one of the most effective pioneers of contemporary Arabic poetry?

In Egypt the poetic compositions of Ḥasan al-Aṭṭār (d. 1835), Ḥasan Fuwaydir (d. 1845), ᶜAlī al-Darwīsh (d. 1853) and other minor poets of the first half of the nineteenth century were merely a continuation of the literary activities of the period of decline. Far-fetched similes, metaphors, allusions, chronograms, amplifications of predecessors' works, and similar rhetorical devices intended to display erudition and mastery of language characterized the bulk of poetry produced by these poets.[47] They remained unaffected by the impact of Muḥammad ᶜAlī's reforms. The professional schools he opened, the

42 Quoted by al-Rāfiᶜī, p. 23.

43 See al-Bārūdī, I: 98 and II: 86-87, 296-297.

44 *Ibid.*, I: 109-110, 207-214 and II: 47-55, 130-135, 256-263, 321-328.

45 *Ibid.*, I: 100-104 and II: 359-360.

46 *Al-Muqtaṭāf*, XXX (February, 1905): 94.

47 See ᶜUmar Dasūqī, *Fī al-Adab al-Ḥadīth*, 2 vols. (Cairo, 1951), I: 38-52.

educational missions he sent to Europe, the movement of translation he created under the direction of Rifāᶜa al-Ṭahṭāwī, the printing press he founded in order to publish the translated works and the official Gazette — all these and other developments that occurred under his reign were too technically oriented to have any effect on the literary activities of the period. Even under the more favorable conditions of Ismāᶜīl's reign, the major poets (with one exception) were left basically untouched by the process of Westernization which reached its peak during that period. In fact, while Egypt's borrowing from Europe's fund of educational methods, science, law, administration, and other fields was taking place, and while the development of the new periodical press along with the growth of the school of Syrian and Egyptian translators was bringing the society closer to Western thought, literary composition — and in particular poetry — was deriving its inspiration from the Arab classical works and not from Western models. "In the sphere of poetry," wrote Gibb, "the continuing classical tradition far outweighed any literary influences from the West down to 1914."[48] But while poets like ᶜAlī al-Laythī (d. 1896), ᶜAlī Abū al-Naṣr (d. 1881), and Maḥmūd Ṣafwat al-Sāᶜātī (d. 1880) were still composing panegyrics, elegies, satires, pleasure songs, and other poetic forms cramped by artifice and overloaded with the traditional rhetorical devices, two other contemporaries, Muḥammad ᶜUthmān Jalāl (1828-1898) and Maḥmūd Sāmī al-Bārūdī were following new trends and trying to innovate. Both were motivated by the same dissatisfaction with the ornamental and inflated style of poetry. Jalāl's revolt against the conventional poetry of his day is reminiscent of Bashshār's or Abū Nuwās's against the traditionalists of their own time, when he says: "And they claim that eloquence could not be better than in a poem which compares the shape of a woman to a spear; The color of a cheek to roses and fire; and the brightness of a face — when it appears — to the morning."[49] The same idea is implied in al-Bārūdī's conception of good poetry: "The best [poetic] language is that whose words harmonize and whose meanings are free from ambiguity."[50]

Despite the differences between the predominantly aristocratic so-

[48] H. A. R. Gibb, "Arabiyya," in *Encyc. of Islam,* 2nd ed., I: 597.
[49] Uthmān Jalāl, *al-ᶜUyūn al-yawāqiẓ,* p. 102, quoted by Dasuqi, I: 90.
[50] Al-Bārūdī, I: 3.

cial origin and audience of al-Bārūdī and the more common social origin and more popular audience of Jalāl, neither of the poets was supported by a patron.

Whether selected, translated or original, their works were mainly intended to express their own thoughts and experiences. This is shown in al-Bārūdī's assertion that he composed his poetry "not seeking any person's favor nor aspiring to material gain. Only natural feelings inspired me."[51]

Jalāl's translations and popular poetry, on the other hand, were motivated by the impact of French literature on his sensibility and by his own desire to amuse and educate his audience.

Here ends, however, their similarities. In searching for their models and poetic mediums, Jalāl looked forward to find himself fascinated by Bernardin de Sainte Pierre, Racine, Lafontaine, and Molière. He made translations of their works either in Arabic verse or in pure Egyptian colloquial. Since the Bulāq printing press was set up by Muḥammad ᶜAlī in 1821, and turned out hundreds of translations from European authors or republished a large number of Arabic masterpieces from the period before the decline, there occurred in Egypt a definite change in literary taste. But such a change was not so drastic as to make Jalāl's complete repudiation of the old literary tradition in favor of the new Western models really tolerable.[52] However, Molière's Egyptian-like humor, and Lafontaine's fables not unlike *Kalīla wa Dimna,* could not have been as alien and novel to his audience as his weak and "vulgar" medium of expression: "Believe me it's none of your business. It is your stepfather's affair."[53] As Gibb says, "The time was scarcely ripe for a step so decisive, but the complete breach with the past which it illustrated was an indication of the spirit of the age."[54]

Not less representative of his age al-Bārūdī, who, though looking

[51] Al-Bārūdī, I: 5-6.

[52] See H. A. R. Gibb, *Studies on the Civilization of Islam,* S. Shaw and W. Polk, eds. (Boston: Beacon Press, 1962), pp. 248-249.

[53] ᶜUthmān Jalāl, quoted by Dasūqī, I: 90.

[54] Gibb, *Studies,* p. 242. Describing this line of development due, in his opinion, to the impact of the West, G. E. von Grunebaum says: "Whether unconsciously or by design, the West has been ever present in the mind of the middle Easterners since Napoleon invaded . . . Egypt. It has been present as a menace, as a helper, as a model." See *Modern Isalm* (Berkeley, 1962), p. 220.

backward instead of thrusting too far ahead, knew how to transcend a dead past for a living and glorious one. This he did in order to revive its literary values, reaffirm them in his own poetical works, and recreate among the Arabic speaking peoples a better taste for the appreciation of their own poetry.

In their common pursuit of genuine reform, al-Bārūdī and ᶜAbduh, his friend, seem to follow, whether unconsciously or by design, the same patterns of action. At the beginning of his fragment of biography ᶜAbduh defines two of his major purposes: "First to liberate thought from the shackles of *taqlīd* and understand religion as it was understood by the elders of the community before dissension appeared; to return, in the acquisition of religious knowledge, to its first sources, and to weigh them in the scales of human reason. . . . My second purpose has been the reform of the way of writing the Arabic language. . . ."[55]

As a poet committed mainly to the cause of literary reform, al-Bārūdī's task involved, like ᶜAbduh's, two major goals; first, to free the conventional poetry prevalent in his time from the shackles of *taqlīd,* and to return, in the acquisition of a genuine poetic taste, to the classical works of the masters of Abbasid period. This task he achieved in the *Mukhtārāt* published in Cairo in four volumes, two in 1909 and two in 1911. This anthology contained 39,593 verses by thirty Abbasid poets. Al-Bārūdī's classification was vital for the renewal of interest in great poets such as Ibn al-Rūmī, al-Maᶜarrī and others who had been almost forgotten. After the *Mukhtārāt* appeared, they became an inexhaustible source of literary appreciation. Moreover, the arrangement of the *Mukhtārāt* in categories with the *Adab* (moral or ethical) subjects first and the occasional subjects such as *Madīḥ* (panegyric) and *Rithā'* (Threnody) second, is a very significant feature of al-Bārūdī's anthology. It marks the beginning of a new trend toward the freer, more personal kind of poetry which appeared also in his own *Dīwān* and was developed later by other poets. Connected with his anthology is his "Kashf al-Ghumma fī Madḥ Sayyid al-Umma," a long poem of 447 verses, in which he expressed his Islamic zeal as well as the religious spirit of his age while imitating al-Būsīrī's famous "Burda."[56] His success in this imitative work led several of

[55] Riḍā, I, 11, quoted by Hourani, p. 140.

[56] Al-Būṣīrī (1213-1295/6) is a distinguished Arab poet of Berber origin. According to the legend he composed his celebrated poem of 172 verses, "al Kawākib

his ardent admirers to prefer his ode to its model,[57] and stimulated Aḥmad Shawqī to compose later his own praise of the prophet in his poem called "Nahj al-Burda" using the same metre and the same rhyme.

The second task al-Bārūdī set himself was to revitalize the poetic language itself — to make an effective medium for the expression of the poet's thoughts and feelings. That he fulfilled this purpose with resounding success is clearly demonstrated in his *Dīwān,* of which only the poems with rhymes "hamza" to "lām" appeared after his death. Whether they are conscious imitations of his models from the classical period, or original compositions embodying his own experiences, al-Bārūdī's poems reveal that he attained an undisputed mastery of the poetic language in its purest and most dynamic classical form.

It was this striking feature of his poetic style that led some major Arab critics like al-ᶜAqqād, Ṭāhā Ḥusayn, Haykal and others to consider his achievement a unique literary event in contemporary Egyptian poetry. Al-ᶜAqqād, for instance, describes his poetic idiom by saying: "He has . . . a distinctive characteristic that has no equal in the history of modern Egyptian literature, and that is that he jumped in poetic expression, in a single leap, from the level of weakness to that of strength. He did this almost suddenly and without the benefits of previous pioneering efforts."[58] Ṭāhā Ḥusayn, on the other hand, who was displeased with the development of poetry in the hands of Ḥāfiẓ and Shawqī, as compared with that of prose, which was moving far ahead in the hands of contemporary writers, has this to say about al-Bārūdī's achievement:

> The literary taste began to change [during the second half of the 19th century]. It was a basic change that manifested itself in two aspects: the first, preferring the colloquial language to that of con-

al-Durriyya fī Madḥ Khayr al-Bariyya" — best known as "al-Burda" — when he was cured of a paralytic stroke by the Prophet's throwing his mantle over his shoulders as he had done on a previous occasion for his own poet, Kaᶜb b. Zuhayr. See "Burda" by R. Basset in *Ency. of Islam.* 2nd ed., I: 1314-1315. Cf. Būsīrī, *Dīwān,* ed. M. Kaylānī (Cairo: al-Babi, 1955).

[57] See Zakī Mubārak, *al-Muwāzana bayn al-Shuᶜarā* (Cairo, 1926), p. 185; M. M. Rashid, "Ḥamāmatā al-Bārūdī," in *al-Thaqāfa,* I (May, 1939): 46. See also A. al-Zayn, "Aḥsan ma Yurwā," *al-Thāqāfa,* I (February, 1939): 34-35, and Muṣtafā Ṣ. al-Rāfiᶜī, "Shiᶜr al-Bārūdī," in *al-Muqtaṭāf,* XXX (March, 1905): 189-195.

[58] Al-ᶜAqqād, p. 121.

> temporary literature; the second, preferring the old language and styles to those of the present age. . . . Prose was proceeding apace with poetry in this movement, but its development was slow. It was slower than the development of poetry. Likewise at the end of the last century and the beginning of this one the poetry of al-Bārūdī appeared Arabic, pure, eloquent and free, while al-Shaykh Muḥammad Abduh's prose was wavering between the eloquence of the old prose and the weakness of the new.[59]

The same appreciation of al-Bārūdī's successful efforts to renovate the poetic language is expressed by H. Haykal in his introduction to the poet's *Dīwān*.

It is hard to determine the reasons for al-Bārūdī's success as a poet during this period. However, three factors at least are worth mentioning. First, he was undoubtedly much more gifted than any other poet of his generation. Second, he was not subjected to the rigid traditional training of his age (prosody, rhetoric, philology, grammar, etc.). As a result, he was able to pursue a freer, more dynamic aesthetic appreciation of what he considered to be genuine Arabic poetry.[60] Third, he was not directly exposed to western literature, and did not therefore channel his energies into imitating its themes, styles, and techniques. At this stage, however, "Western ideas had been too rapidly acquired to have penetrated more than skin-deep,"[61] and it is questionable whether al-Bārūdī could have been more successful than ᶜUthmān Jalāl had he joined the advanced wing of the modernists instead of leading the revivalist literary movement.

Altogether, then, al-Bārūdī was the first poet of distinction who led the one significant new trend in poetry during the formative phase of the literary renaissance in Egypt and the Arab Middle East. He freed the poetic language from the chains of mannerism and provided in his own works the spark needed for its revival. He showed that poetry, in proportion to its vigor and excellence, could affect the sensibility of the community by stimulating its religious and national consciousness. It is very significant that at the time of the Anglo-Egyptian hostilities in

[59] Ṭāhā Ḥusayn, *Ḥāfiẓ wa Shawqī,* 4th ed. (Cairo, 1958), pp. 4-5. Cf. H. Pérès, "Aḥmad Shawqi," in AIEO, II (1936): 313-315.

[60] See Muḥammad Ṣabrī, *Maḥmūd Sāmī al-Bārūdī* (Cairo, 1923), p. 11. Cf. Al-Bārūdī, I, 11.

[61] Gibb, *Studies,* p. 249.

1882, the Egyptian masses were called upon to recite with al-Būkhārī some powerful, soul-stirring poems composed on the occasion of Baghdad's fall. What could be more evocative of the religious and national feelings in the hearts of men during that crisis than a sonorous, declamatory, oratorical ode composed by a distinguished poet? In fact al-Bārūdī's patriotic poems not only reflected the rise of the nationalist movement in Egypt, but also contributed to both the articulation and wider circulation of its main ideas and aspirations. Basic terms such as *ᶜadl* ("justice"), *ḥurriyya* ("freedom"), *shūrā* or *mashūra* ("consultation," "deliberation"), *ḥuqūq* ("rights"), *qawm* ("folk," "people," "nation"), *ḥimā* or *waṭan* ("patrie"), *difāᶜ* ("defense"), and many other formulas deriving their connotations from the constitutionalist and nationalist movements were effectively expressed in his poetry and communicated to this audience. Although he was not the popular poet of the ᶜUrābī Revolt, as Abdallāh al-Nadīm was its orator, many of his poems echo its atmosphere and reveal that the movement was more than the handiwork of a few selfish officers. It was a revolt led by a group of liberals who, either by national sentiment or religious conviction, or both, sought to replace absolute rule by constitutional government, and to defend the rights and liberty of the Egyptian community against foreign domination.[62] No one, perhaps, felt more intensely the crushing defeat of the nationalist movement than al-Bārūdī. He expressed that living experience of defeat in powerful verses that could not have failed to affect the sensibility of his readers.

[62] While fully aware of ᶜUrābī's shortcomings, Aḥmad Luṭfī al-Sayyid nevertheless wrote about his achievement thus: "Were it not for ᶜUrābī, there would have been no Constitution. The Egyptian Constitution of 1882 is his work, accomplished by his own hands, and the result of his courage. ᶜUrābī sought it, not as a military revolutionary, but as a deputy on behalf of the nation which had entrusted him with this task. For the petition demanding the Constitution was signed by the notables and leaders of the nation. And if the military power which was the tool for the execution of the nation's will at Maydān ᶜĀbidīn was not judicially legal, it was, however, legal according to the traditions of nations, for this was the established practice in many countries." See Aḥmad Luṭfī al-Sayyid, *al-Muntakhabāt* I (Cairo, 1937): 252-256.

The Ultimate Origin and the Hereafter in Islam

FRITZ MEIER*

ISLAM is a monotheistic religion. That is to say, it is not satisfied with the natural observation that man does not comprehend the entire web of interrelationships between causes and effects in which he and the world exist and act, but rather that he is imbedded in problems which transcend conscious awareness, i.e., in things transcendental. Nor does Islam stop with the philosophical speculation that everything, both that which is accessible to the consciousness, and the transcendental, ultimately goes back to a *first cause.* It asserts that this latter super-transcendental power *reveals itself* to man in varied ways. It calls this power God and teaches a succession of pronouncements and manifestations of this God from the earliest times on earth to the present day. In addition, however, Islam distinguishes the divine pronouncements according to their different purposes. Not all of them are necessarily meant for the public. Those which are not so designated are called inspirations, while those which are intended for the public are called revelations. The latter can be fragmentary or comprehensive and legislative. They are now all completed and, in contrast to the inspirations, God does not supplement them with others. As a consequence, also the mediators who have received or still receive divine pronouncements are arranged in different ranks. The receivers of inspirations are called friends of God; the receivers of the fragmentary revelations are the prophets; the receivers of comprehensive systems finally are called Messengers of God. Each Messenger of God is also a prophet

* The editor is grateful to Mr. Hans Hoch of the Linguistics Department, University of Illinois, and to Mrs. Hannelone Antonsen for translating Professor Meier's article from German to English.

and a friend of God, but not each prophet and friend of God is at the same time a Messenger of God. Since the revelations are complete, the succession of prophets and God-sent people is completed. The last and final pronouncement of God is the Koran, and the "Seal of the Prophets" and of the Messengers of God is Mohammed who between 610 and 632 A.D. founded Islam in the two Arabic cities of Mekka and Medina, immediately to the south and the north of the Tropic of Cancer. Mohammed considered Biblical figures like Abraham, Moses, and Jesus his predecessors, prophets and Messengers of God who, like he, had transmitted to mankind comprehensive, compulsory laws of God; but he declared that their followers, the Jews and the Christians, had falsified these documents and that he, Mohammed, had come to replace these scriptures by the final and ultimate revelation of God, as set forth in the Koran. In addition, he left behind his own pronouncements which he did not declare to be the Word of God and which, therefore, do not appear in the Koran. These utterances form a corpus of their own and are recognized as additional guiding principles and, as Words of the Prophet (*ḥadīṯh*), in the eyes of his followers, the Muslims, they enjoy a rank not much lower than the Word of God contained in the Koran.

One might think that a religious community like that of Islam, which claims to possess in black and white the ultimate wisdom expressed by God and His infallible messenger, would have no further history of philosophical speculation. A number of objections have to be made against this view. Firstly, the only thing that was relatively firmly established was the Koran, while the aphoristic tradition of the Prophet was subject to great vacillations and augmentations in scope and wording, as well as to obvious falsifications. Secondly, not all inhabitants of the Islamic world have been affected to the same degree by the religious doctrine of Islam. Thirdly, the adherents of Islam did not remain forever untouched by outside influence. Finally, both of the scriptural sources, the Koran (the Word of God) and the aphoristic tradition (the Words of the Prophet) were subject to discussion and interpretation. It is above all this interpretation which was the source for the construction, extension, reconstructions, additions, demolitions, and renovations of the system of Islamic doctrine and which reflects all these developments like a mirror. Or, to put it differently, since everything which was intended to be recognized as Islamic had to be brought into agreement with the evidence of the two scriptures, the changes of view which took place can be observed especially in the interpretations of the two scriptural documents.

In the following I will try to show the place and nature of the problem of the ultimate origin and the hereafter of all living creatures within Islamic monotheism and within Islamic theocentrism. I will attempt to do this from three points of view: from the viewpoint of the orthodox beliefs of the majority of the followers of Islam, from the viewpoint of the "heterodox" additional notions of a minority, and from the viewpoint of a system of endeavors at scientific, i.e., scholastic reasoning.

I

The basic "orthodox" view is about as follows: God is the First and the Last. After He had created Paradise and Hell, as well as the geocentrically interpreted universe, together with all creatures of material and spiritual nature, He created Adam as the last creature "from dry clay and stinking mud" and breathed into him "His spirit." This spirit of God is not interpreted as a part of God, but as a creation and a possession of His. For that reason man does not hold within himself anything divine. God created Eve from a rib of Adam. In addition, while still in Paradise, God made all of Adam's offspring come forth from him and obtained from him the contract that they would recognize Him, God, as their master. This implicitly justifies the further claim of the Koran that man by nature is orthodox and that only by secondary influences is he misdirected to one or another heresy. This belief further constitutes an argument for considering infidels guilty of breach or forgetfulness of contract. The assumption that man is orthodox by nature at the same time rejects the concept of original sin. The Fall of Adam and Eve only had the result that they were driven out of Paradise onto earth which has been given them as a fief. Here, where the law of birth and death rules, their offspring pass in succession through generations until, at an indeterminable date, the world in its entirety will also be taken away again. All human beings will then be brought back to life by God in a second extraordinary act of creation, they will be put before God's court of law, and depending on the preponderance of their good or evil deeds, they will be raised back to the Paradise from which Adam and Eve had been driven out, or they will be cast down to Hell. There will be no excuses, for since Adam's days God has seen to it that again and again prophets and Messengers of God pronounced the guidelines set by God and that everybody had a chance to get to know the right path. Except for the intercession of Mohammed which can release a sinner from Hell into Paradise, God's decision is irrevocable and the fate of man in the hereafter eternal in principle, unless one were to demand that everything that has a beginning must have an end. Though this latter view would be supported by the conception of God as the First and Last, orthodox meaning has it that through an act of God's will the hereafter will with God be everlasting.

Mankind thus appears to have been put into a kind of circular path which originates with God in Paradise and ends with God in Paradise — or in Hell. "We belong to God and we will return to Him." *Mutatis mutandis,* the whole thing is a combination and revision of the Jewish myth of creation and the Christian myth of the hereafter.

Mankind, however, is not the only tie stretching in this way from primeval eternity (*azal*) to final eternity (*abad*). Its course is paralleled by the paths of the other kingdoms of nature: animals, plants, minerals. The same holds true for the angels and the spirits or demons (*ǧinn*). Like the colors of the rainbow they lie on top of each other and stretch from the horizon of the "world-rise" to the horizon of the "world-set." There is only disagreement about the ranking of the angels, demons, and men. Some put the angels and demons *above* men, others *below,* since man is considered the quintessence of nature which contains within itself the essence of all other creatures and since God ordered the angels in Paradise to prostrate themselves before Adam.

Although there are forms of the animal kingdom which come close to man and which thus are at the upper edge of the animal kingdom; and although there are others which just barely manage to remain above the border of the plant kingdom; and although there are likewise plants that are almost animals, and others which barely live above the border of the mineral kingdom; nevertheless, there are no transitions upward or downward. A human being can never become an angel, not even after his death,* nor can he become an animal, even if

* Traditions about Ǧaᶜfar aṭ-Ṭayyār as an angel are an exception.

morally he can be considered a devil or "more erring than cattle" and if for the spiritual eye he may indeed look like a certain animal, depending on the kind of qualities he betrays. Also the bars between minerals, plants, and animals are insurmountable. On the other hand, angels and demons can assume any form they desire; but it is precisely this quality which they would lose if they actually changed over into another class. Only God's hand can overrule this order: in less serious cases he can make animals talk, as in the case of Bileam's ass; in more serious cases he can bring about real transformations. Thus he changed the Israelite breakers of the Sabbath into monkeys. But these are exceptions which by the very fact that they are considered miracles only confirm the rule. There have been different opinions concerning the question whether through crossbreeding between angel and man, or man and demon, mixed creatures can be brought about. Often the Queen of Sheba is considered the daughter of a man and a beautiful demoness; even some entire peoples are regarded to be of similar mixed parentage. In general, however, Islam maintains the theory that every type of creature was fully developed from the very beginning, and that no development from lower to higher forms of existence, from below to above, has taken place, just as there was no opposite development consisting in the degeneration from above to below. Only heterodox doctrines of transformations of the soul and aberrant traditions have occasionally come up with different theories.

Not all classes of creatures, however, share in the exodus from Paradise at the *beginning* of world history and the return to the same place or the banishment to the place located one step below, to Hell, at the *end* of time. Animals, plants, and minerals existed from the very beginning, both in Paradise and on earth. Those in Paradise remain there in eternity, those on earth cease to exist at the time of its destruction, since they were promised neither Paradise nor Hell. True, on judgment day there will be a settlement between those animals that hurt each other, but then they will disintegrate into dust. Only a small sect has postulated compensation in Paradise for the injustice animals suffer from human beings. According to certain traditions, however, there are only birds in Paradise, in addition to horses and camels which serve as means of transportation for the blessed. Also angels live both in Paradise and on earth. It can be assumed that those angels that are assigned to earthly duties will be transferred to different posts in the hereafter. The whole voyage from Paradise to Paradise or to Hell, respectively, thus is carried out only by humans and demons. Both of these are morally responsible and after examination of their actions will either go to eternal bliss or to damnation.

Paradise and Hell are described differently, in a mirror-image sort of way. The basic idea is that of most delightful joy in Paradise and most terrible pain in Hell. Paradise is depicted as a large garden and is mostly named this way or similarly (*ğanna*), just as our New Testament word Paradise has no other meaning than garden. Often we find in its stead the simple word "bliss" (*na*ᶜ*īm*). The climate of Paradise is temperate; in Arab terms, it is cool. Hell, however, has only extreme temperatures, mostly extremely hot, to a lesser extent icy cold. It is for that reason most often referred to as "the fire," "the blaze," etc. Both Paradise and Hell are subdivided into different steps in order to reward or punish the blessed and the sinners according to their different merits. Each of the two ultimate abodes of man is characterized by a mighty tree. The Tree of Paradise is gorgeous, that of Hell terrifying. Paradise and Hell are each traversed by four rivers. The rivers of Paradise are of water, milk, wine, and honey; those of Hell are of dishwater, sewage water, puss, and pitch. Paradise is light and fragrant; Hell is dark and stinks. Paradise has green meadows, shady trees, tasty fruits, gazebos, and ponds; Hell has cliffs, pavilions, abysses, pits, boiling vessels, and instruments of torture. In Paradise the blissful, rejuvenated and beautified, indulge in an eternal drinking party, eat good foods, drink wine, and enjoy the pleasures of love with the eternally young women "with the beautiful and big eyes" who, since they are hetaeras, often are considered to be part of the personnel of Paradise and thus are not thought to die and be resurrected. They are mostly identified as women of this earth who because of their piety have been transferred to Paradise. Beautiful boys serve the blessed. On the other hand, the personnel of Hell consists of persecutors; these most terribly torment the sinners who have been rendered ugly even physically. We are in the possession of numerous exact depictions of the hereafter in collections of pertinent traditional accounts, in apocalypses, and in two famous literary fictions from the eleventh century in the manner of Dante's *Divine Comedy,* one by a Syrian, the other by a Spanish Muslim.

Only on two important, although controversial counts, are Hell and

Paradise not mirror-image opposites, namely, the sight of God and the duration of the hereafter. For all the joys of Paradise are surpassed by the sight of God's face and the hearing of God's voice by means of one's bodily senses, a fact which orthodoxy strongly emphasizes. To this should correspond in Hell the impression made on the sinners by the devil's ugly face and speech. But that is not the case. This correspondence is absent because the devil by no means is the prince of Hell, but rather dies at the end of the world like the rest and then suffers his punishment in Hell. Considering the second point, the duration of Paradise and Hell, two things must be mentioned: (a) Nobody in whom there is even a glimmer of belief in God and Mohammed will remain in Hell forever, but he will after a certain time be raised to Paradise. On the other hand, once in Paradise, no one will ever be subsequently thrown to Hell. (b) Some noted theologists, although they admit that the infidel will remain in Hell "forever," nevertheless consider it possible, even probable, that Hell itself in contradistinction to Paradise, one day will come to an end, since God's mercy is considered greater than his wrath and consequently also the field in which his anger manifests itself one day must end. In either case, then, Hell would have the role of a purgatory whose only purpose is to burn and freeze out sins. Also elsewhere in Islam, proportions are frequently changed in favor of the cheerful, and mercy wins out over justice.

Our presentation so far could give the impression that mankind, after its expulsion from God's presence onto its journey through the temporal world, was abandoned until the Day of Judgment. That is by no means the case. The chain of developments from the first to the last day is bound up with innumerable connections with God. The most notable vertical connections are the periodical revelations to or through the so-called 'Messengers of God', already mentioned, the last of which, the Koran, is literally called 'God's rope'. 'Messenger of God', however, should not be understood as though God sent out someone from on high to the earth. That would be against the horizontal progress of the hereditary process in the natural kingdoms. God, however, "looks into the hearts of men and selects one, whom he sends forth then with his message." Or, as is also maintained, he selected the bearers of his messages already at the beginning of time. Just as man stands in contact downward to the other kingdoms of nature, he also stands either directly or indirectly in contact upward toward God. In addition, God knows no barriers. His power and knowledge permeate everything, are indeed indispensable for the continued existence and development of creation, for the occurrence of all acts and happenings in the world. The atomistic theologians of Islam have divided not only space, but also time into the smallest atomistic particles, which are separated each from the other by a still smaller time vacuum. In order to allow the world to continue to exist, God must exert His creative power in every unimaginably tiny time vacuum anew. The world is therefore in a continuous imperceptible oscillation between existence and nonexistence. If God should cease His creating in one of these time vacuums, the world would suddenly no longer exist. The horizontal causal nexus of the so-called laws of nature is transformed in this scholasticism into a 'habit of creating'. God could at any time let a different effect follow upon a so-called 'cause', because at any given moment His all-powerful hand is involved. The interrelationship between chain and weft is very close in this bold theology, and it is also as close in the less reflective conception of the ordinary Muslim.

Even the broad arch from the origins in primeval eternity to the end in final eternity occasionally appears compressed to a hairpin curve of an individual descent from God's presence and a reascension to Him or, veering off, to Hell. The consciousness of being linked with God bent the ends of the curve sharply upward or one of them sharply downward. The phylogenetic concept is thereby transformed into an ontogenetic one. In this case it is the spirit, and only the spirit, which descends into the body of man before his birth, then with or without its body, strives upward after death, and before the Day of Judgment enters Paradise or Hell. Innumerable stories depict dreamers who see someone deceased already in Paradise. It is the same intermingling of two actually irreconcilable concepts with which we are also familiar from Christianity, when Jesus, on the Cross, promises a sinner that he will be with Him today in Paradise. The contradiction is somewhat alleviated in Islam, however, by the further conception that after death the spirit and the body part and the spirit of the pious one waits inside a bird in Paradise for the resurrection of the body on the Day of Judgment.

The whole basic view of ultimate origins and the hereafter sketched above is hidden in Islamic literature behind a decorative structure of baroque traditions. Baroque is perhaps the right word for it, for aside from the multitude of holy men and angelic beings which appear in it, the sharp contours of the system depicted are frequently altered, deflected, and penetrated by numerous deviations and additions, often of foreign, Jewish, or Christian, origin. The characteristic element is the sweeping style and gestures, the obvious dramatic events and the bizarre characters rather than the simple structure which I have attempted to reveal. In addition, natural philosophical and metaphysical speculations have placed some things in a new light. It is not the features of this baroque façade, nor the reinterpretations of these explicators which I wish to present in the second part, but the additional basic structural changes which the *Shia* has affected in the overall picture.

II

At first, the abbreviated name *Shia* ("party") designates the early Islamic opposition which did not recognize the first three heads of the young Islamic state and wanted to claim as the sole rightful heir and successor to Mohammed his cousin and son-in-law, Ali, who ascended the throne only as the fourth Calif. Even after Ali's death in 661, it insisted that only Ali's offspring, the Alides, could be considered successors to the Prophet. If it had only been a question of this political legitimacy, we would not have to mention it further. Around this claim to legitimacy, however, a theology arose which was intended to support it and thereby arose theories which also place the subject of ultimate origins and the hereafter in a new context.

The decisive change, and we must restrict ourselves to this change alone here, lies in a partial revision of the vertical relationship of God to the world. Moslems in general and the *Shia* agree that down to Mohammed there had been a multitude of so-called prophets (exactly 124,000), among them a small number of so-called 'Messengers of God', who had transmitted detailed revelations of God, and that Mohammed had been the last Prophet and Messenger of God. Whereas, however, Moslems generally accept temporal gaps in the divine inspiration without question, the *Shia* demands an uninterrupted series of divinely inspired authorities from Adam to the Day of Judgment. First of all, it means that the so-called prophets before Mohammed are not randomly strewn in time, but stand in an uninterrupted chronological series. Secondly, if we were to depict in a diagram the pre-Islamic prophets as rays proceeding from God as the center, these rays in the philosophy of the *Shia* would congeal into a disc. To be sure, these inspired authorities after Mohammed cannot be called prophets in the *Shia*, either; their most famous name is 'Leader' (*imām*). The technical term for all of these inspired authorities, whether they are to be listed before or after Mohammed, and among them Mohammed himself is to be reckoned, is 'Arguments' (*ḥuğağ*, *sg.* *ḥuğğa*). The Shi-ites maintain, and have tried to prove by tradition, that this spiritual leadership by the so-called 'Arguments' was transferred by Mohammed to Ali and is passed on in the hereditary succession of the Alides by the selection of a successor by his predecessor. A series of Alides therefore constitutes the 'Arguments' of God from Mohammed down to the Day of Judgment.

Already in the seventh century a dispute arose within the *Shia* concerning the legal Imamat-line and down to the tenth century the Shi-ites broke up into numerous feuding groups, of which only three, however, have persisted to the present: the Fiver, Sevener, and Twelver Shi-ites. The Fivers and Seveners are so called because they diverge with the Fifth or Seventh Imām, whom they recognize, from the line of the Twelver Shi-ites. The Imām of the Fivers is at present fighting in Yemen against the local republicans. He is, however, no descendent of the above-mentioned Fifth Imām, but belongs to another Alide-lineage, for the Fivers' adherents do not have the formally pretentious theory of the Imamat described above, but demand only that the leadership should remain in the Alide line. The Imām of the main group, of the adherents of the Seveners, is the Agha Khan, whose Alidic descent is, however, subject to the greatest doubts. The theology of these Seveners wavers between a theory of the Imamat which is exoterically realistic and one which is esoterically extremistic. The Imamat-theory of the Twelvers appears to be most tightly bound. Since they represent the majority today — since the sixteenth century their confession has been the state religion of Persia, and in addition contains characteristic elements of older Shi-ite groups no longer in existence — it is advisable to take it as a model case.

According to this theory, the so-called 'Arguments', i.e., Messengers of God, prophets, and Imāms, are the viceroys and representatives of God on earth and are omniscient. In this sect, the office and the knowledge is passed on to the particular successor at the time of his selection and at the latest in the last moments of his predecessor's life. Their knowledge is partially recorded in additional secret books, but for the most part it is the inspiration of God. The Holy Ghost, which according to this teaching is not identical with Gabriel, as in "orthodox" Islam, accompanies them, or a divine source of light illuminates things in such a way for them that they recognize everything.

In the teaching of the Shi-ites, the word of God, i.e., especially the Koran, is not considered to be uncreated, as in the teaching of the "orthodox," but its wisdom surpasses human understanding to such an extent that only the Imām is able to plumb its depths. All decisive knowledge therefore comes from the Imām and reaches the people through authoritative instruction (*ta*ᶜ*līm*). Thus the Shi-ite Imām stands at the top of a system of divine wisdom, whose only externally confirmable part is the external wording of the Koran. That is, the Imām for all practical purposes stands above the Koran. The possession of the weapons of the Prophet Mohammed was taken for visible legitimation of the rightful Imām. In fact, however, only the first Imām was actually in power, the so-called executor of the will of the Prophet, Ali (656-661). All others remained purely pontifical califs and had to leave the political leadership of the Islamic community to the real califs. Since, however, the Shi-ite theology we have described arose only after Ali and his direct sons, it is permeated by undertones of pain at the loss of the theocracy and the unbreachable schism between the pontifical and political leadership. With this anguish is combined the hope that these leaders will again unite into one. Indeed, the Shi-ite faith is borne by the express promise that such a unification will come about and the Imām concerned, the 'Master of the Sword', the 'Appearing One', then will "fill the world with justice, just as it is now filled with injustice." Many an Imām was pressed by his followers to "move out" (*ḫurūǧ*), but each consoled them with the promise of one still to come.

The latter has never appeared. When the Eleventh Imām died in 873, and after him neither a successor nor the expected savior arrived, the theory was constructed that his four- or five-year-old son, Mohammed, was the designated Twelfth Imām, but was spirited away into seclusion in a miraculous fashion. What really happened cannot be determined. Until 940, four successive administrators (*wakīl*) led the community. Already before the end of this period, however, the belief became established in the theology of this community that the vanished Twelfth Imām was also the expected savior and would bring about the hoped-for salvation (*farağ*). A fermata (*waqf*) was placed on his life: he was and would remain the last Imām and would live hidden on earth until his victorious return, no matter how long the waiting period might last. In the Middle Ages, the Twelvers kept saddled horses ready day and night at various places where they expected his return, so that he could mount at any time.

The "orthodox" also expect an inspired prince who will rehabilitate a fallen humanity and erect on earth a kind of Paradise. But typical for the *Shia* is the view of God as communicating with man through all time on the narrow ridge of an uninterrupted series of Chosen Ones, each of whom is the 'Only Gate' (*bāb*) and the 'Only Path' (*sabīt*) for spiritual communication between man and God, and the Imāms of Ali's line have the task of further slitting open the heaven of God's secrets until the end of time. The recognition and acceptance of the right Imām is in the articles of faith of the *Shia*. Anyone who dies without having known the Imām dies as an infidel and his works will also not be accepted by God. For him, his fate in the hereafter is therefore also determined.

III

In this third and last section, we will touch upon a question which has been the object of Islam's theological thought for centuries: the question of the type and the area of God's actions in relation to what man can do. The question has been answered variously. Here we will sketch only the "orthodox" view.

One can differentiate between God's will and God's activity. By God's will is understood God's intention and plan. It lies at the basis of development, belongs to the past as God's act, took place before God created the world: God *has* determined, He no longer determines. It is a different matter with God's activity: God created the world and continues to create in and on it in order to carry out what He has determined.

While the determination, from the point of view of the meaning of the word, occurred only in the beginning and from then on in the development of time is realized horizontally, so to speak, God's creativity began with the creation of the world at the beginning of time, but also continues vertically, unless one assumes that God's plan is valid only for a single one of His acts of creation at a time and must be replaced by a new determination each time. There is, however, no mention of a multitude or a repetition of divine acts of determination, of divine plannings, in either the written documents or in their theological evaluation. Apparent changes in the original determination of God are only illusory. When such seems to occur, they themselves are predetermined, belong to the original determination.

From the discrepancy between a single, completed determination and continuing creativity there arises one difficulty: God places upon himself laws, according to which He himself must act later. Indeed, if the determination is also valid for that action and event which is not expressly designated as 'creativity' — and nowhere is determination expressly connected with 'creation' — then even God's judgment concerning the fate of men and spirits in the hereafter on the Day of Judgment is subject to the determination He himself made in primeval eternity. The orthodox belief has accepted this in silence, or has maintained that primeval eternity and final eternity are one, that is, has erased the difference between beginning, course of time, and end.

But let us leave the question of how predetermination must react back toward God *Himself* and focus upon the effect of God's determination and creation on the *world!* "Orthodox" Islamism has upheld the thesis that God determines and creates everything without exception. For if He had not determined everything, His planning and His control would not be all-encompassing and if He did not create everything, then there would be a creator in addition to Him. Let us follow these two lines catechistically.

First of all, the creation: God creates all things, even the flea, but out of a sense of decency one does not call God the creator of the flea, although He is. God also creates all deeds, the good and the bad, but from a sense of decency one does not call Him the creator of evil, although He is. God creates the conscious and unconscious deeds of men, and also the will for them. If one should be able to speak of freedom of choice, and most people speak of it, God creates it also, as well as the decision which is reached. Is there then any active being besides God? This question can likewise be answered both affirmatively and negatively. Anyone who answers affirmatively, i.e., recognizes other active beings in addition to God, must admit, however, at the same time that God is the prime actor, and makes all other active beings active, so that they can act. For this purpose, then, He creates in them, simultaneously with the deed, the ability to act. Before the deed, also before an intellectual deed, no one has the power to do anything. This stresses the absolute and continual dependence of man and all active beings on God. Man possesses no reserves whatever.

Secondly, determination: God's determination is identical with God's will. Everything which God has decided, i.e., wanted or wants, happens. What He does not will, does not happen. What is and happens is God-willed, be it ever so perverse or bad. There is always a wisdom active behind it, which sometimes can even be recognized to a certain extent. But man's insight in this area has certain limitations. God's determination or will must be kept apart from God's wishing, liking, God's 'love', as the scholastic expression, for example, goes, along with their opposites: God's 'hate', and repugnance toward that which He does not want. God's wish, or 'love', are His commandments, His 'hate' is expressed in His prohibitions. What He has commanded, He wishes, likes, and loves. For the observance of those things He loves, i.e., His commandments, He promises a reward, for disregarding them, punishment. God's *will,* therefore, is behind everything that *happens,* is all-encompassing. God's wish or 'love' is behind only those things which He likes, is restricted. God also wills and creates that which He does not desire, they are the object of His 'hate' and displeasure. He gives His help sometimes or to someone, but another time He leaves him, as the technical term goes, in the lurch. He guides the one in the right way, the other he leads astray. Both are His will, but He loves the one, hates the other.

The question arises: Is there any sense at all in striving to do right and good, since God has determined, willed, everything? The orthodox answer is: Yes, there is sense in it. Man does not know in advance what is determined. Not until he has acted does he know what was determined for him. He therefore always has to play one possible will of God against another possible will of God, and it is the divine commands which he is to carry out. Divine commands stand above the passive act of letting all things happen, or the doing of all those things that are fun with the excuse that it is happening by God's will. There were Quietists and Libertines, to be sure, but the theology objected to them most vigorously.

Islam is often called a fatalistic religion. Fatalism is an ambiguous concept which must be explained when used. If it is understood by it that everything is predetermined, then the expression applies to Islam. Instead, however, we have the more explicit term 'doctrine of predestination'. If fatalism is understood to mean that the unavoidable is to be accepted, whether it is something that has already happened or something that is to happen, the expression is once again justified. For this reason, the Moslem should do everything with the reservation: "God willing." If it is understood to mean passively letting things happen as they may under the pretense that God alone watches out for right, or does as He wishes anyway, then it is incorrect. God created the world in such a way that in order to reach a goal one must make use of certain means. In order to harvest, one must sow. In order not to be buried under a falling house, one must repair it. In order to help the poor, one must be concerned with them in one way or another. In order to qualify in the eyes of God, one must fulfill his commandments.

Since, however, the *striving* for deeds and the *success* of the deeds are both also in God's hands, Islamism, when it defines precisely, denies that Paradise can be 'earned'. The deeds themselves are a grace of God. Entrance into Paradise is a second grace, just as on the other hand the failure to do deeds and infidelity are damnation and the expulsion into Hell a second damnation. One may ask: What purpose does the Last Judgment serve? Is it not a farce, a spectacle? Islamic theology does not have these two words. It is called 'argumentation' (*ḥuǧǧa*). God already knows everything, but he wants to assess the deeds of man before he orders him to Paradise or to Hell. In other words, God has man carry out in life what He has decided for him and then shows him on the Day of Judgment in the form of a ledger whether He has decided to send him to Paradise or to Hell — or better, could have decided! For the judgment which God now pronounces is not the logical conclusion to be drawn from the 'argumentation', but rather unpredictable arbitrariness, God's decision which is still impenetrable. If He wants to, according to the Koran, He can forgive everything except polytheism. These are the consequences to which a unification of all powers in a single authority, as Islamic monotheism requires, can and must lead, especially when life is based completely on a dialogue with this authority. God again and again proves Himself alone, but fortunately for mankind, is inclined to overlook shortcomings. His kindness is greater than His righteousness.

"Orthodox" theology also reaches the same conclusion when consulting God's presentation of Himself in the Koran. God has names in the Koran like 'Creator', 'the Righteous One', 'the Wise One', 'the Merciful One', 'the Strict One', etc., ninety-nine such names in all. These point to His qualities of righteousness, mercy, etc., and these qualities involve deeds: God would not be the Creator if He did not create, not strict if He did not act strictly, etc. The deeds, on the other hand, demand products and objects. If God creates, then there must be that which is created; if He is merciful, there must be beings to whom He can be merciful, etc. Thus the here-and-now and the hereafter and everything in them are presented as objects of God's creativity, so to speak as accusatives of His effecting (acting) and affecting (treating). God's attributes, His activity, can be discerned from the creatures, from creation, so to speak. He needs creatures with which He can be strict and others to whom He can be kindly.

In this third section, I have also restricted myself intentionally to a straight-forward middle road in order to make visible a representative line of thought of Islamic theology. The parallelism to Calvinism is obvious. It even includes the rejection of excessive piety and the denigration of an ascetic retreat from the world, but the parallelism ceases at the point where Max Weber ascribes to Calvinism the rise of, or at least the favorable climate for, an 'innerworldly asceticism', i.e., the restriction of pleasure and the release of gainful activity and thereby the rise of a rationalizing spirit of initiative and willingness to work in productive capitalism. Islamic theology never triggered such a development, and certainly never advocated it. In the West, a factor X must have triggered such a development, or in the East, a factor Y must have prevented it. The weak and dangerous points in the theological line of thought we have described are obvious, and at those points one can imagine deviations from the orthodox teaching. Thus there were adherents of an extreme predestination who rejected the use of media and even of supplicatory prayer, even rascals who derived from God's need to forgive sinners a reason for sinning. There were adherents of a moderate predestination who did not differentiate between God's wanting and wishing and therefore ascribed evil (which

God could not have wanted-wished) exclusively to man, and also pantheists who conceived of the creation not merely as the effect, but actually as an aspect and form of God's appearance, etc. Some Islamic mystics extricated themselves from the dilemma by placing *man's love for God above* the striving for a pleasure-filled hereafter, i.e. they addressed themselves directly to God's being, above the two sides of wrath and grace, which God possesses.

They followed God's commandment, not with an eye toward their bliss, but because the one who loves gladly does what the loved one wishes and attempted to accept gratefully and perseveringly everything that God sent them and burdened them with, and by means of such preliminary exercises, to be capable at some future time of being content with whatever God might grant them in the hereafter, even the agony of Hell.

With this we arrive at new, provocative questions, but we have attained our goal. In restrospect we can perhaps permit ourselves the following judgment: The basic concept of the ultimate origins and the hereafter in Islam presented in the first section is not characterized by any particular originality, and as a system is no more satisfying than the corresponding Judeo-Christian one. The Shi-ite additions described in the second section diverge somewhat from the actual aim of Islam toward the glorification of a pontifical dynasty, make salvation in the hereafter strongly dependent on this political affiliation and draw it somewhat into the here-and-now by its marked expectation of a Messiah. But in the scholastic reworking of the problem of God's determination, as we tried to present it in a simplified form, lies one of the most significant accomplishments of Islamic theology.

Arabic Orthography and Some Non-Semitic Languages

C. MOHAMMED NAIM

ARABIC ORTHOGRAPHY

ARABIC ORTHOGRAPHY is a cursive system of writing in which a grapheme[1] of the alphabet is joined with either the preceding or the following grapheme, or with both, as usually is the case, within a written word.[2] It is written from right to left.

Classical Arabic (C.A.) has twenty-nine graphemes, which are used always, and a few diacritics,[3] which are used only for special purposes. Traditional analyses of Arabic orthography usually present an alphabet of twenty-eight letters, as they tend to confuse between *hamzah* and *'alif* due to a special relationship between the two.[4] Three Arabic graphemes, *'alif, yā,* and *wāw,* are regularly used as the "bearer" of *hamzah,* but as the latter two also occur as consonant graphemes, the old grammarians had no problem with them. For the confusion between *'alif* and *hamzah* usually two reasons are given.

1 A grapheme is the smallest distinctive unit in the orthography of any language. It is a unit, as it may consist of a number of allographs, or graphemic variants, which usually have a constant, common phonemic reference, and which are in noncontrastive distribution in the orthography. The graphemes of a writing system may be identical in number and in shape with the letters of its alphabet, but not necessarily so (see Gleason, chap. 21; Pulgram).

2 For the purposes of this study, a written word is defined as a single grapheme, or a combination of more than one grapheme, separated from other such combinations by an arbitrarily fixed space. The arbitrariness being in the size of this space, and not in its position.

3 Graphemes are segmental and linear; diacritics are suprasegmental and nonlinear. A grapheme can occur without a diacritic, but a diacritic cannot occur without a grapheme.

4 For example, Mitchell, p. 7, 87.

1. *'alif* is never used as a consonant letter, whereas the rest of the letters in the alphabet are.

2. Every syllable in C.A. must begin with a consonant, consequently *'alif* never occurs syllable-initial without a *hamzah*. But the above does not show the entire distribution of *'alif*. We must include it in the inventory of C.A. graphemes because — besides its common usage with *hamzah* — it is also used to indicate a long vowel, /ā/, after consonants other than *hamzah*.

The phonemic inventory of C.A. as postulated by scholars contains twenty-eight consonants,[5]

		t	ṭ		k	q	'	
b		d	ḍ	j				
f	θ	s	ṣ	š	x		h	ḥ
	đ	z	ẓ		ḡ			c
m		n						
w	l	r	y,					

six long and short vowels, i, ī, u, ū, a, ā,
and two diphthongs, ai au.
Some of the above symbols may be explained a bit more:

q : voiceless uvular stop;
ṭ, ḍ : velarized alveolar stops, voiceless and voiced;
ṣ, ẓ : velarized alveolar spirants, voiceless and voiced;
ḡ : voiced velar fricative;
ḥ : voiceless pharyngeal fricative;
c : voiced pharyngeal fricative.

Considering that there are thirty-six phonemes and only twenty-nine graphemes, it becomes apparent that there is no one-to-one correspondence between the two systems. The following chart shows the phonemic equivalents for the different graphemes. An asterisk indicates more than one usage.

One immediately notices the major drawback of the Arabic orthography: it fails to account for all the vowels of the language. It does, however, provide — as mentioned earlier — a few diacritics which may be used, either by themselves or in combination with certain

[5] See the bibliography for the several books from which data was gathered.

Name	Grapheme	Phoneme	Name	Grapheme	Phoneme
ʼalif	ا	ā*	ṭā	ط	ṭ
bā	ب	b	ẓā	ظ	ẓ
tā	ت	t	ᶜain	ع	c̄
θā	ث	θ	ḡain	غ	ḡ
jīm	ج	j	fā	ف	f
ḥā	ح	ḥ	qāf	ق	q
xā	خ	x	kāf	ک	k
dāl	د	d	lām	ل	l
đāl	ذ	đ	mīm	م	m
rā	ر	r	nūn	ن	n
zā	ز	z	hā	ه	h
sīn	س	s	wāw	و	w*
šīn	ش	š	yā	ى	y*
ṣād	ص	ṣ	hamzah	ء	ʼ
ḍād	ض	ḍ			

graphemes, to clearly indicate the vowels and the diphthongs, as listed below.

i : the diacritic *kasrah* under the consonant.

ī : the diacritic *kasrah* under the consonant, followed by *yā*.

u : the diacritic *ḍammah* over the consonant.

ū : the diacritic *ḍammah* over the consonant, followed by *wāw*.

a : the diacritic *fatḥah* over the consonant.

ā : the diacritic *fatḥah* over the consonant, followed by *ʼalif*. Also other variants.

ai : the diacritic *fatḥah* over the consonant, followed by *yā* with a *sukūn* over it.

au : the diacritic *fatḥah* over the consonant, followed by *wāw* with a *sukūn* over it.

It must be kept in mind, though, that a full use of these diacritics is made only in the so called "pointed" texts of Arabic; it is more common not to use them for average purposes.

The cursive nature of the C.A. orthography has already been mentioned, but a few features need to be detailed. Within a written word, all graphemes except *hamzah* combine with any preceding grapheme; all graphemes except *hamzah, ʼalif, dāl, đāl, rā, zā,* and *wāw* also combine with any grapheme that follows them. C.A. graphemes can have a maximum of four different variants or allographs, depending upon their position within a written word. The four significant positions are:

1. Initial, i.e., connected only to the following grapheme.
2. Medial, i.e., connected to both the preceding and the following grapheme.
3. Final, i.e., connected only to the preceding grapheme.
4. Independent, i.e., not connected on either side.

Most of the C.A. graphemes have at least two different forms. *hamzah* is different from the rest of the C.A. graphemes in that it does not combine with either the preceding or the following grapheme. As a matter of fact, its distribution is rather complicated, but we need not go into it here.[6]

In summation, and for the purpose of this article, the following points should be noted with reference to the graphemes of Classical Arabic.

1. There is a one-to-one correspondence only between the consonant graphemes and the consonant phonemes.
2. Vowels are indicated unambiguously only in certain special texts; otherwise they are mostly to be guessed from the context.
3. In pointed texts all vowels except /ā/ have single graphemic shapes. /ā/ is generally indicated by a combination of *'alif* and *fatḥah,* but there are also other variants.
4. Certain graphemes do not connect with the grapheme that follows them.
5. Most of the graphemes have positional variants — ranging from two to four — depending upon where they occur in a written word.
6. Many graphemes are similar in shape and differ only in their superscript or subscript dots, which may number from one to three.
7. The graphemes which are similar in shape are not necessarily also similar phonetically.

[6] In this paper, *hamzah* refers to what in Arabic terminology is called *hamzat-ul-qatᶜa.* No reference is implied to what is traditionally called *hamzat-ul-waṣl.* It usually occurs with either of the three graphemes, *'alif, yā,* and *wāw,* which are referred to as its *kursī* or "bearer."

NON-SEMITIC LANGUAGES

With the rise of Islam in the seventh century the Arabs and the Arabic language began to make their mark in other countries of the world. Although not all the converts to Islam were ever able to speak Arabic, it became incumbent upon them to learn at least a little bit of it in order to say their prayers in that language. There were also other numerous reasons for these people to borrow Arabic — and later Persian and Turkish — words into their own languages. Similar reasons also required of these converts to adapt Arabic orthography for their own languages, even in those instances where an earlier system existed.

In what follows we shall study the writing systems of nine languages from among the many which adapted Arabic orthography for their own purposes.[7] Our aim will be to determine how adequately these adapted systems represent the phonemic systems of these languages. The nine languages are: Persian, Kurdish, East Turki, Azerbaijani, Pashto, Sindhi, Urdu, Sulu, and Malay. These do not, by any means, exhaust the number of languages which either now use, or have used in the past, some form of Arabic orthography. Further, it is not implied that these languages borrowed the orthography directly from Arabic in each case; nor is the particular order of presentation intended to suggest a chain of borrowing. We shall consider each language separately, and make comparison between languages only to

Persian:[8] Inventory of phonemes.

Consonants							*Vowels*		
p	t	c	k	q			i	u	
b	d	j	g				e	o	
f	s	š	x		h		a	ɔ	
v	z	ž				ei	ai	ou	ɔi
m	n								
	l	r	y						

[7] Some other languages are, Kashmiri, Balochi, Turki, Spanish of the "aljamiado" literature, and several of the Berber languages of Africa. Professor Denzel Carr of the University of California at Berkeley once showed me specimens of even Japanese and Byelorussian written in an orthography devised from the C.A. orthography.

[8] Ann K. S. Lambton, *Persian Grammar* (Cambridge, 1957).

point out structural similarities, without necessarily implying a simultaneous historical relationship.

Persian consonants not shared[9] with C.A.: /p, c, g, v, ž/.

C.A. consonants not shared with Persian: /ṭ, ḍ, ', Θ, đ, ḡ, ^{c}, ṣ, ẓ, w/.

On comparing the two orthographies we find that all the graphemes of C.A. have been retained in Persian, but the graphemes for the C.A. consonants not shared with Persian have gained new values.

C.A. đ, ẓ, ḍ = z in Persian
Θ, ṣ = s
ṭ = t
ḥ = h
w = v

^{c}*ain* and *hamzah* no longer have consonantal values; in most instances their phonemic equivalent in Persian is a syllable boundary between conjunct vowels. ^{c}*ain* is used only in Arabic loans; *hamzah* is used in non-Arabic words, too, though never initially. An interesting innovation is its use over a final *hā* to indicate the /-i/ ending of various morphological categories. Medially it occurs only with a dotless *yā*.

Arabic loans with a /ḡ/ keep the original spelling; however, at the phonemic level, /ḡ/ and /q/ have fallen together in Persian. Persian only has one phoneme /q/, which has two allophones: a voiced uvular plosive between two back vowels, and a voiceless uvular plosive elsewhere.

Persian consonant phonemes are represented by the graphemes for their closest equivalents in C.A. Those without equivalents are represented by new graphemes created from Arabic models. Such new graphemes are:

Name	Grapheme	Phoneme	Name	Grapheme	Phoneme
pe	پ	p	cim	چ	c
gaf	گ	g	že	ژ	ž

[9] By "shared" we do not imply that phoneme X in Persian is identical with phoneme X in Arabic in both allophony and distribution; we only refer to the fact that both Persian and C.A. have two phonemes which at the phonetic level share certain features, and which are represented in the orthography by one and the same grapheme.

A certain pattern can immediately be discerned. The new graphemes are formed with the help of the diacritics that already existed in C.A. — subscript and superscript dots, and diagonal bars — and the graphemes for the closest equivalents for the Persian phonemes. It may also be noted that the number of dots used in each case is three, which suggests that the new graphemes were all devised at one time, for only two dots would have been enough in the case of *cim* and *že*.

With regard to vowels, we find that the original confusion has continued into Persian, though with some changes. *Hamzah* being no longer significant as a consonant, *'alif* has gained more importance. With, and without, other graphemes and diacritics it indicates various vowels in the initial position. Medially and finally, however, it is the regular grapheme for /ɔ/ only.

/e/ is irregularly indicated by a final *hā*; /o/ is often indicated by *wāw*. In general, however, the three vowels, /e, a, o/, are left unindicated in the orthography. The remaining two vowels, /i, u/, are indicated non-initially by *yā* and *wāw,* respectively, which are also the graphemes for /y/ and /v/. Among the diphthongs, /ei/ and /ai/ are indicated by *yā,* /oi/ by *'alif* and *yā,* /ui/ by *wāw* and *yā,* and /ou/ by *wāw*. The distinction between a diphthong and a sequence of two vowels is indicated by writing a *hamzah* as a syllable boundary.

Kurdish:[10] Inventory of phonemes.

Consonants								*Vowels*		
p	t	c	k	q	'		close	i	î	u
b	d	j	g				open	ɨ		ʉ
f	s	š	x		h	ḥ	close	e		o
v	z	ž	ḡ			ċ	open		ə	
m	n		ŋ						a	
w	l	r	ř	y	ł	ṣ				

(Note: /ł, ṣ/ are velarized consonants.)

Kurdish consonants not shared with C.A.: /p, c, g, v, ž, ŋ, ř, ł/.
C.A. consonants not shared with Kurdish: /ṭ, ḍ, Θ, đ, ẓ/.

All the graphemes of C.A. have been retained, but the graphemes for the C.A. consonants not shared with Kurdish have gained new values.

[10] Ernest N. McCarus, *A Kurdish Grammar* (A.C.L.S., 1958).

C.A. ḍ, đ, ẓ = z in Kurdish
ṭ = t
θ = s

New graphemes have been devised for the Kurdish consonants not shared with C.A. These are:

Grapheme	Phoneme	Grapheme	Phoneme
پ	p	ڤ	v
ڵ	ł	چ	c
ژ	ž	گ	g
ڕ	ṙ		

Though no common pattern can be discerned in the diacritical devices, it is apparent that the new graphemes have been devised from the C.A. graphemes that represented the closest equivalents to the Kurdish phonemes. The graphemes for /p, c, ž, g/ are the same as in Persian. It is interesting to note that the grapheme for Kurdish /v/ has been devised from the C.A. grapheme for /f/, and not from the C.A. grapheme for /w/. Further, it should be noted that no new grapheme has been developed to represent Kurdish phoneme /ŋ/, a velar nasal, which is indicated in the orthography by merely writing together the graphemes for /n/ and /g/. /ŋ/ does not occur initially in Kurdish, and perhaps this gap in its distribution produced the lapse in the orthography. Even the recent script reforms did not change the situation.[11]

According to an earlier grammar, the graphemic representation of vowels in Kurdish was similar in nature to that in the unpointed texts of C.A. and Persian, i.e., rudimentary. A more recent grammar, however, mentions script reforms and gives a chart prepared by a Kurdish grammarian, Mr. Wahby, who seems to have tried to throw out all non-Kurdish elements in the language and who has also tried to pro-

[11] The graphemes for /ł/ and /ṙ/ were established more recently, as they are not mentioned in a grammar published in 1913 (E. B. Soane, *Kurdish Grammar*). Soane does not include /ᶜ, ', ṙ, ł, ṣ/ in his list of Kurdish consonants, which might be due to the fact that he is trying to describe several dialects of Kurdish at one time, whereas the recent grammar deals exclusively with one urban dialect, the Kurdish of Sulaimaniya, Iraq.

vide the orthography with separate graphemes for all phonemes except /ŋ/. He worked out his reforms in 1929, but it has not been possible to establish just how much his reforms are still in vogue. His graphemes for Kurdish vowels are as follows.

Grapheme	Phoneme	Grapheme	Phoneme	Grapheme	Phoneme
سى	i	ى	ɨ	ێ	e
ۆ	ə	ا	a	ي	î
وو	u	و	ʉ	ۆ	o

In this grammar, Ernest McCarus also mentions another system which according to him is "in general use in Iraq today." It is called Ṣidqi's system, and is as follows.

Grapheme	Phoneme	Grapheme	Phoneme	Grapheme	Phoneme
ى	i	—	ɨ	ى	e
ۆ	ə	ا	a	—	î
و	u	و	ʉ	و	o

At the end of his grammar, McCarus has given a few brief texts in Kurdish script, though without mentioning what particular reformed style was being used. A cursory analysis of these texts shows some interesting features in the graphemic representation of vowels, as indicated in the chart below.

Grapheme	Phoneme	Grapheme	Phoneme	Grapheme	Phoneme
ـيي	i	—	ɨ	ي	e
ۆ	ə	ا	a	—	î
وو	u	—	ʉ	و	o

Kurdish seems to be the most sophisticated language, among the many which use some modified form of Arabic orthography, in the extent to which it has sought to evolve a system to represent vowels through linear graphemes and not through the usual method of diacritics. To the extent it could be figured out, the third system seems to share features with both the systems mentioned earlier. The most interesting feature is the use of *hā* for /ə/ in all the three systems. In

C.A. the grapheme *hā* had four different allographs depending upon its position in a written word. Of these, it seems, the final and the independent variants are used exclusively to represent /ə/ in Kurdish. No example of a medial *hā* was found in the texts; it appears that in its Kurdish usage *hā* is never combined with a following grapheme. In other words, while in C.A. *hā* was a connector, in Kurdish it is used as a nonconnector. Also notable is the fact that all the graphemes for Kurdish vowels are used most regularly. Of the three vowels for which no graphemes are given in the third chart, /î/ and /ʉ/ do not have overt graphemic representations, while no word with /ɨ/ was found in these texts.

It should also be mentioned that in these texts no distinction is made between /l/ and /ł/, and /r/ and /ṙ/. No example of /v/ is found either. *hamzah* is used only as a consonant grapheme for /'/; it never indicates syllable boundary as it does, for example, in Persian and Urdu. Instead, conjunct vowels are written together without any intervening grapheme (such examples are, however, infrequent in these texts). *yā* and *wāw* are still used for both vowels and consonants. These texts also show that the digraph *nūn-gāf* for /ŋ/ is not used before *kāf* (/k/), instead, only *nūn* is used in that position.

East Turki:[12] Inventory of phonemes.

Consonants							*Vowels*	
p	t	c	k	q		i	û	u
b	d	j	g			e	ô	o
f	s	š	x		h		â	a
v	z	ž	ḡ					
m	n		ŋ					
	l	r	y					

East Turki (E.T.) consonants not shared with C.A.: /p, c, g, v, ž, ŋ/.

C.A. consonants not shared with E.T.: /ṭ, ḍ, ', ϴ, đ, ṣ, ẓ, ḥ, ᶜ, w/.

All C.A. graphemes are retained in E.T. The graphemes for consonants not shared with E.T. have gained new values.

[12] *A Handbook of the East Turki Language* (University of California Library, Berkeley; title page mutilated). East Turki is another name for modern Uigur as written "in Sinkiang province in western China."

C.A. ḍ, đ, ẓ = z in E.T.
ṭ = t
θ, ṣ = s
w = v
ḥ = h
ᶜ, ʾ = See below.

New graphemes devised for the E.T. phonemes not shared with C.A. are:

Grapheme	Phoneme	Grapheme	Phoneme	Grapheme	Phoneme
پ	p	چ	c	گ	g
ژ	ž	ڭ	ŋ		

The graphemes for /p, c, ž, g/ are the same as in Persian or Kurdish. The interesting innovation is the new grapheme for the velar nasal, /ŋ/. This new grapheme, called *sağir nun,* has the basic shape of C.A. *kāf,* with three additional superscript dots. It is used, however, in free variation with a digraph, consisting of *nūn* and *kāf* (not *nūn* and *gāf,* as in Kurdish).

/f/ is a rather marginal phoneme in E.T. Arabic loans with a /f/ are often pronounced by some speakers as if with a /p/. Often such loans are written with a *pā,* instead of an original *fā.* On the other hand, *fā* is also often used for a /p/ in native E.T. words. This confusion in the use of an original C.A. grapheme is unusual for the languages studied here — on the phonemic level in the second language, two original C.A. graphemes may fall together, but never an original grapheme and a newly devised one, as in the case of E.T.

Though in the above inventory we have listed both /ğ/ and /q/ as separate phonemes, the particular data available to us is not very clear about their exact phonemic nature. A remark under the heading "Vowel Harmony" (p. 26) tells us that "the guttural sounds *q* (unvoiced) and *ğ* (voiced) are used only with back vowels; *k* (unvoiced) and *g* (voiced) are used with front vowels." Contrary examples, however, are found in the main body of the book: */qiliq/* "deed, act," */dukan/* "shop," */ickari/* "inside," */qisqâ/* "short," */qilğil/* "Do!" */kolxoz/* "collective farm." One is tempted to ascribe a morphophonemic nature to the E.T. orthography, but the data is too meager.

ᶜain and *hamzah* no longer have consonantal values; the words in which they occur are pronounced with conjunct vowels. However, only *hamzah* is used to indicate a syllable boundary in native E.T. words.

E.T. has an interesting system of eight vowels, which for the reasons of vowel harmony are first divided into front and back vowels, and later into unrounded and rounded vowels. The E.T. orthography, however, does not clearly indicate these distinctions. "The spelling of East Turki words, both as regards insertion of vowels and handling of consonants, is not standardized. Spelling usage varies not only from text to text but even from sentence to sentence. The tendency is to provide all vowels, to use *hā,* rather than *'alif,* for the sound *â* (except initially), to indicate double consonants by writing the letter twice, to join suffixes to the stem of the words, and to spell the words (even loans) as they are pronounced."[13] The author of that grammar also mentions a reformed Arabic alphabet introduced in Chinese Turkestan, and gives it in a chart, but it is difficult to say anything about it as no explanations or sample texts are given with it. The examples within the book, however, are given in a variety of Arabic orthography, and on page 18 of the book a small text does appear. The following rudimentary conclusions are based on those two sources.

It can be said that, medially and finally, *wāw* is used for rounded vowels and *yā* is used for the unrounded ones. *'alif* is used initially for both rounded and unrounded vowels. At the same time, however, /e, u, û, a, i, â/ are also found unindicated by any particular grapheme.

An interesting feature is the use of the final and the independent variants of *hā* for /â/ in E.T. But this is not done rigorously, and *hā* often occurs in free variation with *'alif* in the medial position. In word-final, however, its use is more regular. The selection of these two particular allographs of *hā* is similar to that found in Kurdish for /ə/.

In the sample text, the phoneme /ŋ/ of E.T. is indicated by a combination of the graphemes *nūn* and *kāf,* while in the main body of the book the new grapheme, *sağir nun,* is used for that purpose. Also, a double consonant is sometimes indicated by writing the grapheme twice, and sometimes by only a single grapheme. As far as it was

[13] *Ibid.,* p. 17.

possible to check, Arabic loans were found to be written in their original spellings.

Azerbaijani:[14] Inventory of phonemes.

Consonants

p	t	c	č	k	ʾ
b	d	j	ǰ	g	
f	s	š		x	h
v	z	ž		ḡ	
m	n				
	l	r	y		

Vowels

i	û	î	u
e	ô		o
ə		a	

Azerbaijani consonants not shared with C.A.: /p, c, č, ǰ, g, ž, v/.

C.A. consonants not shared with Azerbaijani: /q, ṭ, ḍ, Ɵ, đ, ṣ, ẓ, ḥ, ᶜ, w/.

All the graphemes of C.A. are retained in Azerbaijani. The graphemes for the C.A. consonants not shared with Azerbaijani have gained the following values.

C.A. đ, ḍ, ẓ = z in Azerbaijani
Ɵ, ṣ = s
q = g, k
ᶜ = ʾ
w = v
ḥ = h
ṭ = t

New graphemes devised for some of the Azerbaijani consonants not shared with C.A. are:

Grapheme	Phoneme	Grapheme	Phoneme
پ	p	چ	c
گ	ǰ	ژ	ž

The new graphemes for /p, c, ž/ are the same as in Persian for similar consonants. The new grapheme for Azerbaijani /ǰ/ is in Persian the grapheme for /g/, as also in Urdu and Kurdish. Azer-

[14] Fred W. Householder, Jr. and Mansour Lotfi, *Spoken Azerbaijani* (F.S.I., 1953).

baijani has two dorso-palatal stops /č, j̄/, which are in contrast with the simple velar stops /k, g/. Azerbaijani /g/ is indicated by *qāf*, which in the case of Arabic loans — always written in the original spelling — is pronounced as a voiceless velar stop. In other words, the grapheme *qāf* is pronounced as /k/ in Arabic loans, but as /g/ in native Azerbaijani words. That leaves only *kāf*, which is used for both /k/ and /č/ in Azerbaijani.

In the case of vowels, no particular attempt is made to represent them in an unambiguous fashion. The graphemes used are *hā, 'alif, yā,* and *wāw*. The only exception seems to be a final /ə/, which is always indicated by *hā*, though a final *hā* can also represent a final /h/.

Pashto:[15] Inventory of phonemes.

Consonants

p	t		T	k	q	’		
b	d		D	g				
f	s	š	S	x			h	ḥ
	z	ž	Z	ḡ				
m	n		N					
w	l	r	y	R				

Vowels

ii			uu
i			u
ee	e		oo
	a	aa	

(Note: /T, D, S, Z, N, R/ are retroflex consonants. Double vowels are long.)

Pashto consonants not shared with C.A.: /p, T, D, g, S, ž, Z, N, R/.

C.A. consonants not shared with Pashto: /j, ṭ, ḍ, Θ, đ, ṣ, ẓ, ᶜ/.

All the graphemes of C.A. are retained in Pashto. The graphemes for the C.A. consonants not shared with Pashto have gained the following new values.

C.A. ḍ, đ, ẓ = z in Pashto
j = dž
ṭ = t
Θ, ṣ = s
ᶜ = ’

New graphemes adopted for the Pashto consonants not shared with C.A. are:

[15] Herbert Penzl, *A Grammar of Pashto* (A.C.L.S., 1955).

Grapheme	Phoneme	Grapheme	Phoneme	Grapheme	Phoneme
پ	p	ټ	T	ډ	D
گ	g	ښ	S	ژ	ž
ږ	Z	ڼ	N	ړ	R

The graphemes for /p, g, ž/ are the same as in Persian, etc., for similar consonants. The graphemes for the retroflex consonants have been devised — as usual — by modifying the C.A. graphemes for the consonants most similar to the retroflex consonants. The graphemes for /T, D, N, R/ are formed by putting a small circle under the graphemes *tā, dāl, nūn,* and *rā,* respectively. The graphemes for the remaining two retroflex consonants, /S, Z/, do not follow this pattern: for /Z/, a superscript dot is added to *zā,* and in the case of /S/, both a superscript dot and a subscript dot are added to *sīn.*

Pashto alphabet contains, however, a set of six very similar graphemes, out of which four are used for what Penzl analyzes as consonant clusters. These four are:

Grapheme	Consonant Cluster	Grapheme	Consonant Cluster
ج	dž	چ	tš
ځ	dz	څ	ts

The grapheme for /dž/ is the original C.A. *jīm,* used in C.A. and in other languages for single phonemes; the grapheme for /tš/ is the same as in Persian and Kurdish for what in those languages are analyzed as single phonemes. The remaining two graphemes are peculiar to Pashto, but they share the basic shape with the previous two. According to Penzl's analysis, therefore, we find in Pashto alphabet a most rare case of neatly patterned over-differentiation, independent of any influence of the C.A. orthography, and unlike any of the languages considered here. Of course, the presence of these separate graphemes does not require us to analyze these clusters as single phonemes, but it does point out the native grammarian's view of the problem.

ᶜain — used in Arabic loans — is pronounced as a glottal stop; *hamzah* — used in loans as well as in native Pashto words — sometimes represents a glottal stop, but mostly a syllable boundary.

As regards the vowels, the situation in Pashto orthography seems familiarly confusing. *'alif* is used for all initial short vowels and, in combination with *yā* and *wāw,* for initial long vowels, too. Only medially and finally it represents /aa/ exclusively. Both an /a/ and /e/ are indicated in final position by *hā*. Penzl mentions some special graphemes for vowels, but does not give examples of their use in different positions. Further, even from his own statement, it does not appear that their use is regular and common. Some of these graphemes are: (1) *yā* with two subscript dots, one under the other, for /ee/; (2) *yā* with a "short horizontal extension to its left," for a diphthong, /ei/; (3) *yā* with a "superior *hamzah* sign," for another diphthong, /ey/.

One feature needs special mention. This is the use of a grapheme called *yā-i-majhūl*; its distribution is limited, as it is used only for a final /ee/, and only in certain styles of writing. Originally this grapheme was a positional variant of *yā,* conditioned by reasons of calligraphy. We find this grapheme again in Urdu, where it is used regularly for final /e/ and /æ/.

Sindhi:[16] Inventory of phonemes.

Consonants

p	t	T	c	k	
ph	th	Th	ch	kh	
b	d	D	j	g	
bh	dh	Dh	jh	gh	
ḅ		Ḍ	j̣	g̣	
m	n	N	ñ	ŋ	
f	s		š	x	h
v	z			ḡ	
l	r	R	Rh	y	

Vowels

i		u
I		U
e	ə	o
E	a	ɔ

Nasalization: ~

(Note: /ḅ, Ḍ, j̣, g̣/ are implosives. /T, Th, D, Dh, Ḍ, N, R, Rh/ are retroflex consonants. /ph, th, Th, ch, kh, bh, dh, Dh, jh, gh, Rh/ are aspirates.)

Sindhi consonants not shared with C.A.: /p, T, c, ph, th, Th, ch, kh, D, g, bh, dh, Dh, jh, gh, ḅ, Ḍ, j̣, g̣, N, ñ, ŋ, v, R, Rh/.

[16] I am grateful to Dr. Lachman Khubchandani of the Deccan College, Poona, for the data on Sindhi phonemics and graphemics.

C.A. consonants not shared with Sindhi: /Θ, đ, ḥ, q, ṭ, ḍ, ṣ, ẓ, ^{c}, w, ’/.

All the C.A. graphemes are retained in Sindhi. The graphemes for C.A. consonants not shared with Sindhi have gained the following new values.

C.A. đ, ḍ, ẓ = z in Sindhi
Θ, ṣ = s
q = k
ṭ = t
ḥ = h
w = v
^{c}, ’ = no consonantal value; syllable boundary between conjunct vowels.

Sindhi, with its eleven aspirates and four implosives — beside other consonants — had quite a large task of devising new graphemes, as indicated in the chart below.

Grapheme	Phoneme	Grapheme	Phoneme	Grapheme	Phoneme
پ	p	ٽ	T	چ	c
ڦ	ph	ٿ	th	ٺ	Th
ڇ	ch	ک	kh	ڊ	D
گ	g	ڀ	bh	ڌ	dh
ڍ	Dh	جھ	jh	گھ	gh
ٻ	ḅ	ڏ	Ḍ	ڄ	j̣
ڳ	g̣	ڻ	N	ڃ	n̂
ڱ	ŋ	ڙ	R	ڙھ	Rh

We find that most of the new consonantal contrasts are provided for by setting up new graphemes, using C.A. basic shapes and diacritics, especially superscript and subscript dots, ranging in number from one to four. But any attempt to discover some kind of underlying patterns may only lead one to lose faith in human nature.

The use of *kāf* for Sindhi aspirate /kh/ is somewhat unique. While both *kāf* and *qāf* in Arabic loans are pronounced as a voiceless velar unaspirate, /k/, in native Sindhi words *kāf* is used exclusively for /kh/. The unaspirated stop /k/ in native Sindhi words is represented by a special grapheme ڪ, which is based on a calligraphic variant of the initial part of the C.A. *kāf*. In other words, the phonemic value of *kāf* in Sindhi depends not on its graphemic environment but on the historical origin of any particular word.

In the use of dots in the new graphemes one notices a variety of arrangements. Two dots are arranged either horizontally or vertically; three dots are arranged in the shape of a pyramid, with the apex downward (in C.A. graphemes, three dots always appear with the apex upward); and four dots are arranged in a box shape. A new diacritic is a small superscript *ṭā* which combines with the basic shape of *nūn* to form the grapheme for Sindhi /N/, a retroflex nasal. While in Sindhi this superscript is not used in the graphemes for other retroflex consonants, its use for that purpose is regular in Urdu.

Another interesting feature needs our notice. All the new graphemes have been developed, in the usual manner, from the basic shapes of the graphemes that represent the closest C.A. equivalents to the Sindhi phonemes, but two of them indicate a greater awareness of phonetic features on the part of the native grammarians. The palatal nasal /n̂/ is represented by a grapheme that shares its basic shape, not with *nūn,* but with *jīm,* the grapheme for the palatal stop /j/. Likewise, the velar nasal /ŋ/ has the grapheme that shares its basic shape with *gāf* (/g/) and not with *nūn*. The grapheme for the retroflex nasal /N/, however, has been devised from *nūn,* as expected.

Among the aspirates, the graphemes for /jh, gh, Rh/ can be analyzed to be digraphs, as they are merely combinations of the graphemes for the unaspirated consonants /j, g, R/ and another grapheme which is identical in shape with an allograph of *hā* in Sindhi. That particular allograph of *hā* is used for /h/ in all positions except finally after a nonconnector, e.g., after *wāw* or *'alif*. However, as the rest of the aspirated consonants have single graphemes, it is reasonable to set up these combinations as single unit graphemes, rather than analyzing them as containing a grapheme for the unaspirated consonant and a grapheme for aspiration (cf. Urdu).

As usual, Sindhi orthography does not represent overtly and distinctly all the vowels of Sindhi. The three graphemes, *'alif, yā,* and *wāw,* are used singly or in combination to represent all the vowels, resulting in the usual overlapping and ambiguity.

The following description of Urdu is based on my own analysis of Urdu phonemics and graphemics. See the bibliography for more details.

Urdu: Inventory of phonemes.

Consonants

p	t	T	c	k	q	
ph	th	Th	ch	kh		
b	d	D	j	g		
bh	dh	Dh	jh	gh		
f	s		š	x		h
v	z		ž	ḡ		
m	n					
l	r	R	y			

Vowels

i		u
I		U
e	ə	o
æ	a	ɔ

Nasalization: ~

(Note: /T, Th, D, Dh, R/ are retroflex consonants. /ph, th, Th, ch, kh, bh, dh, Dh, jh, gh/ are aspirates.)

Urdu consonants not shared with C.A.: /p, c, T, ph, th, Th, ch, kh, D, g, bh, dh, Dh, jh, gh, v, ž, R/.

C.A. consonants not shared with Urdu: /θ, đ, ṭ, ḍ, ṣ, ẓ, ḥ, ᶜ, ', w/.

All the graphemes of C.A. have been retained in Urdu. The graphemes for C.A. consonants not shared with Urdu have gained the following values.

C.A. đ, ḍ, ẓ = z in Urdu
θ, ṣ = s
ṭ = t
ḥ = h
w = v
ᶜ, ' = See below.

New graphemes for Urdu consonants not shared with C.A.

Grapheme	Phoneme	Grapheme	Phoneme
پ	p	چ	c
ٹ	T	ڈ	D
گ	g	ژ	ž
ڑ	R	ھ	Aspiration

The new graphemes for /p, c, g, ž/ are the same as in Persian, etc. The main problem was to devise graphemes for the retroflex consonants and the aspirates. This was done in an interesting manner.

In Urdu phonemics it is always found more convenient to analyze the aspirates as single units rather than as sequences of two phonemes (consonant + aspiration), but in the orthography a separate grapheme has been devised for aspiration itself which is written after the grapheme for the relevant consonant. This new grapheme is historically just a variant of C.A. *hā,* and we found it being used in this special manner (i.e., to indicate aspiration) in three Sindhi graphemes, too. But, whereas in Urdu it is used in a regular fashion for all aspirates, in Sindhi that was not the case, and hence it could not fruitfully be set up as a separate grapheme in Sindhi. Its name in Urdu is *do-cəšmi he*. The other variants of C.A. *hā* are treated as variants of the grapheme *choTi he* in Urdu, and represent /h/.

Name of the grapheme	Independent	Initial	Medial	Final
C.A. *hā* (/h/)	ه	هـ	ـهـ	ـه
Urdu *choTi he* (/h/)	ہ	ہـ	ـہـ	~
Urdu *do-cəšmi he* (/aspiration/)	ھ		ـھـ	ـھ

The two initial and medial variants of Urdu *choTi he* are interesting, as they use a subscript which is not found elsewhere in the orthography, and also appears to be unique to Urdu among the languages studied here. It should be mentioned here that the *do-cəšmi he* is also regularly used to represent initial /h/ in Urdu type (as opposed to Urdu calligraphy). Thus, on an Urdu typewriter keyboard, there are only three signs to take care of aspiration and /h/.

Sign	Initial	Medial	Final	Independent	Phoneme
ه			√	√	h
ـهـ		√			h
هـ	√				h
ھ		√	√	√	Aspiration

In ordinary calligraphy, however, the contrastive distribution of the two graphemes for two separate phonemes is strictly observed.

Urdu has five retroflex consonants, /T, Th, D, Dh, R/. Of these, the unaspirated ones are represented by three separate graphemes, while the aspirated ones are represented by sequences of *do-cəšmi he* and the grapheme for the relevant unaspirated consonant. The three new graphemes share a superscript in the shape of a small C.A. *ṭā* (cf. the grapheme for Sindhi /N/).[17]

An interesting thing to observe in the history of Urdu orthography is the development of a separate grapheme for /R/. At one stage in the development of Urdu, this consonant was only an allophone of /D/. Both /D/ and /Dh/ had two allophones each, whose distribution neatly compared.

Phoneme	Allophone	Distribution
/D/	[R], a retroflex flap, unaspirated.	i. Between oral vowels. ii. Medially before all consonants except /D, Dh/. iii. Medially after all consonants except /n, D/. iv. Finally after vowels.
	[D], a voiced, retroflex stop, unaspirated.	Elsewhere.
/Dh/	[Rh], a retroflex flap, aspirated.	i. Between oral vowels. ii. Medially before all consonants except /D, Dh/. iii. Finally after vowels.
	[Dh], a voiced, retroflex stop, aspirated.	Elsewhere.

Up until the third quarter of the last century, Urdu orthography indicated both the phonemic and the allophonic contrasts in the following manner.

Allophone	Grapheme or Graphemic Sequence
[D]	ڈ
[R]	ڈ , in free-variation with ڑ
[Dh]	ڈھ
[Rh]	ڈھ , in free-variation with ڑھ

[17] In older manuscripts we also find four superscript dots being used instead of the small ṭā.

But due to increasing borrowing of English words, whose alveolar "t" and "d" were pronounced retroflex in Urdu, a contrast developed between [D] and [R], and they were established as two separate phonemes.[18] The situation with [Dh] and [Rh], however, did not change; they remained in complimentary distribution.

In the orthography, the contrast between /D/ and /R/ was clearly indicated by setting up a separate grapheme for each. This, however, resulted in over-differentiation in the case of [Dh] and [Rh], as the grapheme for /R/, combined with the grapheme for aspiration, came to be used for the latter.

Phoneme	Allophone	Grapheme
/D/	[D]	ڈ
/R/	[R]	ڑ
/Dh/	[Dh]	ڈھ
	[Rh]	ڑھ

In Urdu, *hamzah* indicates syllable boundary between conjunct vowels. ᶜ*ain* occurs only in the Arabic loans, but is never pronounced as a consonant, except in learned, formal speech.

The contrast between oral and nasal vowels is phonemic in Urdu, but the orthography clearly indicates that distinction only word-finally, in which case a dot-less *nūn* indicates nasalization of the final vowel. Elsewhere, *nūn* (with its dot) is used for both nasalization and /n/.

Regarding the vowels the confusion is familiar. *'alif* alone indicates initial /I, ə, U/ as well as medial and final /a/. It combines with *yā* to indicate initial /i, e, æ/, and with *wāw,* to indicate initial /u, o, ɔ/. Medially, short vowels /I, ə, U/ are not indicated, while /e, i, æ/ are indicated by *yā,* and /o, u, ɔ/ by *wāw.* Finally, /u, o, ɔ/ are indicated by *wāw,* /e, æ/ by one variant of C.A. *yā,* and /i/ by another. In terms of Urdu, the two variants of C.A. *yā* are separate graphemes, with their distribution limited to the independent and final positions within the orthography.

[18] At present the contrast between /D/ and /R/ is true also for native Urdu words, e.g., /jəR/ "root" and /khəD/ "chasm, pit"; /lɔ̃Ra/ "penis" and /lɔ̃Da/ "lad, chap."

Name of the Grapheme	Grapheme	Phoneme
choTi ye		Final /i/.
bəRi ye		Final /e, æ/
ye		/y/, medial /i, e, æ/, (with *'alif*) initial /i, e, æ/.

Urdu grapheme *bəRi ye* is identical in shape with the *yā-i-majhūl* of Pashto mentioned earlier.

Sulu:[19] Inventory of phonemes.

Consonants						*Vowels*					
p	t	c	k	'		i	ī			u	ū
b	d	j	g					a	ā		
	s			h							
m	n	ñ	ŋ								
w	l	r	y								

Sulu consonants not shared with C.A.: /p, c, g, ñ, ŋ/.

C.A. consonants not shared with Sulu: /ṭ, q, ḍ, f, Θ, ṣ, š, x, ḥ, đ, z, ẓ, ḡ, ^{c}/.

All the C.A. graphemes are retained in Sulu. The graphemes for C.A. consonants not shared with Sulu have gained diverse new values. Some have only one substitute pronunciation; others have two or three, which are not predictable and depend upon the particular Arabic loan in which they occur, and which, as expected, keeps its original spelling.

C.A. Θ, ṣ, š = s in Sulu	C.A. x = k, h in Sulu
ḥ = h	đ = j, n, s
ṭ = t	z = j, s
q = k	ḍ = d, b, l
f = p	ẓ = l, s
^{c} = '	
ḡ = g	

Sulu consonants not shared with C.A. are indicated either by a new grapheme or by giving a new value to some C.A. grapheme.

[19] C. R. Cameron, *Sulu Writing* (Zamboanga, 1917).

Grapheme	Phoneme	Grapheme	Phoneme
ڤ	p	چ	c
ڭ، ݢ، گ	g	ڽ	ñ
ڠ	ŋ		

The graphemes for /c/ and /ñ/ are identical with the Persian and Urdu graphemes for /c/ and /p/, respectively. The use of C.A. *fā* and *ğain* for Sulu /p/ and /g/ is unique to this language, and was perhaps made possible by the high degree of assimilation of Arabic loans that has occurred in Sulu. Note that the new grapheme for Sulu /ŋ/ shares its basic shape with C.A. *ğain,* and not with *kāf.*

Sulu has a glottal stop and, therefore, uses *hamzah* in more or less the same way as C.A.; though *ᶜain* in Arabic loans is also pronounced as a glottal stop, it is never used in native Sulu words.

The study used for the data on Sulu does not give very exact information regarding the number of vowel phonemes in the language; one can only surmise that there are at least six. These are indicated with the help of diacritics, much the same way as in C.A. From the short specimens of Sulu writing given in the book it appears that the diacritics are used regularly, even in ordinary writing, which is not the case in any other language studied here. In all the other languages, the diacritics are used only in special texts or, for example, to indicate the exact pronunciation of some loan word. The three diacritics used in Sulu are called *hata'as, hababa',* and *dapan,* and are identical with the C.A. *fatḥah, kasrah,* and *ḍammah,* respectively.

An incidental, but most interesting, new development in Sulu is the use of the Arabic numeral for 2 to indicate the reduplication of stems. The name for this sign in Sulu is *aŋkā,* but it cannot be treated as a grapheme in terms of this study. The book gives extensive rules to establish the particular part of the stem that is to be repeated in each instance. An identical sign is found in Malay, too, where it is used in an identical manner and where it is called *aŋka dua.* It should be noted that in Hindi, which uses the Devanagari script, the numeral 2 is used in a similar but limited manner, whereas in Urdu that is not possible.

The following description of Malay is based on information from the books on Malay listed in the bibliography at the end of this chapter.

Malay: Inventory of phonemes.

Consonants						*Vowels*		
p	t	c	k	ʼ		i		u
b	d	j	g				ə	
f	s	š		h		e		o
	z		ḡ				a	
m	n	ñ	ŋ			ai		au
w	l	r	y					

Malay consonants not shared with C.A.: /p, c, g, ñ, ŋ/.

C.A. consonants not shared with Malay: /ṭ, ḍ, q, ϴ, đ, ṣ, ẓ, x, ḥ, ᶜ/.

All the C.A. graphemes have been retained in Malay, and those which represent consonants not shared with Malay have gained diverse values. As in Sulu, some graphemes have one substitute pronunciation, while others have more than one. In the latter cases, the choice of one substitute pronunciation, among many, is not predictable in terms of the phonological environment, but depends entirely upon the morphology of the particular word.

C.A. ϴ, ṣ = s in Malay
ṭ = t
ḥ = h

C.A. ḍ = d, l, z in Malay
q = k, ʼ
đ = j, z, dz
ẓ = l, tl, dz
x = k, h
ᶜ = ʼ

In the inventory of phonemes given above, we have shown /f, z, š, ḡ/ to be distinct phonemes in Malay, but it should be pointed out that they are so only in formal, educated speech. In colloquial Malay, they are replaced by /p, j, s, r/, respectively. Loan words from Arabic are usually written in the original spelling, but often they are given pronunciation spellings, especially when they occur with Malay affixes.

C.A.	Malay	Meaning
غيب /ḡaib/	رائيف /raip/	"absent"
جواب /jawāb/	جواڤن /jawapan/	"reply"
صفت /ṣifat/	مپيڤتكن /məñipatkan/	"quality"
عادل /ādil/	ڤڠاديل /pəŋadil/	"just"

The five Malay consonants not shared with C.A. are indicated by the following graphemes.

Grapheme	Phoneme	Grapheme	Phoneme
ف	p	چ	c
غ	g	پ	ñ
ڠ	ŋ		

The new grapheme for /p/ is often replaced by *fā,* though the reverse is also true, as mentioned earlier. Of the three variant graphemes given for Malay /g/, the one with one superscript dot is more common. But the grapheme for the velar nasal /ŋ/ shares its basic shape with C.A. *ğain,* and not with the Malay graphemes for the velar stops; it is identical with the Sulu grapheme for /ŋ/. The grapheme for Malay /ñ/ has the basic shape of C.A. *nūn;* it has three superscript dots in the final and independent positions, and three subscript dots in the other two positions, possibly to distinguish it from C.A. *θā.*

Grapheme		Independent	Initial	Medial	Final	Phoneme
C.A.	ث	ث	ثـ	ـثـ	ـث	θ
Malay	ڽ	ڽ	پـ	ـپـ	ـڽ	ñ

Compare it with the grapheme for Sulu /ñ/, which shares its basic shape with C.A. *θā,* and has three subscript dots in all positions.

In a few very common words, *hamzah* indicates a final /'/, but usually it is used to indicate syllable boundary between conjunct vowels. What is noteworthy is the fact that in most instances it occurs without a *kursī,* sometimes even in those Arabic loans which have it occurring with a *kursī* in the original spelling.

C.A.	Malay	Meaning
عجائب /^{c}ajā'ib/	عجائيب /^{c}aja'ib/	"wonders"
ملائكة /malā'ika/	ملائيكت /mala'ikat/	"angels"

In Malay, compared with other languages, *hā* is never used to indicate a vowel; only *'alif, yā,* and *wāw* are used for this purpose. *'alif,* alone or in combination with *yā* and *wāw,* indicates all initial vowels.

It also indicates medial /a/. *yā* is used for /i, e, ai/, though /i, e/ are often left unmarked. Likewise, *wāw* is used for /u, o, au/, though /u, o/ are often left unindicated. No attempt is made to indicate /ə/. Thus we are left with a familiar confusion in the representation of vowels. Even the attempts to reform the Malay script seem to seek only to establish rules for predicting the graphemic form of a Malay word, without making sure at the same time that its phonemic form be predictable from the graphemic form.

Malay also uses, like Sulu, the Arabic numeral for 2, to indicate reduplication of words and stems. This sign is called *aŋka dua* in Malay.

Single Form	Reduplicated Form
نڬري /nəgəri/	نڬري٢ /nəgəri-nəgari/
بواه /buah/	بواه٢ من، بواهن٢ /buah-buahan/
بارڠ /baraŋ/	بارڠ٢ مو /baraŋ-baraŋ-mu/

CONCLUSIONS

The purpose of this study was to see how the C.A. orthography was adapted for several non-Semitic languages, and to what extent these adaptations represent the phonemic systems of the borrowing languages. Much of that has been discussed in the sections on specific languages. Below we give what few generalizations we can make regarding these matters.

In each case the borrowing language retained all the graphemes of C.A., listing them in the adapted alphabet, in the original sequence. New graphemes were placed in the alphabet next to the C.A. graphemes with which they shared basic shapes.

The graphemes for the C.A. consonants not shared with the borrowing language gained diverse values, but only rarely were they used outside of Arabic loans (Malay being one exception).

In nearly all the languages, the following C.A. phonemic contrasts were neutralized similarly.

C.A. /đ/, /z/, /ḍ/, and /ẓ/ > /z/
/θ/, /s/, and /ṣ/ > /s/
/t/, and /ṭ/ > /t/
/ḥ/, and /h/ > /h/

Yet, in each instance, only one C.A. grapheme was selected to represent that consonant in native words and in loans from languages other than Arabic. In fact the selections were identical in all the languages: *zā* for /z/, *sīn* for /s/, *tā* for /t/, and *hā* for /h/, phonetic similarity being the obvious reason.

Consonants in the borrowing languages were assigned graphemes which represented the phonetically most similar consonants in C.A. For new consonantal contrasts, the borrowing languages generally set up new graphemes. Only in rare cases was a C.A. grapheme used for such a purpose (*ḡain* for Sulu /g/, for example).

All new graphemes were developed from the basic shapes existing in the C.A. system; even the diacritics were those already in use in C.A. The only somewhat new attempt was to use a small *ṭā* as a diacritic in the graphemes for Urdu retroflex consonants and the Sindhi retroflex nasal. The basic shapes were almost always selected on the basis of phonetic similarity, but no similar attempts were necessarily always made to establish a relationship between the phonetics of the borrowing language and its graphemics. In other words, for example, the graphemes for the palatal consonants in a language do not necessarily show any similarity, in terms of either the basic shape or the diacritics. One of the few exceptions being the graphemes for the retroflex consonants in Urdu.

Except for the possible exception of Kurdish, none of the orthographies examined here discretely represents, or seems to have tried to represent, all the vowels of the particular language. Only a few vowels, in each case, have been given discrete graphemes. In a few cases, calligraphic variants of C.A. graphemes have been set up as separate graphemes to represent separate vowels (e.g., a variant of *hā* for E. Turki /â/ in the final position, or a variant of *yā* for a final /ee/ in Pashto). In all the above orthographies, a number of original C.A. diacritics are used whenever it is felt necessary to indicate discretely all the vowels in a particular word or text.

Ranging a little further away from the original purpose of this study, we can confidently say that the C.A. orthography and the orthographies derived from it, were most economical and efficient for the days when writing meant only calligraphy. In calligraphy it saved space and time if the orthography was cursive, if it discretely indicated all the consonantal contrasts with single graphemes but neglected some of the vowels which could be predicted, and if the letters were written in a nonlinear fashion and were given smaller, special variants for that purpose. But these very qualities of an orthography become its worst shortcomings in these days of typewriter and printing. It is in these areas that attempts to reform the scripts should be made — and, in some cases, are being made. But, if these reforms are expected to truly reflect the genius of the original orthography and also establish a sense of affinity, both historical and cultural, between C.A. and the borrowing language, and among the borrowing languages themselves, then a large scale study, similar in nature to this brief one, should first be made of all the orthographies that have been developed from the C.A. orthography.

Name in C.A.	C.A.	Per.	Kur.	E.T.	Azer.	Pashto	Sindhi	Urdu	Sulu	Mal.
'alif	* ا	* ا	*' ا	* ا	* ا	* ا	* ا	* ا	* ا	* ا
bā	b ب	b ب	b ب	b ب	b ب	b ب	b ب bh ڀ	b ب	b ب	b ب
tā	t ت	t ت	t ت	t ت	t ت	t ت	t ت th ٺ	t ت	t ت	t ت
θā	θ ث	s ث	s ث	s ث	s ث	s ث	s ث T ٽ	s ث	s ث	s ث
		p پ	p پ	p پ	p پ	p پ	p پ ḅ ٻ	p پ	ñ پ	
						T ټ	Th ٿ	T ٹ		
jīm	j ج	j ج	j ج	j ج	j ج	dž ج dz ځ	j ج j̣ ڄ	j ج	j ج	j ج
ḥā	ḥ ح	h ح	ḥ ح	h ح	h ح	ḥ ح	h ح n̂ ح	h ح	h ح	h ح
xā	x خ	x خ	x خ	x خ	x خ	x خ	x خ	x خ	k* خ	k* خ
		c چ	c چ	c چ	c چ	tš چ ts څ	c چ ch ڇ	c چ	c چ	c چ
dāl	d د	d د	d د	d د	d د	d د	d د dh ڌ	d د	d د	d د
đāl	đ ذ	z ذ	z ذ	z ذ	z ذ	z ذ	z ذ ḍ ڏ	z ذ	j* ذ	j* ذ
						D ډ	D ڊ Dh ڍ	D ڈ		
rā	r ر	r ر	r ر	r ر	r ر	r ر	r ر	r ر	r ر	r ر
zā	z ز	z ز	z ز	z ز	z ز	z ز Z ږ	z ز	z ز	j* ز	z* ز
			ṙ ڕ			R ړ	R ڙ	R ڑ		
		ž ژ	ž ژ	ž ژ	ž ژ	ž ژ		ž ژ		
sīn	s س	s س	s س	s س	s س	s س	s س	s س	s س	s س
šīn	š ش	š ش	š ش	š ش	š ش	š ش S ښ	š ش	š ش	š ش	š* ش
ṣād	ṣ ص	s ص	ṣ ص	s ص	s ص	s ص	s ص	s ص	s ص	s ص
ḍād	ḍ ض	ż ض	z ض	z ض	z ض	z ض	z ض	z ض	d* ض	d* ض
ṭā	ṭ ط	t ط	t ط	t ط	t ط	t ط	t ط	t ط	t ط	t ط
ẓā	ẓ ظ	z ظ	z ظ	z ظ	z ظ	z ظ	z ظ	z ظ	l* ظ	l* ظ
ʕain	ʕ ع	ع	ʕ ع	ع	' ع	' ع	ع	ع	' ع	'* ع
ḡain	ḡ غ	ḡ غ	ḡ غ	ḡ غ	ḡ غ	ḡ غ	ḡ غ	ḡ غ	ḡ غ	ḡ* غ
			v ڤ				ph ڦ		ŋ ڠ	ŋ ڠ
fā	f ف	f ف	f ف	f* ف	f ف	f ف	f ف	f ف	p ف	f* ف
qāf	q ق	q ق	q ق	q ق	g* ق	q ق	k ق	q ق	k ق	k* ق
				ŋ ڭ			ŋ ڱ			p ڤ
kāf	k ک	k ک	k ک	k ک	k* ک	k ک	kh ک k	k ک	k ک	k ک
		g گ	g گ	g گ	j̄ گ	g گ	g گ g̣ ڳ	g گ		g ڬ
lām	l ل	l ل	l ل	l ل	l ل	l ل	l ل	l ل	l ل	l ل
mīm	m م	m م	m م	m م	m م	m م	m م	m م	m م	m م
			ɫ ڵ			N ڼ	N ڻ	˜ ں		ñ ڽ
nūn	n ن	n ن	n ن	n ن	n ن	n ن	n ن	n ن	n ن	n ن
hā	h ه	h ه	h ه	h ه	h ه	h ة	h ه gh گھ	h ه	h ه	h ه
			ə ە				Rh ڙھ jh جھ	ھ		
wāw	w* و	v* و	w* و	v* و	v* و	w* و	v* و	v* و	w* و	w* و
yā	y* ي	y* ی	y* ي	y* ی	y* ی	y* ی	y* ي	y* ی	y* ی	y* ي
						ee ې		e ے		
hamzah	' ء	ء	' ء	ء	' ء	' ء	ء	ء	' ء	'* ء

REFERENCES

General

1. I. J. Gelb. *A Study of Writing.* Chicago, 1952.
2. H. A. Gleason. *An Introduction to Descriptive Linguistics.* New York, 1955.
3. Ernest Pulgram. "Phoneme and Grapheme; A Parallel," *Word* VII, no. 1, 1951.

Arabic

4. G. R. Driver. *Semitic Writing.* London, 1948.
5. W. H. T. Gairdner. *The Phonetics of Arabic.* Oxford, 1925.
6. Jochanan Kapliwatsky. *Arabic, Language and Grammar.* 3 vols. Jerusalem, 1957.
7. T. F. Mitchell. *Writing Arabic.* London, 1953.
8. Frank A. Rice. *The Classical Arabic Writing System.* A.C.L.S., 1958.
9. W. Wright. *A Grammar of the Arabic Language.* Cambridge, 1896.

Azerbaijani

10. Fred W. Householder and Mansour Lotfi. *Spoken Azerbaijani.* F.S.I., 1953.
11. D. Francisco-Maria Maggio. *Syntagmaton Linguarum Orientalium, Quæ in Georgiæ Regionibus Audiuntur.* Romæ, 1670.

East Turki

12. *A Handbook of the East Turki Language.* University of California Library at Berkeley; title page mutilated.
13. C. A. Thimm. *Turkish Self-Taught.* London, 1910.

Kurdish

14. Ernest N. McCarus. *A Kurdish Grammar.* A.C.L.S., 1958.
15. E. B. Soane. *Grammar of the Kurmanji or Kurdish Language.* London, 1913.

Malay

16. M. B. Lewis. *Teach Yourself Malay.* London, 1947.

17. M. B. Lewis. *A Handbook of Malay Script.* London, 1954.

18. Rev. W. G. Shellabear. "The Evolution of Malay Spelling," *Journal of the Royal Asiatic Society, Straits Branch* XXXVI, July, 1901.

19. Eduard F. Winckel. *Handbook of the Malay Language.* S. Pasadena, 1944.

20. Richard Winstedt. *Colloquial Malay.* London, 1945.

Pashto

21. Herbert Penzl. *A Grammar of Pashto.* A.C.L.S., 1955.

Persian

22. Ann K. S. Lambton. *Persian Grammar.* Cambridge, 1957.

Sulu

23. C. R. Cameron. *Sulu Writing.* Zamboanga, Philippine Islands, 1917.

Urdu

24. M. A. R. Barker, et al. *A Course in Urdu.* 3 vols. Montreal, 1967.

25. C. M. Naim, et al. *Introductory Urdu.* 2 vols. Mimeo. Chicago, 1965.

Dāniyāl-Nāme: An Exposition of Judeo-Persian

AMNON NETZER

GENERAL INTRODUCTION

THE JUDEO-PERSIAN writings are vast in time and space. They encompass over eleven centuries (from the middle of the eighth century till the beginning of the twentieth century), and their playground is the whole of Persia and Central Asia. It is perhaps a matter of coincidence that the earliest J-P writing is also the earliest written evidence of New Persian language: there is a reference to a fragment of a Persian business letter found at Dandan-Uyliq, near Khotan, in Chinese Turkistan. This letter, which is written in New Persian language and Hebrew characters, probably in the middle of the eighth century, represents the earliest available document in New Persian language of any sort.[1] Although this letter may, to some extent, indicate the cultural integration of Persian Jews in Iran, for our purpose, it cannot be regarded as the beginning of J-P literature.

It is interesting to notice that the Mongol period, one of the most brilliant periods of literature and art in Persia, is also the producer of the greatest J-P poet — Shahin of Shiraz. The name and life of Shahin are known to us by his works. He is glorified by a number of J-P poets who came after him, none of these poets provide us with any biographical data on Shahin, except a scanty account given by Bābā'i Loṭf, another J-P poet (Kashan, 1617-56), who in his work, *Ketāb-e*

[1] This letter was found by an expedition headed by Aurel Stein; see G. Margoliouth, *JRAS*, 1903, 707-760; and also W. B. Henning, *Handbuch Iranistik* I: 79-80.

Anusi,[2] says that he visited Shahin's tomb in Shiraz. Shahin's panygeric to Sultan Abu Saᶜid (d. 1335) puts him in the fourteenth century. Since we find some of his works dated we are able to be more precise in determining Shahin's time: 1327-1358. The second half of the fourteenth century is known as the flourishing period of Persian literature. Toleration displayed by Il-Khanids greatly influenced the spiritual life and cultural betterment of Persian Jews.

For lack of knowledge of Hebrew script, and probably lack of interest too, the Persian *tadhkarāt'* biographical accounts on poets', do not mention the names and the works of any J-P poets. Thanks to the researches of W. Bacher we have some knowledge of Shahin and his works; though Bacher's work cannot be regarded complete since it is based on a portion of Shahin's poetical works — *Musā-nāme, Ardashir-nāme* and *Ezrā-nāme*.[3]

Shahin succeeded in establishing a poetic genre which was enthusiastically followed by the later J-P poets, notably Emrani (ca. 1500)[4] and Kh(w)āje of Bokhara (ca. 1606). Bacher's account on Shahin and Emrani made these two poets known to the western scholars, but Kh(w)āje was relegated to oblivion. Since, in my opinion, Kh(w)āje marks the end of a great period in J-P poetry and his poetic genre and style are representative of those of Shahin and Emrani, it is important to make an observation on the literary aspect of Kh(w)āje's only work — *Dāniyāl-nāme*.

DĀNIYĀL-NĀME

This is the name of the British Museum manuscript Or. 4743 containing a text of sixty-five octave folios in the Persian language in Hebrew characters.[5] Since it is a unique text which has never been published, a brief account is necessary to describe its form and content.

The author of the text calls his work by the Hebrew name שיר חדש 'a new song',[6] probably taken from the passage 'sing unto Lord a new

[2] MS ENA 401. Unless otherwise indicated MSS mentioned in this article belong to the Jewish Theological Seminary of America in New York.

[3] W. Bacher, *Zwi Jüdisch-Persische Dichter Schahin und Imrani* (Strassburg, 1908), pp. 7-165.

[4] *Ibid.*, pp. 166-206.

[5] G. Margoliouth, *Catalogue of the Hebrew and Samaritan Manuscripts in the British Museum* (London, 1909), p. 269.

[6] MS f.65b.

song'.[7] The folio 2b bears the title *Dāniyāl-nāme* 'the book of Daniel' according to which the text is known.[8]

Basically, the main part of this MS is a verification of the Book of Daniel developed, paraphrased, and expanded by the author. The MS contains 2174 distichs in the form of *mathnavi,* divided into eighty-eight chapters of various length. The meter is *hazaj-e mosaddas-e maḥdhuf*: (from right to left: — — ∪ — — — ∪ — — — ∪), a relatively convenient meter for composing long poems.

The Hebrew characters, except in a few cases, are not vocalized in the text. In general, the transcription of Persian words into Hebrew characters is not carefully done. In this regard, the following transliteration, with inconsistency in usage of diacritical marks, is used throughout the MS:

ג for ج چ غ گ

צ for چ ص

ז for ذ ز ژ ض ظ

ס for ث س ص

The copyist called himself Elyahu Eshaq ben Mordekhai.[9] He is not mentioned in the J-P MSS which I have examined in the libraries of the Jewish Theological Seminary of America in New York, the British Museum in London, the Bibliothèque Nationale in Paris, K. K. Hofbibliothek in Vienna, the Vatican, and the Machon Ben-Zvi in Jerusalem. According to the colophon (f. 65b) the scribe copied the MS on Friday the first of the month Adar in the year התקעו corresponding to A.D. 1816.[10] Also according to him the text was copied for a certain Mordekhai ben Ababa Mikhal, probably a Rabbi. The last distich in the MS belongs to the copyist who says: "Elyahu ben

[7] See Isa. 42:10; also see Ps. 33:3.

[8] See also the colophon on f.1b. The owner of the MS calls it *fārsi-ye Dāniyāl* 'Daniel in Persian'. This work, *Dāniyāl-nāme,* should not be confused with the prose work in J-P called *Qeṣṣe-ye Dāniyāl,* described by Zotenberg in his article "Geschichte Daniels" in *Archiv für wissenschaftliche des Alten Testaments* (1869) III: 385-427.

[9] MS f.65b.

[10] E. N. Adler confused this date with the date of the composition of the work, see "Bokhara," *Jewish Encyclopaedia.* He made the same mistake in *Jewish Quarterly Review* VII: 119.

Eshaq has hope from the threshold of Truth of witnessing salvation."

The MS begins with the distich:

בבאם לא מכאן אَגאז כרדם / בחמדש לב צֿה גֿונְה באז כרדם

"I have begun (this work) with the name of the Placeless (God), in praising Him, I have opened my lips like buds."

And ends with the distich:

דוכם אז צד בוׄד אז כׄאגְה תא חאל / כׄודׄיא משיח בפרסתו אמסאל

'From the (time of) Kh(w)āje till now a hundred less two (years have passed). O God, send the Messiah this year.'

AUTHORSHIP AND DATE

On the title folio the author's name appears as Bakh(w)āje Bokharai. He often addresses himself as Kh(w)āje or Kh(w)ājegi throughout the work. According to R. Levy, who gives a short account of the text in *Jewish Studies in Memory of George A. Kohut,* the author of *Dāniyāl-nāme* is Amina.[11] Levy mistakenly translates the title folio (f.2b) as ". . . from the narrative of ? (*sic*) to Kh(w)aja Bukharai" for the Persian *az gofte-ye Bakh(w)āje Bokhārāi.* First, in many J-P as well as Persian works *az gofte* means composed or versified by; secondly, the first syllable of the name Bakh(w)āje is not the preposition *be* 'to', but a short form of the Hebrew *aba*[12] 'father' as *bu* is a short form of the Arabic *abu* 'father'. Levy says, "The Kh(w)aje, whoever he may be, appears consciously to have adopted material originally composed by one Amina and to have fashioned it into a new work of his own. . . ." This conclusion of Levy is incorrect. The fifty-sixth verse of the last chapter (f.65b), which for the first and only time mentions Amina, says: "Amina has edited it (the poem); it is necessary that you should mention him also."

There is internal as well as external evidence indicating that Amina is not the author of the present work. First, the *Dāniyāl-nāme* is *az gofte-ye* 'composed by' Bakh(w)āje of Bokhara and the name

[11] Eds. S. Baron and A. Marx (New York, 1935), pp. 423-428. W. Fischel says, "It is quite likely that a Daniel Apocalypse, *Daniel Nama,* of Khodja Bukhari (1705) goes back to this Amina," "Israel in Iran" in *The Jews: Their History and Religion,* ed. L. Finkelstein (New York, 1960), p. 844.

[12] MSS: ENA 185 f.103, ENA 161 f.222b, ENA 1388 f.20a, et al. In addition, among the Jews of Isfahan and Kashan Bakh(w)āje means grandfather.

Kh(w)āje occurs many times throughout the text. Secondly, the distich mentioning Amina refers to him as someone who did *dastkāri* 'editing'. Thirdly, this editing of Amina took place ninety-eight years after the date of the composition of the original MS. This fact is indicated in the last distich of the text. According to folio 65b (vs 51), the *Dāniyāl-nāme* was completed in the year 1918 of the Seleucid era, "One thousand and nine hundred and eighteen, O my love, had passed from the era of Alexander, King of Kings, when this superb poetry was finished and was accepted by the elite and became famous among the commons." The year 1918 corresponds to A.D. 1606; *do kam az ṣad* 'a hundred years less two years' i.e., ninety-eight years later gives us the date A.D. 1704.

In line 56, we read more clearly that the editing of the work by Amina took place in *do alf ast az Sekandar ba shesh o dah,* 'It is two thousand and sixteen (years) since Alexander'; this date 2016 = A.D. 1704, precisely agrees with the date of Benyamin ben Mishael, a J-P poet, whose pen name is Amina.[13] There are several works of Amina extant, the best of which is his *Eḥterāz-nāme* 'the book of precaution'. It is characteristic of Amina to mention his pen name as many times as possible in his works.

KH(W)ĀJE, HIS THOUGHTS AND ATTITUDES

No information is available as to the actual status and the life of this poet in the Jewish community of his area, nor has anything been written about him in the works of Jews and non-Jews in Persia. His *nesbe* as Bokharai together with the pronunciation and usage of several words specific to the Tajik dialect, clearly show that Kh(w)āje was a native of Bokhara. From the fact that he possessed the linguistic qualifications required for composing the *Dāniyāl-nāme,* and his references to Biblical and rabbinical literature, Shahin, David Kimhi, Sa^{c}diya Ga^{c}on and the Persian poet Ferdausi, one may infer that he belonged to the class of 'the learned', and as such was well acquainted with the traditional interpretation of the Book of Daniel. Religious teachings deduced from the Book of Daniel, and the thoughts and views expressed by the author throughout the work, to some extent, throw light on the attitudes and the Weltanschauung of the poet.

[13] About Amina see MSS ENA 140 f.25b, ACC. 324 F.59, ENA 581 f.13b.

To understand the poet, one must rely exclusively on internal evidence. According to some of this evidence, which has no connection with the Book of Daniel, he was already known as *ahl-e naẓm*[14] 'a poet' among his people, but except for *Dāniyāl-nāme* we possess none of his poems. Kh(w)āje acknowledges Shahin's superiority and says he is inspired by Shahin though, "Being like a weak sparrow he cannot fly like Shahin."[15] Then he adds, "If it is possible for you follow him (Shahin)." The author has confidence that his work will have an effect on its readers and he goes one step further and compares himself with Ferdausi, "I shall be satisfied with this much from my friends, that at reading it (the poem) they will remember me. Then they will say, 'Bravo! Bravo! His words remind us of Ferdausi'."[16]

The author's view of the world is altogether pessimistic. In chapter four where he explains the reasons for composing the *Dāniyāl-nāme,* he speaks against this "perishable and mean world." He is looking for inspiration to help him accomplish his work, therefore he needs to detach himself from this world:

> O Kh(w)āje, if you have a taste for poetry,
> You should then refrain from thinking of this world.
> You should not be captive by worldly bonds.
> You should erase from the board of your chest,
> All loves of this mean world and affections
>   for the inverted-wheel.
> Keep away (your skirt) from this transient world,
> You should not get around it as long as you can.
> For in it there are naught but grains and snares—
> You might eventually be trapped by them before
>   attaining your desire.[17]

The author's views on the world are best expressed in Chapter eighty-seven. The world is perishable and is not to be trusted:

> How long will you attach yourself to this world,
> And neglect the affairs of the hereafter?
> Today, hold back from it,
> So that tomorrow you will be proud.

[14] MS f.7a 21-22.
[15] MS f.6b. Shahin also means falcon.
[16] MS f.65b 54-55.
[17] MS f.7a 30-34.

She is not worth being faithful to,
For she (only) appears like a bride.
When she removes the veil from her face,
Then you become aware of her condition.
Every moment she decorates herself
In order to deceive the people anew.
It is better that you resign from the world
and retire in seclusion.[18]

Reading the above lines together with Chapter three where, lamenting and supplicating, the poet asks God to uproot wordly love from his heart and replace it with His love, one is tempted to think that he was indeed oriented toward Sufiism:

O God, uproot the love of this world from my heart,
Which you molded in my clay in the beginning,
So that I shall place your love in my heart,
And my anguish and burning (love) for you will increase.[19]

Then he follows the footsteps of the Persian mystic poets by saying:

You blew wind (spirit) in my nose[20]
Until out of my anguish, I became aware of the Path.
By your favor, I became alive from that moment,
And became your slave through my heart and soul.
In the beginning you molded in my nature,
The singing of poems and the verve of poetry.[21]

He speaks of *vaṣl-e yār* 'union with the Friend' and of the prophets who gave up their lives for love of God. He wants to give up his life for *Jānān* 'Beloved'. He is *majun-e Ḥeyrān* 'a bewildered madman' and he begs God by all the prophets and lovers to guide him toward Himself, "May you show me the Path toward you, I have no other begging but this from your threshold."[22]

Fatalistic trends and tones, which are very strong in Persian mystic and epic poetry, are also found in the *Dāniyāl-nāme*. Speaking of the war between the combined armies of Cyrus and Darius on the one hand and Belshazzar on the other hand, the author says:

[18] MS ff.63b-64a.
[19] MS ff.5b-6a.
[20] I took the word *damāgh* meaning nose and not brain; cf. Gen.2:7.
[21] MS f.6a 15-17.
[22] MS f.65b 48.

The star of their (Cyrus' and Darius') fortune was lit.
The sky wore armour to help them.
Because of their luck and fortune,
The Moon became their shield-holder.
Dark night became so illuminated for them,
That one would say their sleeping fortune awoke.
When misfortune was subtracted from the fortune
of the kings,
At that hour, happiness became their mate.
The decree of fate (wanted) the gate (of Baghdad)
not to be broken.
Thereupon the gate was not closed that night.
When the stars help someone,
They open the gates to him in secret.
Because of the evil-deeds of the cruel wheel
Suddenly at dawn
The gate-keeper was taken by sleep in such a way
That one would say he had never slept in his life.
When suddenly fortune turns away from someone,
He will become bewildered, miserable and go astray.[23]

Heaven (*falak*) is treacherous, unstable and faithless: Man can never be sure of its benevolence, never rely upon it. On the death of Darius in the battlefield, the author says:

O Heaven you do nothing but injure hearts.
You never intend to help anyone.
Even if for a few times it (Heaven) helps,
What is the use, it (Heaven) is not persistent.
Even if it is faithful for one or two days,
On the fourth or fifth day, the faithfulness vanishes.[24]

The author's conception of God is that of Judaism. God is transcendent, omnipotent, merciful, and at the time of necessity, fierce and cruel. The entire first chapter is dedicated to praising God who created the whole universe, the prophets, mankind, animals and vegetation. He is *lāmakān* 'placeless' and has no beginning and end. He performed all the miracles recorded in the Old Testament and rabbinical literature. God also named Moses *Kalimollah* 'conversant with God'.[25]

[23] MS f.38a.
[24] MS f.5a 1-3.
[25] This is the reason for Jews of Persia being called Kalimi.

The author is grateful to God who endowed him with talent to compose poetry.

In Chapter two, the author praises Moses, *Kalimollah rosul-e dhāt-e bi chun* 'the conversant with God, the messenger of the indescribable Essence'. Moses "the proof and the leader of the people of Yeshurun was so *gostākh* 'daring' with God that there was none like him."

> One would say he was a placeless falcon,
> Happy fortune and co-dweller with the *Simorgh.*[26]
> He was a pearl in the encircling ocean of Truth;
> He was as a jewel in the dark night.
> Neither like kings possessed he tools of mastership,
> Nor claimed he prophetship like a prophet.
> He spoke to God with the same language.
> Who among the prophets had this rank?

The author then goes on to describe the story of Genesis and the miracles performed by Moses.

In Chapter three, under the heading *monājāt-e in bande-ye pāymāl bedargāh-e Dholjalāl* 'supplication of this down-trodden slave to the threshold of the Exalted', he regrets his past evil deeds. He asks God not to put him to shame on the day of resurrection but help him complete his work.

Other themes treated in *Dāniyāl-nāme* are *tavakkol* 'trust in God', *ṣadaqe* 'alms-giving' and *madhammat-e sharāb* 'condemnation of wine'. Like the above themes and concepts, also these themes contain the author's personal views and have no connection with the Book of Daniel.

Chapter twenty-seven is dedicated to the teaching of *tavakkol* 'trust in God'. In the author's view, everyone must believe in *tavakkol. Khalilollah* 'Abraham' had *tavakkol* therefore he escaped from the furnace.[27] Wise men must rely upon *tavakkol.*

Alms-giving to dervishes[28] is considered very important by the author. In Chapter thirty-three, he firmly demands that everyone give

[26] A legendary bird in Iranian mythology.

[27] This is a reference to the story of Abraham and Nimrod which is found in rabbinical and Islamic literature; see Jellinek, *Beth ha-Midrash* (Jerusalem, 1938) I: 25-34; Thaᶜalabi, *Qeṣaṣ al-Anbiyā* (Cairo, 1912), pp. 45-47; cf. Quran, 21: 59-67.

[28] Possibly the poor among the Jews.

alms to dervishes. Giving alms to dervishes is considered as "giving loans to Exalted Truth." It is interesting that the author, using Islamic terminology, says that alms-giving is one of *aḥkām-e shariᶜat* 'religious commands'.

In Chapter forty-five, *dar bayān-e madhammat-e mey va sharr-e u guyad,* 'on the condemnation of wine and its ills' the author finds himself in a difficult position. At the beginning of this chapter, one may get the impression that wine is a prohibited drink. He gives a series of examples of Biblical figures who drank wine and performed evil deeds. Adam drank it and became mortal instead of eternal.[29] Noah planted vines therefore God called him the man of the desert.[30] Lot drank wine in the cave and then made love to his daughters.[31] Had Joseph's brothers not drunk wine, they would not have attempted to kill Joseph.[32] Had the sons of Aaron not drunk wine, they would not have been burned to death.[33] Then the author realizes that it is against the Jewish custom to prohibit the drinking of wine, and say:

> From time to time drink a little of it (wine),
> Not every day, but once in a month or year.
> Feasts cannot be without it.
> It decreases sadness from the heart and increases happiness.
> Twice it is nice that you should become drunken;
> Once on *purim*[34] and again on the feast of *sukka.*[35]
> It is superb to do *qedusha*[36] with it on the seventh (Sabbath),
> Except for *habdala*[37] it is not nice (to drink wine).

[29] See *Sanhedrin,* 70; *Pirqe Rabbi Eliᶜezer,* 23.

[30] See Gen. 9:20; *Midrash Bereshit Rabba,* eds. J. Theodor and Ch. Albeck (Jerusalem, 1965) 36:3; *Midrash Tanhuma ha-Qadum ve ha-Yashan,* ed Buber (Wilna, 1885) 1:46; *Pirqe Rabbi Eliᶜezer,* 23. In these sources Noah is called the man of the soil and not the man of the desert.

[31] Gen. 19:30-36.

[32] See the note on *Midrash Bereshit Rabba,* 84:12, "His (Joseph's) brethren did not go to feed their father's flock in Shechem (Gen. 37:12), they went there to eat and drink (wine)."

[33] See *Midrash Rabba, Veyiqra Rabba,* 12:1.

[34] Jewish feast celebrated annually on the 14th of Adar, in commemoration of the deliverance of the Persian Jews from the plot of Haman to exterminate them, as recorded in the Book of Esther.

[35] The feast of tabernacles the celebration of which begins on the 15th day of the 7th month (Tishri) and lasts for nine days, see Lev. 23:34; Deut. 16:13, 16; 31:10.

[36] I.e., holiness; the benediction which refers to the Sabbath or a festival.

[37] I.e., Separation, distinction; the rabbinical term for the benedictions and

O Kh(w)āje, if you find wine, drink a little for the
sake of health.
Anyway, do not entirely turn away from it;
If you drink it wisely, you shall not have harm.[38]

LITERARY EVALUATION

Dāniyāl-nāme can best be described as a narrative poem using epic and mystic conventions of classical Persian literature and containing religio-messianic and moral teaching.

This genre of poetry (in J-P) was established by Shahin, the greatest J-P poet, at the beginning of the fourteenth century. One of the dominant themes in the narrative of *Dāniyāl-nāme* as well as in other J-P narratives based on Biblical stories aims at showing in detail how foreign rulers, one after another, have acknowledged the God of Israel or shown special favor to His servants. Shahin, Emrani, and Kh(w)āje Bokharai, writing in different periods, undertook to emphasize this notion.[39]

In these narratives what one is given is Jewish religious teaching, testifying to the strength of the Jewish faith. It does not matter whether the historical content of these narratives agrees with the true and accepted history of Persia; what is important is the religious point of view and the heritage of the Jewish people. It appears that the Persian Jews were not interested in the history of Persia for its own sake, but only as a source of material for Jewish theology. None of the Jewish writers of Persia ever inquired into or questioned the accuracy of the dates, names, events and the succession of Persian kings presented in their works.

In *Dāniyāl-nāme* Cyrus (550-530 B.C.) is king of Persia and he is a contemporary of Darius (522-486 B.C.) who is king of "Iraq."[40] They combine their armies and fight against Belshazzar, King of Babylon. After defeating Belshazzar, Darius at the age of sixty-two sits on the throne of "Baghdad." Then, suddenly, an enemy appears from

prayers by which a division is made between times of varying degrees of holiness, e.g., between Sabbath and work-day.

38 MS ff.33a-33b.

39 See Shahin's *Ardeshir-nāme,* MSS ENA 396, ACC. 40919; and Emrani's *Fatḥ-nāme,* MS 298.

40 See Dan. 9:1.

"Farangestan" and puts an end to Darius' life. Cyrus, defending his "father-in-law," Darius, defeats the enemy and thus becomes the ruler of Persia, "Iraq and Baghdad." The one place where the author attempts to correct the incredible historical facts in his work is when he names Darius' father, called Ahasuerus; the author remarks, ". . . but not that Ahasuerus the King of Susa at the time of Haman" (f.57bl-4).

Media is identified with Iraq, and the author never questions the historicity of Darius ruling it before Cyrus. Most of the action in *Dāniyāl-nāme* takes place in Babylon, conceived and referred to as Baghdad by the author. Except for a few occasions where Jerusalem, Media (Iraq), and Persia are mentioned, Baghdad remains the only setting of the story. Baghdad in the author's view, replacing Babylon, has symbolic and historic significance. It signifies the captivity, exile, and dispersion of the Jewish people. The author does not describe locations except with epithets used metaphorically, e.g., "the bride of the cities" for Jerusalem.

The author's main purpose and message are shown in the part which is an inaccurate translation of the Book of Daniel from the Hebrew-Aramaic original. However, his sense of organization and artistic talent are displayed in the part not directly connected with the Book of Daniel. The main body of the first part, dealing with historical and legendary events, is written in the epic style but never reaches the level of true epic poetry. It is interesting to note that although an abundance of historical reminiscences and a mass of soul-stirring legends lay in the storehouse of Jewish literature, none of them was woven into true J-P epic poetry. The Jewish poets of Persia often treated such subjects as Abraham and Isaac and sacrifice on Mount Moriah,[41] the dramatic stories of Jacob and Joseph,[42] Moses and the Exodus,[43] the entrance of Joshua into the land of Cannaan,[44] Esther and Mordekhai,[45] the Meccabees,[46] the Hanukka festival,[47] Hanna

[41] MSS ENA 573 and 581.

[42] MSS ENA 2332.

[43] MS ENA 514.

[44] MS ENA 298.

[45] MSS ACC. 40919 and ENA 396.

[46] Paris MS 130, see Zotenberg's *Catalogue des Manuscrits Hébreux de la Bibliothèque Nationale* (Paris, 1866).

[47] MS ACC. 324.

and her seven sons,[48] Eldād-e Dāni,[49] and Khodādād.[50] These, however, are poems in epic style.

Although the Old Testament offered a variety of themes and subjects to the Jewish poets or Persia, the stern character of Jewish monotheism prevented the rise of hero-worship, without which epic poetry is impossible. The Books of Joshua, Esther, Ezra, and Daniel presented ample opportunities for the Jewish poets of Persia who, in utilizing these Biblical sources, created significant narrative poetry with an epic coloring and heroic mood. Shahin, who attempted to produce a series of poems from the whole range of Biblical literature, was indeed the champion of this branch of poetry and the spiritual ancestor of most of the J-P poets.

Kh(w)āje made extensive use of Persian epic conventions to describe battlefields and wars between Iranian and Babylonian Kings. Here the influence of *Shāh-nāme* is clearly detectable. Horses gallop swiftly on the battlefield like *dud* 'smoke'. Some of these horses are even called *rakhsh* after Rostam's horse. Legendary Iranian heroes and kings who play no specific role in *Dāniyāl-nāme* are mentioned; they are there to embellish the poem and add an epic flavor to the work.

In the following passages, Belshazzar prepares for war against Darius and Cyrus. He needs heroic warriors to defeat the combined armies of the Persians. By giving gold and silver, Belshazzar successfully gathers the type of warriors he needs:

> In stature everyone was like a tall cypress,
> With a strong body like ivory or box-wood.
> In strength everyone was like Esfandiyar,
> On the day of battle and on battle-field, like a
> kingly horseman.
> With powerful arms, neck and shoulders,
> He was like young Sohrab or Rostam son of Zal.
> Everyone in hosemanship was like Bizhan
> Who was unique in ancient times.
> Each one brave on the day of battle,
> Like Bahman and Sam son of Nariman.

[48] MS ENA 188.
[49] MS ENA 52.
[50] MS ENA 434.

In manliness, each was greater than
Borzu, Faramarz and Fereydun.[51]

As in the *Shāh-nāme,* in the *Dāniyāl-nāme* are magnificent descriptions of sunrises and sunsets before and after battles:

When the peacock of the sky disappeared from sight,
The black crow suddenly ran out of its cage.
Light went and darkness came to the world
Which wore black in mourning.
One would say that, suddenly out of anguish, the
face of the sun was covered
With the tresses of night.
In short, light replaced darkness,
Thus Joseph of Canaan rose from the Nile.
The world was illuminated by the rising sun,
Like the furnace which became a garden of flowers
for Abraham.[52]

Not only does he borrow the poetic language, metaphors, and similes from *Shāh-nāme,* but he also finds it necessary to borrow from it the names of weapons and other instruments used on the battlefield. *Tigh* 'sword', *Khanjar* 'dagger', *shamshir* 'scimitar', *gorz* 'mace', *tabarzin* 'battle-axe' are some of the weapons used in *Dāniyāl-nāme. Babr-e bayān* 'armor of Rostam made of tiger skin', *mehmiz* 'spur', *fetrāk* 'saddle-strap', and a group of wind and string musical instruments employed to announce the commencement of war are also found in the text. The following is a description of the preparation for war which was to take place between Belshazzar and the combined armies of Darius and Cyrus:

In revenge against each other, the two armies
Continued to wear coats of mail.
All sat in the saddle
And took their horses beneath their thighs.
Those young men arrayed themselves
Opposite each other to wage war.
In that crowd, from every place
Darafsh-e jāvdāni 'eternal banners' were set up.

[51] MS f.30a 6-9.
[52] MS ff.30b26-31b33.

The sound of drums, harps, horns and trumpets
Rose from everywhere in that commotion.[53]

The combined armies of Darius and Cyrus are now victoriously approaching the gate of Baghdad where Belshazzar has fortified himself. The celestial planets joyously come to the aid of Darius and Cyrus. Here, though the images are the conventional ones of Persian poetry, Kh(w)āje displays his powerful imagination and skill in composing the following lines:

The stars of their fortune (Darius' and Cyrus')
were shining;
The sky wore armor to aid them.
Saturn went to adorn herself,
Jupiter[54] became the customer of those two kings.
Mars, with the intention of shedding the enemy's blood,
Girded on his sharp dagger in that moment.
From the east, Sun, like a passionate peacock,
Rose with lances in her hands.
Because of her destiny, Moon perforce
Became their shield-holder.
Venus stood shoulder to shoulder with them,
And came to wage war against the enemy.
Thus she approached him (Belshazzar) with a psaltery
To bring him into the war with tricks.
Mercury also joined them,
In the form of a lucky star, he took up his position[55]

Nevertheless, Belshazzar defeated the combined armies of Darius and Cyrus. As is common in *Shāh-nāme* were after *razm* 'war' there is *bazm* 'feast', Belshazzar after this victory arranges a royal banquet:

In that moment, the cup-bearers of the Prince
Carried wine to every gathering.
When several cups had gone the rounds,
There rose the voices of musicians from every direction.
The King had continuously before him
A thousand alluring and beautiful girls.
Each was the fame of the firmament;

[53] MS f.31a 4-7.
[54] *Moshtari* which also means customer.
[55] MS f.38a 4-11.

In beauty unique in the two worlds.
In a sense, their ruby (wine) was the food of their souls:
Sometimes it was life-giving and sometimes life-taking.
If one drank a swallow of it,
He would not think of Khezr and the water of life.[56]

There are also elegies in the *Dāniyāl-nāme* which pretend to complete the circle in the poet's work, which was meant to resemble the great Persian epics. Like Ferdausi, Kh(w)āje laments the death of kings and eulogizes them. He blames Fate and the treacherous world for these calamities. Also like Ferdausi, the author draws his morals from these events and preaches *neku nāmi* '(having) a good name' since, "a man with a good name shall never die." The following are a few lines from the elegy on the death of Belshazzar, executed by order of Darius:

Then with one blow the fearless executioner
Cast the prince's head to the earth.
His rosy face became purple,
His white body became saffron-colored.
He set forth into the desert of annihilation,
One would say he never existed.
Heaven gave his dust to the wind in such a manner,
As if he has never been born of his mother.
The eyes of the people were full of tears,
Which streamed like seas from their (eyes') corners.
Heaven in mourning for that handsome one
Donned cerulean dress.
The Dawn is red because of his blood,
Auroras are rosy from the blood of martyres.
The clouds weep a rain of tears lamenting him:
They mourn him with many moans.
Even if one rules for a hundred years,
It is worth nothing at the moment in which he perishes.[57]

There is a short elegy on the death of Darius (f.50a), and some excellent verses of lamentation (f.39a) where Belshazzar's mother perceives the forthcoming death of her son. The combined armies of Darius and Cyrus are heading toward the palace. Recognizing the catastrophe, Belshazzar's mother runs to her son:

[56] MS ff.32a5-32b10.
[57] MS f.40b 17-30.

She hurried several times around her son,
And embraced his sapling-like body.
Tears flowed from her eyes,
She kissed his head and face in anguish.
She said to him, O soul of my world!
May there be no life for me without you:
Life does not befit me without you.
You are the soul of my tired body.
In the garden, You are my flower,
You are my new-grown bloom.
You are my enchanted mirror
In which your picture gives me light and serenity.
You are like a cypress in the garden,
May your shade stay on my head.
O my son! You are the light of my eyes
Measured in the scale of wisdom.
You have no likeness in beauty;
You are like a *Ṭubā* tree[58] in the garden.
Since I have no offspring
Nor a beloved except you,
May I be sacrificed to your bow-like eyebrows,
And take on myself the affliction of your magic eyes.[59]

Words, expressions, and epithets, which in most cases describe the author's inner feelings or the inner qualities of the characters in *Dāniyāl-nāme,* are borrowed from Persian mystic writings and, in a few cases, from Islamic theology. Most of the lines composed in this style have a lyrical inclination. This may greatly affect the flow and the continuity of the movement in the narrative, but, on the other hand, it facilitates our understanding of the author and his Weltanschauung. The following words and expressions are gleaned from all sections of the work:

a. God is referred to as *lāmakān* 'Placeless', *vahāb* 'Bestower', *dust* 'Friend', *sobḥān* 'The Praised', *parde-dān* 'The Knower (of what is behind) the curtain', *Kebriyā* 'The Great (God)', Allah, *dāvar* 'The Judge', and *Yazdān.* God is never referred to as *Elohim* or *Adonai.*

b. Connected with the above, are religio-mystic epithets which are

[58] According to Islamic tradition a tree in paradise whose branches and fruits reach every house.

[59] MS ff.29a18-39b28.

given to the Biblical characters and very rarely to the Irano-Babylonian kings and heros. Thus Moses is 'conversant with God', the leader of the human race, the proof of the people of Yeshurun, the messenger of His indescribable Essence, the depository of His secrets, the placeless falcon, co-dweller with *Simorgh,* the pearl of the ocean of truth, the jewel of the dark night, and the light of revelation. After Moses, Daniel receives the longest list of epithets: the exalted old man, confident of God, the anguished one, the righteous, dervish and traveler of the Path. Abraham is God's friend; Jacob is the high point of the horizons; Joshua is the chief of the heroes; Solomon is King of Kings, the world-conqueror and the subduer of demons and fairies. So are Uriah the lion, Azariah the man of God's Path, Jeremiah the sad old man, and David the man with a pleasant voice.

c. The following words and expressions used throughout *Dāniyāl-nāme* bring this work closer to the Sufi poetry of Classical Persian: *dhekr* 'recollecting (the name of God)', *Khānqāh* 'Sufi monastery', *tavakkol* 'trust in God', *vaṣl-e yār* 'union with the Friend', *ᶜEshq-e u* 'His love', *dalq-e dervish* 'dervish's garment', *nokte-dāni* 'knowing subtleties', *rāz-e eshārat* 'the secret of hints', *pirān-e rāh-e deyr* 'the old men of the Path of monastery', *ostāde-e ṭariqat* 'master of the Path', *morshed* 'the Sufi guide', *tashhid kardan* 'to be slain for God's sake', *ruz-e qiyāmat* 'the day of resurrection', *aḥkām-e shariᶜat* 'the religious laws (of the Muslims)', *nur-e Islām* 'the light of Islam,' *dār-e ṭubā* 'the tree of Tuba', *Ṣobḥ-e Ṣādeq* 'the true morning', *Sālek-e rāh* 'the traveler of the Path'.

Speaking of the characters in *Dāniyāl-nāme* it must be emphasized that though *Dāniyāl-nāme* is in general a fictitious creation it is carried out in the frame of the Biblical narrative of the Book of Daniel. As such all the characters are those mentioned in the Book of Daniel but they are portrayed freely by the author.

The characters in *Dāniyāl-nāme,* excluding those in the prologue and epilogue, and those who take no part in the action of the stories, e.g., Rostam, Zal, Nariman, etc., are of two types. First, the characters who play a secondary role and whose appearance on the scene is temporary. Such characters are Hananiah, Mishael, and Azariah, the three friends of Daniel; *vakil-e khādem* 'the chief of the servants' who takes care of Daniel and his friends; the angel Gabriel who descends from heaven to accompany Daniel's friends into the fiery furnace, or to converse with Daniel; and the Messiah with whom Daniel conducts a dialogue. These secondary characters, whose actions in the narrative are important, are not given detailed descriptions. The author neglects to portray their physical appearance, and gives short epithets to describe their inner qualities.

Daniel's friends are extremely loyal to their faith, for which they preferred to be cast into the fiery furnace. *Vakil-e Khādem* who was helpful to Daniel and his friends, when they refused to eat the King's food, is referred to as *pākize-bonyād* 'good natured'.

Gabriel is given no description except that he is called *mallākh-e khodāyi* 'Divine angel', flying "like the bird of the sky." The Messiah descends from the clouds of the heaven. He is like a human being, shining like a candle and as beautiful as a flower.

Secondly, there are the chief characters of *Dāniyāl-nāme,* the hero and protagonist of which remains Daniel. Others are Nebuchadnezzar, Belshazzar, Cyrus and Darius. The relationship between Daniel and the Babylonian Kings, Nebuchadnessar and Belshazzar, is one of conflict. Of the Iranian Kings, Darius is the less favored; he is an expedient and harsh king who is cruel to his enemies. Cyrus is a good-hearted king who is willing to spare his enemies' lives. Finally it is Cyrus who establishes his reign over Persia, Media and Babylon and enjoys a long reign. Most of the significant action evolves around these five characters. The only character with whom the author has a complete feeling of empathy is Daniel.

In general, there is in *Dāniyāl-nāme* very little extended description of characters. There are some details of physical appearance, particularly of stature. In one place Daniel described as *nāzok-chashm* 'narrow-eyed' kind of beauty admired in author's area — Central Asia. The details given are for the most part general, regularly conveyed by similes.

To evaluate the style and the language of *Dāniyāl-nāme,* in addition to what has been said above, one must distinguish between those sections which are directly paraphrased from the Hebrew-Aramaic text, and those sections which are the author's own creation. There are stylistic, lexicographic and syntactic differences between these two sections.

The explanation for this difference is that the author tries very hard to translate those passages of the Book of Daniel as literally as he can. In this way he limits himself in his choice of words and figures of speech to embellish his poetry. Obviously, this restriction does not exist when the poet takes liberty in introducing fictional episodes, irrelevant to the Book of Daniel, such as the description of the battles between Iranian and Babylonian kings or his feeling toward his own poetry.[60]

There are many examples of these two sections throughout the work. Sometimes the two are interwoven. The poetry of the second section, based on Kh(w)āje's imagination, is rich in figurative speech and firm in its structure. The language is highly expressive and imaginative. Indeed, it is this part of the work which increases the effect and value of *Dāniyāl-nāme* as a literary creation.

As a creative artist, the poet does more than report a Biblical event or teach a fact. He reacts to life both intellectually and emotionally. Kh(w)āje's understanding of love, truth, justice, friendship, life and death and other fundamental virtues is expressive of his philosophy, or of his intellectual attitude toward life — more specifically, his interpretation of that aspect of experience which is the subject of a particular theme.

It is highly desirable that J-P poetry be "studied," analyzed and evaluated for the fullest understanding of subject matter, techniques, or even artistic refinements of diction, imagery, symbols and the like. Persian Jews have had a different cultural background compared to their Persian compatriots. It has to be admitted that J-P poetry in its artistic texture of diction is, compared to much classical Persian poetry, a poetry which reads with flow and ease. The difficulty of J-P poetry lies in its "obscurity" when it contains Biblical, Talmudic, and theological allusions and implications. Here, these allusions and implications together with the usage of Hebrew and Aramaic words may appear both obscure and cacophonic to an unfamiliar reader. Even though the language and literary conventions in *Dāniyāl-nāme* as well as in other J-P poetry are those of classical Persian poetry, their communicability is enhanced when they are read against the background of the Jewish heritage.

[60] E.g., ff.64a1-65a45 in the MS.

Some Socio-Religious Themes in Modern Persian Fiction

GIRDHARI L. TIKKU

TWENTIETH-CENTURY PERSIA experienced great political and social change. Politically the efforts for a democratic system culminated in the establishment of a Constitutional Monarchy (1906), dethronement of the Qajars (1921) and the inauguration of a new dynasty (Pahlavi in 1925), the abdication of the Pahlavi King Reza Shah and his exile (1941), and the near loss of political identity during the two World Wars. The counterpart in the literary effort, which started in the nineteenth century, has its landmarks in the introduction of the Litho Press (1812), the telegraph line connecting Iran with Europe and India (1864), and the establishment of the *Dār al-Funūn* ("House of Knowledge") in 1851 for the introduction of modern military sciences and Western languages. These developments in politics and literature were connected with the social system in Iran and with the introduction of technology and economic colonization by the West. These conditions in Iran were in some degree similar to those in the surrounding countries.

Neighboring Turkey had its political and social problems: a choice between offering a home for all Muslims, a position which cut across the boundaries of nationhood and thus weakened geographically oriented political identity, or the acceptance of the notion of a political sovereignty; the social problem was an adjustment to political change, reality and technology. This confrontation saw the emergence of Turkey as a democratic state with a goal of modernization, with general acceptance of the European notion of nationalism. This new phenomenon also created a desire to search into the past for a new identity.

In India a struggle was going on for the acquisition of a new identity, and religious institutions as well as religious dogmas were being screened in the light of Western ideas and the impact of Western dominance. This effort was carried on in political and literary spheres. In short, the effort was, in the social sense, aimed at purging the religious dogma of its superstition and mal-practice, which necessarily meant a search into the past. A similar reform was attempted by Amanullah in Afghanistan.

Within this general framework of political reality in and around Iran, we shall try to see the development of Persian prose and its role in the criticism of the Persian social system. But before doing so it may be stated that criticism of social evils both in a serious sense and in a sarcastic fashion has been given attention throughout Persian literature. Whether it be in the realm of mysticism, treatises, or poetry; whether in the realm of Machiavellian treatises or the miraculous anecdotes of the Sufi masters; whether in the realm of social codebooks or in satirical anecdotes, Persian literature abounds in criticism of the social structure, if not from a dogmatic point of view, then from the point of view of actual practice. Job descriptions and behavioral codes for kings, prime ministers, religious leaders, courtesans, are found in the most popular books. The treatment given these subjects has generally been subtle to protect the author and only sometimes ruthlessly blunt. The nuance of pun and acceptance of the symbolic use of imagery made possible, even under the severest of political controls, the expression of these criticisms.

After the introduction of the printing press, the newspapers whether published in the country (first in Tehran during the reign of Fath-Ali Shah [1797-1835]), or outside of Iran by exiles or expatriates in Istanbul, Calcutta, Cairo, Paris, London, and Berlin, opened a new forum for political and sociological discussion. During the 1905-1908 period the number of newspapers in Tehran alone counted more than one hundred. One of the results of journalism was the introduction of simple and popular language. In addition to these newspapers, a large number of literary and social magazines were started and these served as a medium for the publication of essays and short stories by Persian writers which dealt with a broad spectrum of social and religious issues.

The discussions in social, political, and literary fields contained many opinions, ranging from the total severance of identity with the Islamic heritage and the rooting of all evils in Islam, to the other extreme of blaming all evils on the political disintegration of an Islamic State and the abrogation af all non-Islamic elements.

Within this background this paper shall concern itself only with some religio-social themes in contemporary Persian fiction in general, and specifically, with a given period of 1921 to 1960, and then again limiting itself to three topics: the character of the *Ḥājjī* in Persian fiction; the character of *Ākhund, Mullā, Shaykh* or *Mudīr*; and the treatment of the institution of *Zakāt*. This paper shall further restrict itself to four writers: M. A. Jamalzada, Sadiq Hidayat, Jalal Al-i Ahmad and F. M. Esfandiary. The year 1921 has purposely been chosen to coincide with the date of publication of Jamalzada's book *Yakī Būd Yakī Nabūd* ("Once Upon a Time" . . .), which is a landmark in the history of the short story in Persian.

However, regarding the use of themes dealt with in this article it must be stated that two important books dealing with the character *of Ḥājjī* were published, *Adventures of Hajji Baba of Isfahan* by Morrier in 1824 (probably translated in 1905), and the *Siyāhatnāma-i Ibrāhīm Bīg* by Zayn al-Abidin (d.1910) in three volumes (1903, 1907 and 1909). Both of these dealt with the hypocrisy and dissimulation of the *Mullā* and other religious leaders in very bitter terms. The whole emphasis from a social point of view was the exposure of the corrupt practices of the *Mullā* and the Dervish — whose action seemed far from the idealistic picture of them in Iranian heritage. Another important step in this direction was the writings of Taliboff which dealt mainly with the introduction of scientific things, which "smacked of atheism and were prohibited by the religious leaders." To this should be added another important journal published from Baku under the title of *Mullā Naṣr ud-Dīn,* the famous character dealing with the situations of life with the gift of prudence and wit rather than with the knowledge of theology. The main theme of the articles in this journal was to ridicule the reactionary character of the Islamic society. It should nevertheless be mentioned that the role played by the Ulema in the revolutionary movement of Iran was great, and prior to actual assumption of power, the religious leaders "went out of their way to promote education and the enlightenment of the people."

The reason for selecting these four authors is to present four different points of view. Jamalzada, born in an orthodox family and educated outside of Iran in Western schools, approaches the problem from a sympathetic yet satirical point of view, and though living most of his life in Europe (Switzerland), commands a vision of the inner life of the religious system. Sadiq Hidayat (d.1951), a patriotic Iranian, is a great agnostic and has little sympathy for Islam or its institutions. Jalal Al-i Ahmad (d.1969), like Jamalzada, brought up in an orthodox environment, is a great critic of the mal-practices of the religious institution and at the same time a supporter of maintaining identity with Islam and its institutions, which he considers to be the best safeguard against westernization or west-toxication. He is, therefore, for reform of Islamic institutions. The last author, Esfandiary (b.1930) brought up in a well-to-do family of Iran and educated and trained in Western tradition is a believer in the ultimate triumph over all social problems through the control of technology. He is living in the United States as an expatriate writer from Iran.

Jamalzada, in his book *Yakī Būd Yakī Nabūd* (Tehran, 1339/1960) has six short stories "Fārsī Shakarast" ("Persian Is Sweet"), "Rajal-i Siyāsī" ("Political Elite"), "Dustī-yi Khāla Khirsä" ("Friendship of Aunt Bear"), "Dard-i Dil-i Mullā Qurbān ᶜAlī" ("Grievances of Mulla Qurban Ali"), "Bila Dīg Bila Chughandar" ("Everyone to His Deserts"), and "Vīlān ud-Daula" ("The Vagrant of the State"). In his first story located in an Iranian prison, we are exposed to the plight of a simple Iranian in the company of a pompous *Shaykh* and a Frenchified young man, both of whom are out of touch with the language of the Iranian commoner and the level of his understanding. The second story deals with the abuse of the public support for political office by the brash and the ignorant, one of them Haj(ji) Ali and the other *Shaykh* Jaffar. The story begins thus:

> You ask me how I became a politician and rose my head taller than others. You should know that . . . four years ago I was a carder, and my work entailed carding. In a day I would earn 2 *rials* or 10 *rials* and in the evening I would somehow bring home one *man-sangak* bread, five *seer* meat. But my defective minded wife would every night reprimand me and say: "Hey, go and squat on your feet and shake your balls; card the cotton and return home in the evening with the spider-knit beard and hair. While our neighbor Haj Ali, who a

> year ago did not have as much as a sigh to trade with a wail, has gradually become some man and found a place in social intercourse; and says his wife that one of these days he shall become a representative of the parliament with a monthly salary of 100 *tomans,* two *rials* for transportation (*charkhī*) and a thousand salutations. But you should till your grave card the cotton! Ah! I wish your hat had some feathers as well." ("Rajal-i Siyāsī," p. 38)

It then moves through the miraculous success of *Shaykh* Jaffar and the offering of bribes by the senior politicians who want to buy him and the final exit of Jaffar from politics and a life of peace away from public attention.

In the story "Bila Dīg Bila Chughandar" ("Everyone to His Deserts"), the author satirically deals with the class structure in Iran — narrated through the mouth of a European bath attendant, whom fortune had made for a short while a foreign adviser to the Ministry of Posts in Iran and who wondered why he became so despite all his ignorance. He divides the classes into three: the Yellow-Capped, the White-Capped and the Black-Capped, representing respectively the common simple believers, who labored for the maintenance of the other classes, the clergy (White-Capped ones) and the nobility (Black-Capped ones) who ruled the country. The description of the White-Capped ones is given in the words:

> These White-Capped are known as *Shaykhs* or *Ākhunds*; and they command great reverence from the people. Since their mark of identification is the headgear, they tie round their head as much of white cloth as they can procure; (their head) resembles a minaret on whose top is the nest of the stork. One day when I secretly inquired from one Iranian the reason for their covering their head in this fashion, I was told that just as you tie a bandage round a finger once it gets deformed, these people also, most probably, because of the damage to their brain, want to prevent any free air from reaching their brain. . . .
>
> During my entire stay in Iran I wanted to know the nature of their work and the occupation of these White-Capped ones, but never succeeded. No matter what, their occupation must be private which they perform away from the sight of the people; I think it a handicraft, for people generally kiss their hands. One day when I told an Iranian acquaintance that their profession, which I do not know, must be artistic, he agreed with me and added: "Yes, it is a great art

under whose shadow the country of Iran lives and survives, and but for this art the wheels of affairs would stop and the chain of affairs would break. And this art is corruption."

("Bila Dīg Bila Chughandar," pp. 108-109)

It was these and other remarks about the clergy that caused strong opposition.

The last story in this book is ironically entitled *"Vīlān ud-Daula"* ("The Vagrant of the State"), which deals with the life of a special class of people, whom the author describes in these words: *"Vīlān ud-Daula"* is one of those herbs which sprouts only in Iran, and bears a fruit named "A Pea for every Pottage." Then in a brief four-page story he relates the problems of this vagrant who is a busy-body, a Mr. Everywhere and Everything, moving from one house to another, sleeping wherever he reaches at dusk, wearing whatever is given him by the people, and eating whenever he is offered a thing. The hero, finally unable to live with this sort of life, buys on loan a few grams of opium, eats them before staying the night in a mosque, and writes a will with pen and ink borrowed from a mosque-scribe. The will reads:

After fifty years of wandering (loafing) and homelessness I go from this transient world, even though I know not if anyone will recognize my corpse. All through I gave nothing but headache and trouble to my acquaintances. Were I not sure that the sympathy generally showed by them towards me far exceeded and still exceeds my bashfulness and humble gratitude, I would spend this last breath of my life in penitence. But they have acted on the principles of humanitarianism and depend not on apologies of me and the likes. Even now I request them as they wished not during my life to see my head without a home, after my death to memorize my bitter, wandering and eternally vagabondic life in this world, by engraving the following verse of my teacher and guide, Baba Tahir Uryan, upon my tombstone, if any:

All the ants and the snakes have a nest
The helpless me does not even have a ruined abode!

("Vīlān ud-Daula," p. 119)

Jamalzada deals, in this short story, with a complex social problem. Within the concept of *Zakāt* such people as the "Vīlān ud-Daula" would be catered to by the society. Members of the Islamic society were supposed to give donations, up to a certain percentage of their income, for catering to the needs of the poor and the disabled members of society. This institution in its deteriorated form created a class of social parasites of which "Vīlān ud-Daula" would be one. Thematically, Jamalzada deals with this important religio-social issue more by inference than by direct reference.

Because of the commotion caused in Iran when the book first appeared in print and perhaps because of misunderstanding, the religious people took the criticisms as personal assault rather than as a dramatization of the need for reform in the political, religious, and social institutions in the country. The commotion caused Jamalzada to quit writing for more than twenty years.

But in 1945, immediately after the end of World War II, came an era of freedom of the press and the publication of two important books from the standpoint of this discussion: *Dīd u Bāzdīd* by Jalal Al-i Ahmad and *Ḥājjī Āghā* by Sadiq Hidayat.

The first book is a collection of short-stories dealing with the criticism of the religious institutions, the great hypocrisy of the religious leaders, and the problem of a superstitious society. It contains twelve short stories (one of which is already translated into English) and in most of them there is reference to an *Ākhund,* a *Mullā,* or a *Shaykh,* and the treatment given these characters is not flattering at all. Perhaps to clarify the intention of such caricaturization of these characters, Al-i Ahmad at one place introduces dialogue between a father and a son who are witnessing a conjurer's tricks (*Ma^{c}rika,* literally "a place where a trickster gathers people to perform"), in this case a *Shaykh* selling printed prayers to people, threatening or imploring the spectators to buy his prayers for self-preservation and success. The inquisitive son asks his father if he (the *Shaykh*) wrote these prayers himself:

> The father replied: "No dear. He gets these printed at the press. A...[gha] *Shaykh* Muhammad, is not a *Shaykh.* But there are many people in this town who call themselves *Shaykhs.* If we discount the turban-wearers, the young bazaar dealers, who during their business dealings with chic and well-dressed women never lift their eyes from the merchandise spread on their counters; the crafty ostensive brokers, who before and after every prayer, crunchingly brush their cavitied

teeth with wooden brushes, gifts from the desert of Hejaz, and believe that this act, in addition to the abidance of the religious precepts, wards off their bodies from seventy diseases, the simplest of whom is leprosy; or the bearded government employees, who in the sacred months (Muharram) sprout from everywhere, wearing nothing but a robe and almost naked, mourn in gatherings, and offer additional supplications after the mandated prayers in the mosque; or in a mourning assembly read the whole of the Koran . . . (a practice in Islam to commemorate the dead) . . . and many others are called *Shaykh. A. . . Shaykh* Muhammad is also one of such persons."

The picture of a *Shaykh* is given in the story "Lamassaba" ("The Heretics") and more by implication, than directly, their behavior criticized. This criticism of the rank and file of the religious leaders is very much in line with the treatment given by Jamalzada. The last of the stories in this collection is entitled "Dū Murda" ("Two Dead Men"); it is brief and brought as a contrast to show the class discrimination between people even after they are dead. One of them was a great social figure, whose funeral is well attended and which causes the stoppage of traffic; and the other a poor man, who dies with one hand and one leg in the stream. The interesting thing about the death of the second person is the report made of his death by two police officers, which reminds one of the will of "Vīlān ud-Daula" and also of the police report of the death of Daryoush in Esfandiary's *The Identity Card.* The description reads:

Two policemen, with two large sheets of paper, arrived, and pushed the crowd aside. First they removed the torn gunny cloth, the only other dress other than his trousers, from his shoulders; they shook it and since nothing fell from it, put it aside; and the policeman who held the paper and pen in hand, after writing the routine type formula of report, added: one torn gunny cloth.

The other policeman had started searching, and the first policeman wrote under the columns one after the other:

· One half-used American match.
· five crushed cigarettes; folded in a newspaper.
· money — two and a half Rials.
· a bound-type identity card, without a picture.
· a rusted pencil-sharpening blade.
No more.

The policeman wanted to sign the report, but the other policeman whose head was still hanging low and who still searched the pockets of the trousers, said:

· and one trouser.

They added one trouser to the list, and thereafter both of them signed the report. And . . . in this fashion closed the file of the life of one human being.

Sadiq Hidayat's *Ḥājjī Āghā* (1945) is a novelette, perhaps not a very well knit story, but a fascinating treatment of the character of a *Ḥājjī,* "whose prototype might be found nowhere except in the Persian society of the time." This novelette comes in line with the earlier characterization of the *Ḥājjī,* dating back to the nineteenth and early twentieth centuries, and more vividly in the caricature drawings of Jamalzada. Similar portrayals exist of *Shaykh* Hasan in the two novels of Hijazi, *Humā* (1927) and *Zībā* (1931), which made these two novels very popular.

Perhaps because of the more relaxed press after the occupation of the country by the Allies, and the promises of freedom after the War, the intelligentsia had become more optimistic. Sadiq's treatment of such a theme in such humorous manner and his interest in social change evidence a sense of hope in him and in others. Sadiq portrays the *Ḥājjī* as the cleverest of the rogues who is able to play ball with all sorts of people and all changed circumstances. The only real failure in *Ḥājjī*'s life is the rebuke given him by the poet and the severance of his son from the heritage. Through these two disappointments the author indicates that in the very difficult task of reforming a society, whose institutions are preserved because everyone is greedy and because civic or moral values have not evolved, the artist (who has a larger vision of life) and perhaps the foreign-trained students (son of the *Ḥājjī* and his group) alone can make a dent. What is really interesting in *Ḥājjī Āghā* is that when *Ḥājjī* is caught by situations where his formula does not work, his weak character is exposed. Two classical examples, except that of the confrontation with the poet, are the admissions he makes before going to the hospital for an operation: (The first is from the Persian text of *Ḥājjī Āghā* and the other from Hasan Kamshad's *Modern Persian Prose Literature,* Cambridge, 1966.)

No it is no longer funny; knife and flesh are no friends. . . . There they shall prick me with a needle. I shall be unconscious, they shall well use the knife . . . Akh, Akh, Akh. . . . I do not know if I shall have the time to utter a sigh or not. . . . What shall suddenly happen to me? I shall have no link with my body . . . a frame shall be lying there without any feeling or movement; I shall not recognize it; but my soul shall see everything and know everything! . . . Ah, Ah. But all my recollections, all my life rests with this body. When I recognize not my body, ha! What shall remain for me? What thing can have a meaning for me? Only regret! God forbid! No, I do not want that after me I see all these beautiful women, these sumptuous meals in this world, with an avaricious eye. So, what was the good of all this toil? Do you understand Murad? No, No . . . I do not want to die. (*Ḥājjī Āghā,* pp. 113-114)

There are two classes of people in the world: the exploiters and the exploited. If you don't want to be exploited try to exploit others. You do not need much education, it is a handicap in life, makes you soft in the head. . . . Be impudent, don't let yourself be forgotten. Boast and show off as much as you can. . . . Do not be afraid of abuse, humiliation or slander. . . . When kicked out from one door enter with a smile from another. . . . Be impudent, insolent and stupid, for it is sometimes necessary to pretend stupidity — it helps. This is the type of man our country requires today. . . . Faith, morals, religion and the rest are mere hypocrisy, though faith is essential for the common man: it serves as a muzzle, and without it society turns into a nest of vipers; everywhere you put your hand it stings. . . . Be an opportunist. Try to establish connections with the holders of high offices. Agree with everybody, no matter what his opinion is, so that you may attract his utmost favour. I want you to grow up as a man of the world independent of people. Books, lectures, and things of this sort are not worth a penny. Imagine you are living in a den of thieves, turn your eyes away and you are robbed. All you need to learn are a few foreign words, a few pompous expressions and you can sit back and take it easy! I give lessons to all these ministers and deputies. What is important is to show them that you are a smart crook, that you can't be caught easily and that you are one of them, willing to negotiate. . . . But most important of all is money. If you happen to have money in this world then you will also have pride, credit, honesty, virtue, and everything else. People adore you, you will be considered intelligent and patriotic, they will flatter you, they

> will do everything for you. . . . The educated engineer takes pride in operating your machine, the architect truckles to you to build your house, the poet licks the dust and writes your eulogy, the painter who has starved all his life paints your portrait, the journalists, deputies, ministers will all stand ready to do your bidding. . . . These scoundrels are all slaves to money. Do you know why knowledge and education are of no use in life? Because when you have got them you still have to serve the rich people. . . . (Kamshad, pp. 193-194)

Al-i Ahmad's *Mudīr-i Madrasa* ("The School Principal," 1958)[1] is in my opinion a continuation of the criticisms which the author started against the *Ākhunds* and the religious leaders as also against the religious institutions. Himself a teacher, the author gives a realistic portrayal of not only the difficulties and preoccupations of a school principal in the set-up of the country, but also of the underlying social malaise of the country, the hypocrisy, and the power lust of various classes of people.

Al-i Ahmad takes us through the experiences of a schoolteacher, who in order to escape the drudgery of teaching wants to become a principal. The principal's difficulties include the charlatanism of the school caretaker, problems of shoes and lavatory for the pupils, lack of gravel for the sidewalks, difficulties with the local community association, the political involvement of his teachers and their financial problems, the sickness of his colleague's mother, the involvement of the teachers with the Justice Department, in addition to bureaucratic bot-

[1] Al-i Ahmad was brought up in a religious environment, cut off from his family, and after attending the *Dār al-Funūn* became a teacher in 1947. He joined the Tudeh Party and became its active member. In 1943 he started actively working for religious reform and one of his works regarding the reform of religion was burnt by the religious zealots. In 1947 he parted company with the Tudeh Party and joined a Socialist group for the reason that the Tudeh wanted to reform itself on Stalinist ideology. Thereafter he withdrew from political activities and devoted himself to the translation of the works of Camus, Gide, and Dostoevsky; and in 1950 he got married. With the coming of Mussadiq he joined the Third Front but withdrew from the Front after the fall of Mussadiq in 1953. After 1953 Al-i Ahmad, having been cut off from his family, the Communists after the War, and the political manipulations in his country, started working on the contradictions that existed in the social traditions of Iran, and on the influences of Western thought, which in his opinion was turning Iran into a colony of the West. This resulted in the publication of *Garb Zadagī* ("West-toxication," 1962). His *Mudīr-i Madrasa* is scheduled to appear in English translation (by the author) in *Select Modern Persian Fiction* (Columbia University Press, forthcoming).

tlenecks in the education department. Finally, he resigns from the principalship.

This work, as he told me last year (February, 1969), was published from the notes he had taken during one of his teaching assignments and reflects, though in a microscopic fashion, the situation in the Iranian educational system and the overall social condition of that period in his country.

I have so far recounted the themes dealing with the *Mullā, Ḥājjī, Ākhund, Mudīr* and *Zakāt*. These themes have been dealt with by Jamalzada in his *Yakī Būd Yakī Nabūd,* and subsequently by Sadiq Hidayat and Al-i Ahmad. The character of *Ḥājjī,* touched upon by Jamalzada, was first dealt with at great length by Hidayat in his novel *Ḥājjī Āghā.* The purpose seems to have been to show the great discrepancy between the public and the private image of the *Ḥājjī,* and to bring out the irrelevance of the institution itself. Hidayat, unlike Jamalzada, who was harsh on the Islamic institutions per se, was generally skeptical of religion itself. Thus while depicting the *Ḥājjī*'s character he denies the possibility of the *Ḥājjī* being a humanitarian and so dramatizes the social damage done by him. Buried in the thought of self-aggrandizement and concept of leadership, the *Ḥājjī* lives a life of comfortable seclusion and delusion, not necessarily ignorance. In spite of being made aware of his puniness and pettiness, those surrounding him are numbed by their economic dependence on him. The ignorant *Ḥājjī* is also portrayed in the role of the maker of economic and political policies of the country. In this role he more or less is portrayed in the garb of the *Ḥājjī* or *Shaykh* Jaffar in Jamalzada's "Rajal-i Siyāsī." The same treatment is given him and the *Ākhund* and the *Mullā* by Al-i Ahmad, in the stories we have quoted. Although of much later date, *Mudīr-i Madrasa* contains an almost caricatural description of the *Ḥājjī,* who is shown to influence the educational and social life of the country for his personal gain.

Institutionally *Ākhund* and *Mullā* were used in the Islamic sense, among other things, for teachers in religious schools who were assumed to have had some training in a *madrasa* or religious school. Jamalzada severely criticizes them, because in a sense they, as symbols of an institution, have failed to live up to the definition given them in Islam. With him the problem is that given proper reform the institution should be able to revitalize itself. Jamalzada sees a hope for the redemption of the institution. In my opinion, even Al-i Ahmad, early in his career, tried to publicize the need for reform.

Perhaps like Jamalzada, having progressed from the concept of bringing a coherence between the symbol and the idealistic function of the institution, and after trying to get rid of the symbol and to revitalize the institution, he moved to the exposure of the illiterate ignorant scribe, the teacher, the judge, the lawyer and the government prosecutor. Then, it would seem, he concentrated on the role of a schoolteacher within the changed society, and presented the difficulties inherent in the assimilation of new concepts. The good intentions and the great endurance of the school principal was not enough to make him carve out a healthy institution — valuable in the social sense — from the all-oppressive, chaotic surroundings, whether of civic citizens or of the governmental bureaucracy. The school principal's attempt ends in failure, in giving up and giving in to the environment. As we know from the subsequent writings of Al-i Ahmad, the drive in him thereafter moved to preserving the old national tradition and to voicing opposition to hasty Westernization, which would lead to the death of what was the best Iranian without assuring the acquisition of the best Western elements. Al-i Ahmad spent the rest of his life as a spokesman for what would superficially appear to be a conservative outlook.

When Jamalzada started writing after the war and produced, in two years, two books, *Qutlashan-Dīvān* (1946) and *Ṣaḥrā-yi Maḥshar* ("Plains of Resurrection," 1947), he took again to social criticism. In the first work, the story of a struggle between a *Hajj Shaykh,* a wholesale dealer, and a cunning opportunist, the author tries to empathize with the *Hajj Shaykh* and then with the cunning and greedy person. Perhaps this was a retreat from the earlier criticisms of religious leaders. But in the second work, written as a fantasy or a view of the day of resurrection, the religious leaders are treated with no mercy, for the sins they committed are heavier than their good. The interesting thing is that the poets and artists are allowed to go free, for their sins are the result of their honest ignorance. It is primarily the actions of people that are the criteria of justice. Omar Khayyam's verse on the *Shaykh* and the harlot is quoted and Paradise is given the poet and the harlot, not the *Shaykh.* Jamalzada's other works which appeared after World War II, particularly *Sar u Tah-i Yak Karbās* ("All of a Pattern," 1956) and the section under *"Jahanum-i Taᶜṣṣub"* ("The Hell of Fanaticism"), deal with the hypocrisy of the *Ākhunds.* Jamalzada has gradually moved out of the controversy of religious characters and institutions.

F. M. Esfandiary's[2] two novels, *The Beggar* (1965) and *The Identity Card* (1966) reveal two aspects of the problem of social and religious themes, touched upon in this article. The first novel, properly called "a parable of justice," applicable universally, is important for the insight it lends to a rather parochial problem of what happens to a society in the Middle Eastern setting, which having retained only the symbol, loses the concept which necessitated the symbol. I am tempted to see the concept of justice meted to Ali as a deterioration of the institution of *Zakāt,* which in the modern sense is a sort of social insurance. Esfandiary exhibits artistic skill in portraying in extremely human terms the desire of Ali to achieve his manhood and belonging. Ali's helplessness and fraility, which should have been a cause of his being helped under the institution of *Zakāt,* prove to be the very reason for his maltreatment. Ali's character resembles that of Sadeq Hedayat's ("David, the Hunchback") who as a helpless creature is tortured by society and humiliated by women to whom he makes offers of marriage.

On the surface, *The Identity Card* is a running commentary on Iran, particularly of Tehran, showing the innumerable twists and turns of bureaucracy, the facade of outer polish, the lack of a system to allocate responsibility to those chosen or commanded to be the leaders in various spheres of life, and the resultant penalty this system imposes on the hero.

The Identity Card also deals with the dilemma of a modern man in society which has a great gap between its professed beliefs and its actual practices, a society which pushes the burden of responsibility from the lower level to the highest, to the Almighty God in the final

[2] F. M. Esfandiary is an Iranian, born in 1930. He attended Iranian, Arab, English, and French schools. In 1948 he was a member of an Iranian team at the Olympic Games in London. He served on the United Nations Conciliation Commission for Palestine, and left the U.N. to devote full time to writing. He writes in both Iranian and English. His third book in English, other than the two mentioned above, is *The Day of Sacrifice.*

analysis. In a very tangential sense this echoes the ideas of a vagrant, a "Vīlān ud-Daula," who must, in the struggle to find a compromise between the tradition and the changed life, end his life voluntarily or accidentally to become an acceptable identity in his own country. The report of his death, given below, reminds us of Al-i Ahmad's death-report already quoted.

> The cause of this man's death is unknown. He looks Iranian and is circumcised. But the only document found in his pocket is foreign and has only numbers on it. Some notes written in a foreign language include a brief letter from abroad (without envelope) dated the year 1964. No identity papers were found on him, and his name and nationality are not known.
>
> This man's body was kept here three days. But no relative or friend or foreign embassy came to claim him.
>
> Teheran Police 9 Azar 1343
> (Esfandiary, p. 236)

In this interpretation of selected literary works, I have imposed an arbitrary pattern on the evolution of these themes in modern Persian fiction and on the approaches of the authors over a period of about forty years. I have attempted to show how these authors have moved from cursory exposure to mature reflection. If we believe that a given age has a number of creative possibilities and consider literature as the epitome of these possibilities, then this essay should be seen as an effort to trace a pattern of one fundamental expression of Iranian society.

On Land Disputes in Eastern Turkey

NUR YALMAN

Diyarbekir'in bir müddetdenberi iktisaden ilerlememesine, ahlakan geri gitmesine sebeb-i asli zira'atin bu halet-i maraziyyesidir. Vilayetimizde hakiki zira'at yok gibidir. Bu bed-baht memleketde fa'al ve devamlı yalnız bir meşgale vardır: Arazi münaza'aları.

(The principal reason for the lack of economic development and the moral regression in Diyarbakir for some time is this miserable state of agriculture. There is almost no real agriculture in our province. There is only one active and continuous concern in this unfortunate country: land disputes.) Ziya Gökalp, in Beysanoglu, 1956:125

INTRODUCTION

On 9 Aug. 1966 the major papers in Turkey reported with banner headlines that in yet another blood feud some more members of the Bucak family in Urfa had been killed. This brought the total dead to 17 for this family. The news was shocking, though not unusual, and there was little analysis of what was behind the incident. In fact, the case had a long history. On 30 Nov. 1965 *Cumhuriyet* had reported that three persons had been gunned down and killed by Sten-gun fire outside a mosque as they were returning from a circumcision festivity. Two of them were of the Bucak family.

Those interested in these matters could see that the case was no different from that reported in *Hürriyet* 18 Oct. 1964 concerning the Mayor of Viransehir, again in the Southeast, where it was stated that the Mayor had needed the protection of an entire gendarme unit in order to "plough" his "own" land. There were pictures of the "farm" of the Mayor with his tractors and other machinery and many armed men, all of which looked more like the courtyard of a fortified guerrilla stronghold than a sleepy and innocent rural landscape. A few days later on 24 Oct. 1964, however, *Milliyet* reported that the Mayor, who was being protected by the forces of the state, had now been arrested for the murder of the nephew of his rival. Much later on 5 Jan. 1965 *Yeni Gazete* reported that the Mayor had finally been induced to pay 73,000TL (about £2500) in blood money to his rival, the leader of the Surufan tribe, whereupon the unit of gendarmes, 38 men strong, had returned to their quarters and the matter was closed for the time being.

Again around this period, on 8 Nov. 1964, another incident had occurred between two villages near Cermik because of a land dispute, and some people had been killed. The gendarmes moved into action against one of the villages, and this was extensively reported in *Cumhuriyet*. It caused terrible embarrassment for the Minister of Interior at the time, but the presence of gendarmes did not prevent the killing of a farmer from one of these villages by men roaming in the mountains bent on vengeance against the rival village (*Cumhuriyet,* 1 Dec. 1964). The same paper reported on 4 Dec. 1964 that the villagers concerned had now decided to migrate out of the area to escape any further reprisals.

I am not concerned with the general roots of violence in Eastern Turkey, which would involve a major investigation of the culture and the social structure of the area. Matters such as the blood feud, concepts of honor, the notions of manliness and aggressiveness are not issues which can be superficially related to this or that material cause. I am here only concerned with those aspects of violence which are related to disputes regarding land and, in particular, with landlord-tenant relations.

Among educated circles in the cities of Turkey, and in the press, one often hears simple and glib solutions suggested for the social problems of these provinces only vaguely known to the public. These often attribute all the blame for the violence and trouble to a class of persons called Aga, a term which carries the connotation of Gentleman and Landowner in the countryside. In the cities the Aga is seen as a tyrant and despot outside the law who holds the innocent and frightened peasants under his arbitrary power. There are elements of truth in these accusations as well as serious misconceptions about the circumstances in which villagers in the Turkish countryside live.

In this paper, the social features and the history of the land problems in the Southeastern region, the worst area for land violence by general consent, will be first discussed. This will provide the background to deal with the present social and economic conditions, as well as the technological factors which have profoundly disturbed the social fabric of the area. Specific cases will then be provided to indicate the various alternative solutions to the deep-seated disputes. The last section will deal with the dynamics of the rise and fall of Aga power in the Southeast.

SOCIAL FEATURES

The southeastern provinces of Turkey, where Diyarbakır is situated, have certain special features which affect our problem. The region presents an ethnographically composite picture. There are various linguistic and confessional groups which exist as separate communities. The major language is Kurdish with its two mutually unintelligible dialects, Zaza and Kormanco. The districts to the North — Bingol, Siirt, Muş — speak Zaza and those south and east speak Kormanco. In fact there appear to be great variations in dialect even within these major groups; and the villagers, at least around the Western mountains near Elbistan, complain of the difficulties of communication between different valleys. There are no such problems in the plains. Turkish is the administrative language; and the bilingual elements (Turkish-Kurdish), though widespread in the population, are mainly to be found among the wealthy families and the civil servants in the towns and cities. Near Diyarbakır there are also some settled Turkmen villagers, so called since they speak Turkish and are Alevi.

Other languages are Armenian, Assyrian, Arabic, and some Circassian. Assyrian in particular is spoken by a large community of Syrian Christians in the region of Mardin. Armenian is largely confined to a small group in Diyarbakır. Arabic speakers, too, are not very numerous in the Diyarbakır region but are to be found further south and west.

The confessional picture is more varied and more important, particularly among the Muslim population. It includes such curious groups as the Yezidi, allegedly Devil Worshippers. The main division is between Sunni and Alevi communities. There are great Alevi communities (their languages are Turkish and/or Kurdish depending on the region) to the west near Elbistan and Malatya, as well as to the north in Tunceli and Muş, Sivas and Erzincan. Apart from the Turkmen (Alevi), the major groups in the Diyarbakır region are the subdivisions of Sunni communities, in particular, the Shafi, Hanefi, and Maliki schools. Although the Sunni subdivisions are not so important as to be barriers to intermarriage — which the Sunni/Alevi barrier is — and although the members of the different schools may attend the same mosques, they are significant in drawing attention to the ethnic picture of the region. The Hanefi in the Diyarbakır area are mainly the Turkish speaking upper-class landlord or administrative elements. The Shafi are the majority of the Kurdish-speaking village population. The Maliki are, again in general, the Arabic-speaking groups in the area. I did not meet the Hinbeli school.[1]

The Hanefi-Shafi distinction is one of very long standing. The Ulu Cami in Diyarbakır is traditionally divided between the Shafi and Hanefi groups for prayer; and the famous Gök Medrese in Mardin was organized so as to teach both schools of law in the right and the left wings of the building. The Hanefi-Shafi distinctions appear in special gestures at prayer, special customs for the formation of communities (e.g., the Shafi have to be at least 40 in number to make up a proper *cemaat,* prayer group, in the mosques), certain distinctive funeral customs, and some important taboos concerning pollution. Under the last heading, for instance, there is the Shafi taboo about touching women under any circumstances. The male is polluted by the female touch and has to renew his ablutions before attending to his prayers.

This linguistic and confessional diversity should not obscure the remarkable cultural uniformity of southeastern Turkey. The structure of the family, the nature of the blood feud, the concepts of honor and shame, and virginity, the complex customs concerning marriage, marriage payments and their manner and size are all nearly identical among the Sunni sections of the population. The Kurdish-Turkish linguistic division does not appear at this cultural level. The *rites de*

[1] This is not a standard pattern: there are Kurdish-speaking Hanefi tribes (such as the Drijan in Malatya) in other regions.

passage are also identical, and the special customs of "circumcision kinship" (*kirve,* somewhat similar to God-parenthood) are to be found in almost all elements of the population.[2] It is this fundamental identity of culture which permits intermarriage between Turkish and Kurdish-speaking elements freely. This cultural bond, established over many centuries and firmly reinforced by religious convictions, is undoubtedly the best insurance against the subtle tendencies of Kurdish irredentism which appear to be confined to some multilingual (largely western educated) Kurdish intellectuals in Diyarbakır.

HISTORY OF LAND TENURE IN THE SOUTHEAST

The legal foundation of the agrarian system of Diyarbakır lies in the recesses of Ottoman economic history.[3] It is claimed in Diyarbakır that the present titles to the large landed estates so characteristic of the province are based on Ottoman *ferman* probably of the nineteenth century. It might, therefore, be useful to recall the outlines of legal developments of land tenure toward the end of the Ottoman Empire.

There appears to have been little uniformity in such arrangements before the nineteenth century in the different regions of the Empire. The basic division of land into *miri* (domain, belonging to the state) and *mülk* (freehold) was generally recognized, though *mülk* (freehold), it appears, was relatively rare before the nineteenth century. Usually *mülk* was confined to building land in the towns, and *miri* was farm land. These distinctions, however, permitted considerable latitude on the part of the holders of an estate. The Eastern regions of Anatolia appear to have been governed as separate *derebeylik* (baronial domains) which owed allegiance to the Empire and paid certain annual taxes to the treasury. Indeed, according to one historian, ". . . the derebeys had become a kind of feudal vassal-princes ruling over autonomous, hereditary principalities. . . . By the beginning of the nineteenth century almost the whole of Anatolia was in the hands of the various *derebey* families — only two eyalets, Karaman and Anadolu, remaining under the direct administration of the Porte" (Lewis, 441).

[2] I established the existence of such ritual kinship by *kirve* connection as between Hanefi Turkish-speakers and Yezidi (Devil Worshipper) villages around Diyarbakır. I have also met them as far north as Sivas and west as Kayseri.

[3] For XV and XVI centuries, see Barkan, 1945.

The legal background of nineteenth-century developments is particularly interesting. Before the nineteenth century, *timar* and *zeamet* (types of feudal fiefs) had formed the basis for considerable sections of the Ottoman military organization. Selim III started the procedure whereby the treasury simply took over *timars* so as to provide revenues for the new army which he was in the process of creating. Some people considered this action to be manifest tyranny on the part of the Sultan, and it is hardly surprising that Selim's reforms earned the hostility of the existing military establishment. The procedure was continued by Mahmud II since it proved useful as a method both of undermining the old establishment and, at least in theory, for providing new revenues for the treasury. In fact, all *timars* were revoked in 1831, though apparently the revenues turned out to be disappointing.

After the revocation of the *timar* system, it appears that there were increasing sales of *miri* land as *mülk,* again in order to increase the revenues of the treasury in the nineteenth century. The purchaser was given a deed called *tapu temessükü,* which in theory gave no legal rights of freehold ownership but only a lease of revenues. But, in fact, the rights of these purchasers were steadily extended. Lewis remarks that the trend of agrarian laws of the Tanzimat period transformed these leases into something barely distinguishable from freehold. The *tapu temessükü* became a title deed, and the laws were successively modified to permit the inheritance of these estates by sons and daughters and other relatives.

Lewis also notes that together with these fundamental changes in the land structure of the Empire, there increasingly developed a kind of rich landlord class standing between the peasantry and the government officials in many districts. They were enriched by the high prices which agricultural exports from the Empire fetched in the world markets, though apparently the condition of the peasantry was not improved.

It is dubious, in fact, to what extent such laws as the revocation of *timars* of 1831 were really effective in the outlying parts of the Empire. Gökalp writes, "Although forms of *zeamet* like *sipahilik, yurtluk, ocaklık* have been formally legally abolished, they are in actuality and in fact still in existence" (my translation). Gökalp, who knew his native Diyarbakır very well, was writing this in 1909.

There were evidently difficulties in curbing the power of locally powerful families. There was a land law of 1858, for instance, which prohibited the acquisition of a whole populated village as an estate by an individual. In 1966, as we shall see, the object of this law had still not been achieved even under the Republic. In 1866 we read that a *Firkai Islahiye* (Improvement Division) was sent into the Adana-Maraş region to curb the power of local lords and to bring them more firmly under Ottoman control and jurisdiction. Its results were again local and temporary, and the social organization of the Southeast was not affected.

These legal developments of the nineteenth century, which were intended to increase the power of central authority and to dismantle the feudal land structure of the Empire, in fact, had unforeseen effects on the agrarian system. They seem to have accomplished exactly the opposite of what had been intended. The *ferman* of the Sultan, which in the past entitled the holder of an estate to draw only a certain share of the produce from the land alloted to him, now, probably under the influence of European land codes, turned him into a landlord with full freehold tenure.[4] This important development, which undermined the traditional agrarian system in which the farmer had a certain security of tenure conditional on his paying his dues, is one which has been insufficiently studied by historians and not properly understood by the Turkish courts.

The traditional system would appear to be more akin to the Persian land-tenure system in which landlord and tenant are bound together in a skein of mutual rights and obligations. Hence, it is understandable why Ottoman jurists considered all the land to belong ultimately to the

[4] Barth reports similar developments for the Suleymaniye area in Irak:

> When Baban rule (i.e., Pasha's of the Baban family — the area was a Pasalik of the Ottoman Empire) was broken in 1851 . . . all land, unless otherwise registered, was decreed to belong to the Ottoman Sultan. Though the rule existed that no whole village should be registered as the property of any single person, this and other rules were generally overlooked. Thus leaders of *tiras* (tribal sections), *Begs*, or in fact any other person who could bribe a few witnesses, registered large tracts of land as their personal property. Although actual power was of course necessary to make these formal transactions effective as far as the collecting of tax was concerned, the result was that a category of landowner emerged for which there were no clear traditional precedents. . . . As a result, the field was left open to individual exploitation on a much larger scale than in Baban times, and the only effective checks were the . . . threats to the personal safety of the exploiter (Barth, 1953:53).

Conditions in Turkey followed similar developments.

Ottoman Treasury as *miri* since no individual had full possession of the land but only certain rights in connection with the land.

The development of this traditional system into one of freehold by certain influential persons in the nineteenth century turned the tenant farmer into a serf and the landlord into a person who could arbitrarily alter the lives and conditions of entire villages. It may be remarked, however, that as long as security of tenure was not guaranteed by the central administration, the hold of the tenants on the land, even under traditional systems such as the Persian, does not seem to have been very considerable (Lambton, 1953:295-305). In the Diyarbakır case, too, it may well be questionable as to what tenure the tenant farmer possessed when the area — pre-nineteenth century — was under *derebey* rule.

In any case, at the end of the nineteenth century, much of the land belonged by legal title (*tapu temessükü*) to influential families and personages who had had foresight and power to register it in their names. And this is, indeed, what is now claimed in Diyarbakır. They paid the traditional Islamic *Ashar* (now admitted to be an excellent tax after years of revilement) of 1/10 to the treasury and may have paid another tenth to the landlord.[5] At other times the rights of the landlord appear to have been 1/8, a figure considerably smaller than similar arrangements in Persia (Lambton, 1953:314-315).

These ratios, which represent a certain economic balance between the landlord and the tenant farmer, have come down to the present day and continue in some places to this day. I think it can be argued that without a major change in the technology of agricultural production, these ratios of land returns between landlord and tenant would have been difficult to alter. One should recall that the yields are low in the province to begin with. The areas to be cultivated are truly vast. The distances before motor transport were formidable.[6] Law and order were (and are) difficult to establish. In such circumstances,

[5] See remarks of Gökalp, "The Ashar tax regulations forbid members of councils and government employees from becoming tax farmers. In the despotic period, this regulation had no effect. Civil servants and councillors would not hesitate to engage in tax farming under pseudonyms. As the influence on the administration was the tool of vengeance of such people, no hero could have the temerity to attempt to take over one of their villages" (my translation) (Beysanoglu, 1956:103).

[6] In 1909 the distance from Diyarbakır to Viransehir is said to have been 20 hours. It is now two or three hours by bus (Beysanoglu, 1956).

the chances of the absentee landlord, who had to depend entirely upon the labor of the tenant farmer in order to get the land cultivated at all, to draw any greater percentage of the return on land would have been small.

Another factor which would have weakened the ability of the landlord to place much pressure on the farmers would have been the low density of population in the Diyarbakır district. I think that relative to the fertility of the land, it was low to begin with and became even lower as a result of the many wars in which the Empire was involved at the turn of the century. The Armenian exodus, too, must be recalled as a factor in these considerations. Therefore, whatever the legal changes in the title situation from the nineteenth century on, it is likely that there would have been few real changes in the landlord-farmer economic balance unless these were accompanied by changes in agricultural technology and physical communications. These, we know, did not alter much until recent years.

The nature of the title deed (*tapu*), itself, is also in question. On unsurveyed, undulating, almost featureless land, how can proper boundaries be fixed and legally maintained except on trust and/or force of arms? In this part of the country, as indeed elsewhere, a slight ridge, an outcrop of rock, a tree, a white stone or anything else that appears prominent are used as markers. Over the years some of these disappear or are altered. The small ridges which mark the boundary between two fields are especially vulnerable: they can simply be ploughed over. Then all depends on the witnesses and their memory. Needless to say, the boundaries on some title deeds are so vague and unclear that with proper witnesses, whose support can be marshaled by special means, these deeds can be made to apply practically anywhere. However, one alleviating factor may be noted: for this region at least, it could be maintained that until very recently there was little pressure on the land, and disputes were less concerned with exact boundaries than with leadership and control over villages as a whole.[7]

[7] Stirling also reports that there was no land shortage in the region in which he worked until very recently. Pierce's observations for the same region confirm this view. There is recorded evidence for some parts of the southeast, at least, that the population in the 1870's was higher than it is now. (See *Kara-Amid,* September, 1956 for Cermik history, p. 281.)

THE AGA SYSTEM

The Aga system in the southeast of Turkey must also be understood in its historical and cultural perspective among Kurdish populations in areas which were part of the Ottoman Empire. The numerous studies of the social organization of the Kurds all underline the fundamental importance of the institutions of leadership around the Aga or Seyh. These institutions center around the traditional and well-known pattern of the guest house and in their general outlines are similar to the traditions of social status and leadership in Anatolian villages further west (Stirling). The traditional position of the Aga in the tribal context is competently analyzed by Leach who draws attention to the importance of constant generosity and benevolence of the leader to maintain his position in the group. His observations reflect the popular saying in Diyarbakır, "Agalık vermekle, Yigidlik vurmakla olur." ("You must give to be an Aga, and you must kill to be a Hero.")

Barth, working in the Suleymaniye district in Iraq, has drawn attention to certain important differences between the organization of Nomad groups and the social patterns to be seen in settled villages. He observes that the fundamental social division between serfs (*meskjin*) and freemen, which is fundamental in the settled regions, is not to be seen among the nomads. The social divisions in settled areas appear to be sharper, and for instance, important marriage barriers are set up between the ordinary members of the village and the kin groups of the Aga. These patterns, too, are to be seen in many parts of Eastern Anatolia where villagers regard certain important families with impressive historical roots as *"Ocak sahibi"* (hearth-holders) and refrain from intermarriage with them out of respect for their exalted status and as an indication of their allegiance to the family.

It is very important for reformers to realize that these institutions of leadership are deeply rooted traditional forms with the weight and respect of centuries of local and Islamic culture behind them. They cannot be regarded, as they have been, as the individual quirks of ambitious men. And, indeed, it is not surprising that a similar system of social division between the aristocratic families and the villagers exists in the villages around Diyarbakır. A distinction should be noted: there is a difference between the allegiance to certain families, who have traditional ritual status as learned and pious people and who act as peacemakers (*Seyhs*), and to the Aga, whose position depends more directly on his worldly power, influence, and effectiveness which are all related, of course, to the extent of his estate. I am not concerned with *Seyh's* and the *Tarikat* organization in this context, but I should note that they are a vital and fundamental feature of the social organization of this region. The spread of their influence is summed up by the Diyarbakır saying, "Seyhi olmıyanın, Seyhi seytandır." ("The *Seyh* of him who has no *Seyh* is Satan.") It needs hardly to be added that these men are by no means the ignorant nonentities they are so often represented to be by westernized groups in Turkey but are the important and greatly respected repositories of local customary law and morality.

These remarks on the traditional social organization of this region should also make it clear that there is an important hiatus between the legal arrangements of the nation at large, emanating out of Ankara, and the stubborn facts of respected local traditions. The aristocratic distinctions of Aga, Bey, Seyh, etc., were all abolished by law in the early days of the Republic, but they clearly continue in the structure of local communities. We shall see that there are good sociological reasons which make these institutions viable in the face of fierce opposition from the administration. Let me merely underline here that the difference between the legal systems of the nation and the customary law and morality of local society is one which is obviously related to the westernization of the upper and governing classes of Turkey and has had the most serious and far-reaching consequences in dividing the administration from the population at large. This division, formerly very obvious in the major cities, has now reached the villages as well, and some of the deep problems which it raises in terms of family structure have been noted by Stirling. It also remains, of course, the major problem in Turkish politics.

These cultural differences which exist everywhere in Turkey are further exacerbated in the Diyarbakır region by the fact that the administration and the population speak two different languages. It is essential for small villagers in their dealings with government officials to utilize intermediaries who understand the intricacies of the administration as well as the language of its officials. Similarly, the administrators, themselves, become dependent upon local notables who can interpret their views to the population at large.[8]

It will be readily seen that any local person who can demonstrate his influence and power over the local administration will quickly develop a following who will then use him as a spokesman for their requests. As Ziya Gökalp so perspicaciously observed in his article, "Timar ve Zeamet," the Aga institution fills this vital gap in the communications between the local population and the administration in the Diyarbakır region (Beysanoglu, 1956:107-108). The question for reformers, therefore, cannot be one of doing away with the individual Aga, which only causes local distress and annoyance, but is a matter of modernizing administrative procedures and developing better communications in the widest sense.

THE ECONOMICS OF AGRICULTURE

Diyarbakır is almost at the center of the vast rolling plains of the fertile crescent. As one drives through it in the summer, it gives the impression of a great desert crossed near the city of Diyarbakır by the Tigris River and further to the West by the Euphrates. The impression of the desert is a vivid one since during the summer there is almost no vegetation visible on this immense dusty plain except near the Tigris or its tributaries where great human effort has produced small oases here and there. The impression is wrong. This region undoubtedly possesses some of the most fertile and productive agricultural land in Turkey.

The settlement pattern is not unlike Central Anatolia. There are the great cities of Diyarbakır, Urfa, Mardin, with small villages around them and, in about two or three hours' drive from the cities, smaller centers — Bismil, Ergani, Siverek, Cermik, and others — with a marketplace, some administrative buildings, and a few lodgings for civil servants. These, too, are surrounded by the small villages where most of the population lives. The small villages consisting of a cluster of flat roofed, sun-baked brick houses are highly nucleated and closely integrated communities.

The economic life of the region centers around dry wheat farming.

8 This was so under the Ottomans as well. (See Gökalp in Beysanoglu, 1956: 107-108.)

Irrigated lands are few (there is not a single dam on the great rivers of the Tigris and Euphrates), and there is a certain amount of vegetables and fruit grown where the water situation is favorable.

The yields on seed sown tend to be low on unirrigated lands. A yield of five to tenfold is considered to be normal, and anything above 10 to 15 is regarded as exceptionally high. The *dönüm* is the unit of land measure (about 33 x 33 m.). Since it is a traditional measure it sometimes differs also; Barth speaks of it as 50 x 50 m. Again according to local custom, the *dönüm* is sown with one *ölçek* of seed. The *ölçek* is reckoned to be 20 kg. These figures apply if the land is to be sown broadcast by hand. If sown by tractor apparently about 13 kg. of seed is sufficient for one *dönüm* of land. The yield of the *dönüm* appears to be between 100 kg. to 130 kg. of wheat. At the going rate in 1965 of 70 kurus per kg., the monetary return on one *dönüm* of land was about 70 to 90 TL in a relatively good year.[9] It can, of course, be much lower depending on the vagaries of the weather. The cultivation pattern of the land is to work it every other year so that it can be left fallow between cultivation years. This means in effect that 70 TL is the return not from one but two *dönüms* of land.

Taking these figures into consideration it becomes clear that with the present technical equipment and traditional methods, immense acreages of land have to be utilized to achieve these modest returns. One is first surprised when villagers speak of 1,000 and 10,000 or 100,000 *dönüms* of land, each of which would signify a fortune anywhere in Western Turkey; but in the area of Diyarbakır, "real land" is said to be of the order of 200,000 to 300,000 *dönüms*. It hardly needs to be emphasized that the organization of labor, the preparation, cultivation, and above all harvesting of these far-flung lands becomes a problem of the first magnitude which must be kept in mind in all discussions of social problems in this region.

In the Diyarbakır region there are three categories of persons involved in dry farming. The farmers, the landlords, and the agents. The landlords are referred to as Aga (or Bey, if they are educated), and the agents have various titles such as Kahya, Nazır, or Kethuda. The relations between these groups have been changing, and the difficulties between them will be further discussed below. Traditional

[9] 15 TL = $1 (1970).

arrangements were worked out for the subsistence needs of tenant farmers in dry farming. The *hane* (household), it was reckoned, needs about 30-40 *dönüms* of land per annum to handle its minimal food requirements. Including fallow land, this is almost 100 *dönüms* per household. (These figures do not include the share to be given the landlord which may be as low as 1/8 or as high as 1/2 depending upon arrangements.)

From the point of view of the landlords, land is always spoken of as "villages." It appears, indeed, that 15 to 20 landlord families control much of the land in the region. The present land situation of one of these families felt to be the most powerful and important one in the area may be described as follows.[10]

The Mafarkınzade family has a long history of power in the region. They are frequently mentioned in the nineteenth century. At the present time, the family has two branches: Branch I (Necip) and Branch II (Fazıl). Between them, the entire family owned five villages. These have now been divided between the branches so that each branch has two villages each, and they share the fifth village which in some ways is the most valuable.

The size of the family population involved in this ownership picture is considerable. Thus, Necip, who died sometime ago, had two daughters, both of whom are married with children. They are both married to Ankara people, one of whom is a Professor at the University, and neither of them have the ability to handle the lands. So the two and one-half villages are in fact handled by a Kahya of Necip who sends their monetary income to the daughters.

In the Fazıl Branch, Fazıl is dead. He had four sons and two daughters who survived him. Of these only one son and daughter have remained behind in Diyarbakır to look after family affairs. One son has often been a MP for Diyarbakır in one of the parties most fervent in the advocation of land reform; the other two have left the family affairs to the eldest son who resides in the city and have taken jobs in Istanbul and Ankara. The daughter is also married into one of the landlord families which has had a member as MP for the same party from this region. The other daughter lives in Istanbul. The handling of the estate is almost entirely in the hands of the two eldest sons who

[10] All names in the cases which follow are fictional.

have taken a village each and share the income of the fifth village. One of them, the more progressive son, has been feeling that it will be difficult to retain hold of these estates against the pressure of land reform from the population and has been trying to sell his "village" to the villagers. I will return to this problem below.

Let me say a little more about the shared village to indicate the relations between landlords and tenants more precisely.

The village of Seydo is within an hour of Diyarbakır. The total amount of land around it is reckoned to be almost 30,000 *dönüms* which appears as much less on the title deeds. In the past it was usual practice, well known in all parts of Anatolia, to register the acreage of the lands as far below their real extent to avoid the grain taxes, *aşar*. Since there is now no grain tax, the acreages are being enlarged again in order to forestall any claims by the treasury on the land as public property.

I had estimates of the value of Seydo from various informants, some of whom were interested in showing it to be very worthless (i.e., members of the landlord's family) and others who claimed it to be very valuable (the enemies of the Mafarkınzade family). On one estimate it was said to be worth 300,000 TL (i.e., 10 TL per *dönüm*) and on the other 2,000,000 TL (i.e., 60 or 70 TL per *dönüm*). It should be recalled, however, that only about 2/3 of Seydo is cultivable, the rest being rocky land and mountains, and also that some parts of Seydo, about 500 *dönüms,* have a good water supply and are irrigable. An abstract value of about 1,000,000 TL appears reasonable. The figure is abstract, since for various reasons to be discussed below, buyers are not to be found at these figures.

In 1965 Seydo consisted of about 32 households. Most of them had been brought in during the last 30 years by the landlords from various parts of Eastern Turkey. Their origins were as follows: 6 households were local, 4 had come in from neighboring villages, 6 from Mazı Dag near Mardin, 4 from Çınar district, 1 from Hazro, 3 from Mardin, 1 from far away Muş, 1 from Lice, 2 from Derik, 3 from Bingol, and 1 household from Kayseri was the family of a gendarme charged with peacekeeping in the village. All except the gendarme were Shafi. This is not, of course, the typical situation in the region but indicates the kind of social group which may be established as a result of the initiative of the landlords. It goes without saying that this village built entirely upon the land of landlords and without common social backgrounds was completely dependent on the landlords for its very existence.

Even so, there had been trouble in the village since the farmers had discovered that out of the 30,000 *dönüms* only a fraction had been legally registered on the title deeds and had applied to the Land Commission in order to have the rest of the land registered as public property, which could then be issued out to them on a freehold basis. I will return to the way this dispute was handled below. Suffice it to say that the village consisted of settled laborers whose relationship to the landlords, educated in Istanbul, Ankara, and abroad, could fairly be described as serfs.

IRRIGATION

Although the Tigris flowed freely through the province, attempts at private irrigation schemes were few.[11] Almost all irrigation work is handled by the State Irrigation Department (DSI). As a contrast to the traditional forms of cultivation, and as an example of what is possible and what is achieved in improving land utilization in this region, the net effects of irrigation should be mentioned.

The DSI has a small irrigation project near Nusaybin which has had an extraordinary impact on the area. The project is a simple one. One of the tributaries of the Tigris is controlled and some of its water is diverted into irrigation channels which reach far out into the countryside. When I was in the Nusaybin area in 1964, the tertiary channels were still under construction by the relatively new office of Toprak-Su (a different government department charged with land

[11] I have mentioned that notwithstanding the low yields on wheat, the land in the region is very fertile. There were some who experimented with growing other products on the land. One such experiment was with grapes. One landlord reported that he had tried growing grapes on some of his mediocre land with some irrigation possibilities. The return was about 2 tons per *dönüm*. At 50 to 60 krs. per kilo, this means a return of about 500 to 600 TL per *dönüm*, which is almost ten times that of wheat. He decided, however, not to continue the experiment. It was too difficult he said since looking after vineyards demanded skill and constant attention. People and their animals had to be kept out of the land by guards. The marketing of fresh fruit was also not as simple a matter as cereals. As a result he dropped the scheme and returned to the well-tried, simple forms of dry wheat farming. The incident shows the difficulty of overcoming traditional forms of land utilization, which are well integrated into deeply rooted social forms. However, as we shall see below, the resistance is not insurmountable.

improvement and preservation, curiously enough independent from the Waterworks DSI). In the village of Kentli, which the channels had touched, the effects of irrigation were truly revolutionary. This had been a village of 20 households, which had had extreme water shortage. There had been barely enough water for humans let alone for animals. Most of the villages in this area went up to the Yayla's with their flocks in the hot months. As far as dry wheat farming was concerned, they had been accustomed to work on 5 to 1 yields. Land values before the irrigation scheme were around 10 TL per *dönüm* near the village.

The arrival of irrigation made it possible to switch first from wheat to rice farming. There were specialized rice farmers from as far afield as Antep and Maraş who came into the area and simply rented the fields from the villagers. The returns on rice were irresistible. The crop gives a noteworthy yield of 60 to 1 in good fields, and the farmer may get 400 to 500 kg. of rice per *dönüm.* At 60 krs. this means a return of 200 to 300 TL per *dönüm.* On a relatively tiny holding of say 100 *dönüm* of one household, this return is a fortune.

However, the methods of rice cultivation in these irrigation projects when compared with those of Ceylon — which are bad enough compared to Japan — are indescribably primitive. The outsiders from Maraş and Antep had no interest in preserving the land. The rich topsoil which had never had irrigation, and which was obviously responsible for the high return, was immediately eroded. Great crevasses 16 to 20 feet deep were produced. And as the years passed the yield began to fall. Irrigation handled in this irresponsible manner is like putting a superb modern instrument into the hands of a child.

After the yield began to fall in rice cultivation, the farmers turned toward cotton. Around the village of Kentli 200 to 300 kg. per *dönüm* was the usual yield. At the Antep price of 1.20 to 2.00 TL per kilo, cotton meant a return of 400 to 600 TL per *dönüm,* which is an even more unbelievable figure for a small villager holding about 100 *dönüms* of land.

In the village of Kentli, which was a village of small holders in the past, the effect of these abundant channels of gold has been to increase the population of the village from 20 to 180 households in about 6 years by immigration from the neighboring villages. At first, land to build houses for these newcomers, who came to work as laborers for the newly rich landlords, was given to them free. He could then build his own *dam* (house) as he wished. Recently even house land has become valuable and is no longer freely provided.

Needless to add, the value of the land has risen from 20 to 700-1000 TL. The rents rose similarly keeping pace with the rice in the productivity of the land.

It should be added that this remarkable irrigation scheme, provided entirely free by the DSI to the people of the area, had almost no financial returns for the DSI. It is true that there is a minimal payment for the water, but this is a symbolic amount. The DSI decided on and handled the project entirely on technical and engineering grounds without the least consideration for the human factors or social effects which were involved.

The irrigation project of Nusaybin indicates the kind of fundamental changes in the size and nature of village communities which can be effected almost incidentally by technological improvements. It also shows the extraordinary lack of concern and communication between a highly technical but effective arm of government (that is the DSI) and the villages which it affects. Finally, it also indicates the inspiring prospects which are possible by irrigation on the Tigris and Euphrates on the vast lands of the Southeast, which could alter the balance between population and land in Turkey in an extremely positive manner.[12]

THE INTRODUCTION OF TRACTORS

Having placed the economic picture in the correct perspective, we should consider the main form of cultivation in greater detail.

[12] It is rare for Irrigation Departments to be so unconcerned with the immediate social effects of their activities. In the large Gal Oya Colonization scheme in Ceylon, both the catchment and the irrigation area of the dam were taken over by a public organization which was charged with the equitable distribution of land and the general organization and administration of the entire project. In Turkey, too, it would be far better for all concerned, and definitely better for the activities of the DSI, to appropriate all the land involved before commencement of engineering activities. The irrigated land, now many times more valuable, could then be returned to the people of the area in a more equitable manner, in smaller lots, and if necessary against certain payments. This would not only be more fair, but the DSI would then be able to undertake more projects and extend its operations which are vital for most of Turkish agriculture.

In the traditional form of land tenure, it was suggested, the landlord was entitled to 1/8 or 1/10 of the crop. It should be understood that this depended upon a certain balance between landlord and the tenant. Had certain new factors not entered into the scheme to disturb this balance, the changes in legislation regarding land tenure or the political winds of Ankara and Istanbul would not have seriously affected the economic conditions in the province. In traditional agriculture the landlord needed the tenant to cultivate the land, and the tenant needed the protection of the landlord. I feel that the dependence of the landlord upon the peasants under the traditional forms of cultivation is such that he would have been loath to alienate the tenants by trying to press for higher shares of the crop. Given the unsettled nature of the region, the relatively low population, the low yields, and the immense acreages which need to be cultivated, it seems clear that the landlord would have found it difficult to put much pressure on the tenant.

Around 1950 this social and economic balance between the landlord and tenant was destroyed. The introduction of tractors into large-scale dry farming fundamentally affected the agrarian structure of Eastern Anatolia. I shall provide examples of the specific nature of these changes. It needs merely to be observed that a powerful tractor can cultivate about 10,000 *dönüms* in the wide open plains around Diyarbakır. At a conservative estimate this means the replacement of at least 50 farmers working with oxen and ploughshares. The benefits to the landlord are immense. If he cultivates 5,000 *dönüms,* which would present no difficulties, he could count on a sale of 350,000 TL worth of wheat without heavy expenses and without needing to share the produce with an entire villageful of subsistence farmers.

From the point of view of the villagers, the introduction of tractors, together with the delayed effects of Ottoman legislation concerning title in the nineteenth century described above, has been disastrous. It is now extremely important for the villagers not to permit, if possible, the claims of the landlord to operate the land with tractors, or in desperation to frighten him and induce him to stay away from the land as usual in the towns. But if the landlord, himself, can be frightened, there are others who will not be. There are also tough men who act as agents of the landlords, who can frighten the villagers, and this simple equation of tractors against villagers is the terrible story of much of Diyarbakır in recent years.

Many combinations of balancing the situation are possible. The village may permit the landlord to work only a section of the land by tractors, reserving the rest for themselves. The landlord may win and permit only a small section of the land to be farmed by the village and increase his acreage as he increases his power. The landlord may use some of the villagers as his agents and allow them to cultivate the land with tractors and push their fellow villagers gradually out. The villagers may claim to the land commission that the title deed is counterfeited and that the land is really public land which should be divided among villagers, or again, the land commission may be bribed and the witnesses frightened by some tough men so that the landlord may once again win the legal battle. All these possible permutations are to be seen in the countryside around Diyarbakır. What is not visible is a firm policy on the part of the many past governments in Turkey to settle the desperate problems of the area. Given the extreme complexity of the situation, and the difficulty of administering the region for a variety of reasons, the courts, themselves, merely become pawns to be manipulated in the complex game of gaining more and more land and power.

I shall provide some actual cases to indicate the tactics which are used by various parties in the present desperate circumstances.

LAND DISPUTES

1. *The Case of Abdullah Bey.* The father of Abdullah Bey had been a member of the Committee of Union and Progress (*Ittihatcı*) and had used his influence to buy a village near Silvan. This village had provided him with some small income in the form of rent for many years. He had two sons, one of whom was mentally deranged; the other, Abdullah Bey, had attended the Law Faculty at Istanbul University where he had been an undistinguished student. His father died soon after his return to Diyarbakır, and the weight of family responsibility was transferred to him. While he was away, and during the illness of the father, it had been difficult to check up on the income from the village; but Abdullah Bey suspected that it was beginning to dry up, since the villagers complained of bad harvests, bad weather and locusts,

and other natural calamities. Abdullah Bey had been to the village numerous times with his father, and although it was on the banks of the Tigris, he had always thought it to be a desert-like place. Having little to do in Diyarbakır he decided that he would go into cultivation himself on the lands of his father.

This decision was understandably unpopular in the village. A landlord had never lived in the village and had never before cultivated the land on his own account. When the villagers heard that Abdullah Bey intended to bring in his own tractor and harvester combine, they became greatly alarmed. Delegations came to Abdullah Bey to tell him of the great dangers involved in living in the village. They spoke of bandits in the area and the general insecurity of the region and mildly threatened him. None of this affected Abdullah Bey. He took some ten trustworthy men with him, all armed to the teeth, and one day simply drove into the village with his group. He was allowed to build a residence for himself on the outskirts of the village. When he first took his tractor into the land, there was a shooting incident and one of his drivers was wounded. Abdullah Bey shot back and wounded one of the villagers. There was a sullen period of a few months. More dogs were brought into Abdullah Bey's compound, and its walls climbed higher and higher.

Abdullah Bey took over about 4,000 *dönüms* of land (his own estimate) out of a claimed total of 14,000. Whatever the total size, however, cultivable land evidently became scarce for the villagers. Tensions rose in the village, and the village itself split into two parts, one of which went further down the Tigris and settled at a distance of 25 minutes walk from the main village. Relations between the two very closely related villages (children of brothers) was by no means cordial. The next year a variety of tensions gave rise to a shooting incident in the main village. A man was killed at night in the fields. People pretended not to know who had killed this person, but at first the village tried to pin the murder on Abdullah Bey. The gendarmes came in. Abdullah Bey's men had already threatened the villagers against being false witnesses and lying to get Abdullah Bey involved in the courts. There was not enough evidence; one faction of the village gave evidence in favor of Abdullah Bey, and the case against him was dismissed. The second faction in the village suspecting that their kinsman had been killed by the other members of the village also moved out of the village and settled 20 minutes walking distance on top of a hill a little way upstream from the residence of Abdullah Bey.

The murderer was never caught. I could not piece the details of the story together, but the group which moved out suspected that either Abdullah Bey or, more probably, a member of the main village had killed this man. In the latter case, there had been a refusal to permit the marriage of the deceased's daughter to another person in the village, and there were some serious suspicions.

Abdullah Bey said that the village had now accepted his presence in the vicinity and conditions were relatively peaceful. I asked him whether he would permit me to visit the village. He agreed but told me that I would have to travel under armed guard through certain parts. In any case, I was able to spend some time with this remarkable person.

The village is about two hours drive in a jeep from Silvan. The land is spectacular with treeless rolling hills and wide horizons with a few inhabited spots here and there. We crossed the Tigris, a remarkable blue contrasting with the red-baked earth around us. A large rectangular mass appeared in the distance between some small hillocks. The driver pointed to the large rectangle which was becoming more clearly visible and said that this was the castle of Abdullah Bey.

His residence was, indeed, a castle. Walls about 20 feet high encircled a large rectangle. As we approached, an elaborate orchard became visible behind the walls inside the domain. The entrance to the rectangle was through a great heavy wooden portal which had clearly been constructed for defense purposes. Inside the doorway in the courtyard of the residence five or six large dogs were prowling around. There were basic unexpected amenities, like running water, and even a shower available. Abdullah Bey took us around the garage where the pride of the place, the various agricultural machinery, was neatly displayed. The garden had a fountain in it with a refreshing pond. We sat near it. There were even some peacocks walking on the walls to complete the scene. Apparently peacocks, too, make excellent guards.

Sitting inside the walls, it might have been possible for the outsider to forget the hostility which so clearly surrounded this residence. If momentarily forgotten, however, it would be quickly brought to mind by the double revolvers which the host always carried about on his belt.

It appeared that the establishment of Abdullah Bey in the midst of the village — the "castle" was in fact ten minutes walk from the main village — had meant some important changes. The main village was now on fairly good terms with Abdullah Bey whom they respected. Even in Diyarbakır it was rare for a landlord to be so personally involved in constant danger. The two hamlets away from the main village, however, were not on good terms. Abdullah Bey gave the main village just enough land to subsist on. The others, however, were not given any land. They had tried to plough some land near one of the borders. This time Abdullah Bey had brought the land commission and had found the right witnesses and had established his own claim to this ploughed land. This year he would allow them to work it; but next year he would not permit it again.

The effect of these developments had been considerable in the village. The scarcity of land had evidently been one of the contributing factors for the splits in the village. When the latest split occurred after the murder case, about ten households had moved to the hilltop upstream where they had built houses. Now, however, eight of these had given up the struggle against the other section of the village and Abdullah Bey and had migrated into Diyarbakır as casual laborers. There had been some others from the other section of the village downstream, and the muhtar of the main village remarked that the person to whom he had given his sister and who lived on the hilltop now had a "black heart" — that he was brooding of vengeance. It would be best for him, too, to go to Diyarbakır. He was, however, still holding on.

I left Abdullah Bey's domain with relief but misgivings. We were again escorted out by four fully armed riflemen. There was no doubt that no one would take any chances in this delicate situation. The friends of Abdullah Bey in Diyarbakır among civil servants, judges, and other relatively high ranking personages admired him but thought him to be somewhat foolhardy to risk so much in the village. On the other hand, Abdullah Bey had cars, residences in Diyarbakır, friends in Istanbul and Ankara, and a very considerable income which was often spent in a quick and carefree manner to make up for the tensions of his working existence.

The case of Abdullah Bey is by no means unique. Similar cases were constantly brought to my attention while working in Diyarbakır. I will mention a few others.

2. *Çınar Case.* The uncle of Kemal Bey has a village in the Çınar district. Four years ago they heard in Diyarbakır that some people from Çınar had come up with a title deed (*tapu*) which established their claims to about 7,000 *dönüms* of land in the village. They had already made connections inside the village and had a number of supporters who were to be paid off later. According to Kemal Bey, their intentions were to attempt to establish these claims for the small section of 7,000 *dönüms,* then depending on their success, they would go on from there by surreptitiously enlarging their borders and cowing the village population and the owners.

Their supporters in the village immediately came and informed them of the movements of the Çınar group. As matters progressed, it became clear to Kemal Bey's family that they had surmised the tactics correctly, and the new group had asked the courts to come and decide the legality of their title deed. Kemal Bey decided not to leave anything to chance. He knew that there had been a good deal of trouble between this section of the village in Çınar and another village in Derik. The hostilities arising from a blood feud had only recently been suppressed. Kemal Bey went to these Derik people, made them some promises, and indicated to them what their enemies were doing in Çınar. On the day of the court case when the judge came into the village to interview the witnesses of either side in the fields about the boundaries, Kemal Bey had 100 armed men from Derik with him. Some were in the fields and some in the village. The people from Çınar also had their bodyguard, but they were cowed by the danger of restarting the old blood feud with their traditional enemies. Conditions were tense as the judge interviewed the witnesses who gave evidence as they were told; the *muhtar* (village headman) was the critical witness. Much depended on his testimony concerning the ownership of the land. He recoiled from the armed conflict and gave evidence in favor of Kemal Bey. The people from Çınar lost their claims to a section of the village. Each village has its enemies; to control the village, the landlord must be able to manipulate these enmities.

In the Silvan and Çınar cases cited above, the landlords happened to win. The contest ends by no means always in favor of the landlord, and I came across numerous instances in which other parties won the dangerous game.

3. *Yusuf Aga.* Consider the village of Yusuf Aga. It is a village of 15,000 *dönüms* of dry land and about 600-700 *dönüms* of irrigated land. Its value in terms of going prices would be about 450,000 TL for the dry land and about 600,000 TL for the irrigated land. Yusuf Aga's sons have been educated in Ankara and do not want to be involved in land troubles, so they wanted to rent the annually cultivated land (i.e., about 8,000 *dönüms*) at 30 TL, which would bring in at least 240,000 TL. But here the villagers had the upper hand. Since the landlord was weak and ineffectual, they would not let him or anybody else even come into the village. They already threatened that whoever dared to come in would be killed. There were, hence, no takers of the village on a rental basis even though the annual revenue of the village would be about 500,000 TL on the dry lands and another 100,000 TL, at least, on the irrigated lands. Moreover, the family of Yusuf Aga had been trying to sell this village with a potential annual revenue of about 600,000 TL for 350,000 to 400,000 TL, and as yet there had been no courageous Abdullah Beys to gamble their luck on this village.

Note, that as far as Yusuf Aga was concerned, there were no possible legal solutions to his problems. The proper legal alternative of winning a court case and then attempting to evict an entire village off the land with the gendarmes is entirely unrealistic, and the only alternative that is left is self-help and violence.

There were, indeed, other cases of villagers gaining the upper hand against the landlords. Especially where the landlords were people from outside Diyarbakır, they were easily threatened and subdued. They could find no local supporters and no witnesses in their favor when the courts or the land commission came into the village to decide on the legality of the title deeds.

4. *The Case of Sakıd.* The landlord Sakıd had had enough trouble with his villagers and wanted to sell the village to others. He found a group of farmers who had migrated out from their own village because of a blood feud; they were looking for another place to settle. He came

to an agreement with them to sell his land for the first installment of 150,000 TL. They would then pay 80,000 and 70,000 TL in the next two years. His own village, knowing that they would then lose their lands, however, would not agree to the deal and instead started threatening him. It became clear that the deal would give rise to much trouble on all sides. Sakıd then sold his share to the village itself, for 200,000 TL payable in three years.

5. *The Case of Nüzhet Bey.* In a case similar to Abdullah Bey related earlier, Nüzhet Bey had established a farm (*çiftlik*) on his own land near his village. He was investing in irrigation facilities himself and had many plans for improving the land. Inevitably again, this was to be at the expense of the village. One day he was found dead of food poisoning. His death was attributed to some poisoned honey sent from the village as a gift. It could not be proven, but the land reverted back to village use.

In some cases the landlords made special arrangements to retain the control of the village. If reliable persons could be won over among the villagers, the landlord had an easier time.

6. *The Case of Şinasi Bey.* Şinasi Bey bought the title to his village during the time of the Armenian troubles in Diyarbakır. At that time he protected an important Armenian family and was able to get the village from them at a low price. He now has an Armenian agent (*nazır*) and another group of 4 or 5 tough men who handle the affairs of the village. He shares the revenue 50/50 with the *nazır*. To make things doubly safe, he has married off his sister to a small tribe, which comes down from the mountains to winter in the region. The tribe has about 60 to 80 armed men who can be called upon in case of trouble. There has been no trouble for a long time in his village.

The predominant impression one received from these complex dynamics of land tenure is the serious lacunae in legal and executive machinery to keep law and order and establish justice in the area. The impression is, of course, strongly confirmed by all parties in Diyarbakır. The following case illustrates it abundantly.

7. *The Ergani Case.* Two Agas were involved in adjacent property. One was strong and "eating" the land of the other Aga or, in other

words, was utilizing the land without the permission of the weak Aga. The weak Aga died. One of his sons was being educated in Ankara and lived there with his mother; the other son, annoyed at the situation and being cowed by the powerful Aga, started looking for "partners." Having found some, he entered into "his" land with a tractor and tried to cultivate it. The men of the strong Aga attacked them, and the case was referred to the courts. The young man, very annoyed that the Aga would summon witnesses and further his claims in the court, got prepared and in a melee outside the courthouse shot and killed the powerful Aga. He then escaped into the mountains. The gendarmes went out to get him but gave up after a while. Now, he cannot return and give himself up, since even though he might be able to get off with a light sentence, the sons of the Aga would certainly kill him in revenge for the death of their father. In this situation, his brother in Ankara, too, is no longer safe and has had to return to Ergani where his armed men can protect him. Moreover, while the killer is at large, the family of the Aga cannot take any action, since they would certainly have to pay for it immediately, while the killer — already outside the law and with little to lose — continues to roam around. A brief stalemate which has, therefore, been reached, all parties agree, can only be settled by the weak family paying off the family of the dead powerful Aga by a grant of land called "blood land" to settle the feud before it goes on much longer.

Incidentally, the killer is in fact no longer in the mountains. Since some time has passed over the incident, the gendarmes are no longer after him with zeal. Moreover, he has already paid off these gendarmes suitably so that now he can risk staying in his own home during the night and keeping out of sight during the day.

The importance of self-help when the authorities are helpless comes through in the next two cases.

8. *The Case of Nihat.* The village belongs to Nihat, but some other farmers are alleged to have about 300 *dönüms* in the village. Nihat uses the entire land and gives nothing to these others. They decide to act. They enter into the village with a number of riflemen, take over one of the empty houses, and start some arguments and shooting. Some people are wounded. Nihat takes the case to the courts and brings in gendarmes, who are paid a daily wage by the landlord to remain in-

side the village and keep the peace. In the meanwhile, the trouble-makers have taken over 2,000 *dönüms* of land which they are using while the court case continues. Their intention is to frighten away the other villagers and Nihat so that they can lay claim to the entire village.

9. *Village on Siverek Road.* Villagers reported to Mehmet that his grandmother had some land in the village and that this was recorded in the title deeds. Mehmet took some men and a tractor and entered upon the fields with the men who discovered "his" land. The second faction in the village went to another powerful man, Hasan, who lives in Diyarbakır, and complained to him. Hasan, who has connections among the authorities, tried to catch Mehmet and his men by reporting to the gendarmes that Mehmet and his group were armed and were hiding guns in the village house. The gendarmes raided the village house, but the guns were already hidden by Mehmet's men. They found nothing and returned to Diyarbakır. Mehmet continued to work the land allegedly inherited from his grandmother. The confrontation continues. Note here that according to local custom in Diyarbakır, women never inherit landed property: Mehmet's grandmother would have had no customary claims on the land. However, according to present Turkish laws, women do have rights, and Mehmet may be able to further some arguments in his favor. But the issue will probably be settled by the strength of will and nerves of steel of the opposing parties.

The disastrous effects of all this disputation on the improvement of agriculture is so obvious that it only needs the briefest mention. When nobody knows to whom the land will eventually belong, when the landlord cannot safely plan a course of action, and the villager is under threat of eviction, long-term improvements or any capital expenditure is naturally out of the question. This is one of the reasons one hardly ever sees any trees planted in the villages, let alone elsewhere.

It should certainly not be thought that the villager is incapable of capital expenditure for land improvement. Quite on the contrary, the excellent orchard of Abdullah Bey was watered by a motor pump which simply pumped up the water from the Tigris to his castle. This simple pump had created an oasis out of the desert. Its cost was about 2,500 TL. Was a village of 100 households incapable of buying some pumps to ease the water situation? Let me merely mention that the bride-price (*kalend*) of a village girl among the Shafi population of Diyarbakır starts at 5,000 TL. This is the cost of the girl to the shepherd. A man of means would have to pay 10,000 TL or much more. The lack of incentive for capital improvements cannot be sought in the general povery of the villager but must be seen in connection with the insecurity of tenure.

POPULATION MOVEMENTS

I have drawn attention in this discussion of the issues involved in land disputes to two related matters, that is (1) the use of tractors by the landlord which have permitted him to break his dependence on tenant farmers, and (2) the economic incentives of the landlord to take over the cultivation of dry farming and dispossess the tenant farmers entirely. In the case of Abdullah Bey the effect of his entry into the village was particularly evident in that tensions rose inside the village community, and in the case of the last group which split off from the village, 9 out of 10 households had left the area permanently to settle in Diyarbakır.

When villagers migrate like this, sometimes no trace of the dispossessed may be left behind. The very land on which they build their sun-baked brick houses is taken over by the landlord. When the tenant farmers move, the tractors come in and raze the dwellings. A group of village houses can be broken and ploughed into dry farming wheat fields in a very short time. There are rarely even any trees in the villages to act as tell-tale marks of where a residential area once stood.

We may observe that if the entry of tractors has the effect of pushing tenant farmers out of the land to the towns, this should be reflected in the population statistics for the province.

Karpat notes that the number of tractors in Turkey rose from 2,227 in the period 1946-1950 to a staggering 40,000 in 1955 (Karpat, 1959:99-100). The immediate effects of this important development, though obvious in the great movement into towns all over Turkey, have not been linked to mechanized farming in any direct manner. This link seems particularly well indicated in the Diyarbakır province which for ecological reasons is ideal for tractor farming. Consider Table I, which shows the population increases for the province as a whole as well as the city of Diyarbakır. Between 1950 and 1960 the

TABLE I

Population Increase in Diyarbakır

Year	*Town* *Rate of Increase* (000)	(%)		*Province* *Rate of Increase* (000)	(%)	
1927	30.4	100		194.3	100	
1950	45.0	150	116	293.7	152	55
1955	61.0	203		343.9	177	
1960	79.8	266		401.8	207	

population of the city has risen more than twice as fast as the figures for the province (55 compared to 116).

Note in Table II, however, that the percentage of men to women has remained the same in the town, indicating that the predominant mode of migrant labor, whereby the men move into towns and cities for casual work and leave their womenfolk behind in the villages, has not materially altered. Of course, the sudden increase in the population of the city has meant an inevitable increase in the slum population. In absolute terms Diyarbakır has increased from 30,000 in 1927 to about 80,000 in 1960.

It could, of course, be maintained that the effects of tractors have been even more drastic than these local figures suggest because at least a certain number of the dispossessed farmers may not have stopped at Diyarbakır but may have moved on to swell the large numbers of such landless migrant labor in Gaziantep, Adana, and thence in Ankara and Istanbul. All this is plausible and should be further investigated. What must be underlined here is that in this movement of peasants into towns and cities in Turkey, there are vital forces which push them out of their traditional locations as well as those factors like industrialization or better communications, which have usually been said to draw the villagers to the larger population centers.

THE RISE OF NEW LANDLORDS

I have drawn the outlines of the general context in which land is cultivated in the Diyarbakır region. It should not be thought that only a handful of powerful men are in control of the situation and

TABLE II

Percentage of Men to Women in Diyarbakır

	Town				*Province (Total Population in Province)*		
Year	*Men* (000)	*Women* (000)	*Total* (000)	*Year*	*Men* (000)	*Women* (000)	*Total* (000)
1927	17.6 (57.5%)	13 (42.6%)	30.7 (100.0%)	1927	97.3	96.9	194.3
1960	45.2 (56.6%)	34.6 (43.3%)	79.8 (100.0%)	1960	208.6	193.2	401.8

From Beysanoglu, *Diyarbakır Cografyasi.*

that it is only these Agas and their feuds which affect land ownership in the countryside. On the contrary, my impression working in Diyarbakır was that the landlord system was one open to new talent at least in the art of confrontation and feuding. New Agas appear to arise from humble and unlikely conditions. The lot of the powerful Agas is not always a secure and enviable one. I will discuss the case of one man on the way up to show how this is possible.

The Case of Kara Ahmet. Kara Ahmet, a past member of the Naksibendi *Tarikat* (brotherhood), the founder of the Risale-i Nur Society (a secret religious right-wing group), and presently a member of the Kadiriya *Tarikat,* is a noteworthy man by any standards. He invited me to his village near Seydo one day and I was able to piece together his remarkable achievements. He is an intense looking man of about 50 with the manner of an authoritarian, who soon after we met, showed me the two fine pistols he carried on either side. He was wearing a tie and coat and, apart from his bearing, would have appeared like any other man from one of the small towns of Anatolia. He spoke of the terrible violence of Diyarbakır and remarked that things were getting much worse, particularly with all the agitation concerning Agas and landless villagers in Parliament and in the newspapers, which was trickling down to the smallest villages and making everybody restless. Since he had many enemies himself, and feared for his life, he nowadays always went around with a fully armed bodyguard of two men. In fact, his enemies had recently grown so bold as to telephone his home one day (a week before we met) and tell his wife and children the news that he had been killed sitting in his office by five men who had riddled him with bullets. His wife had fainted and could hardly believe her eyes when she found him alive. Kara Ahmet had some guesses but did not know (or would not tell me) which among his enemies had the courage to try such a messy trick on him.

He was born on one of the villages of the important Mafarkınzade family mentioned above. It was a matter of luck that Necip Bey had taken a liking to him and had taken him home to be brought up with them. By the time he was 16 he was already acting as a minor overseer for the Mafarkınzade estates. His first serious trouble was the time when the inhabitants of Seydo complained to the land commission and requested a cadastral survey to establish and separate the lands of the Mafarkınzade family in the village. They reported that out of the total estates of 30,000 *dönüms* only 7,000 were legally inscribed in the title deed and that the rest being public land (owned by the treasury) should be distributed among them. Kara Ahmet was 18 at the time but had taken his guns and gone to speak to the villagers. Later when the cadastral survey came into the village, there were simply no witnesses to give any evidence; and the land commission decided that the villagers were evidently not interested in treasury land and permitted the legal enlargement of the lands of the Mafarkınzade to the entire 30,000-*dönüm* estate. The sons of the family, grown men at the time, had recoiled from the task accomplished so simply by Kara Ahmet.

Later a similar instance took place on the same land. Kara Ahmet was again sent along as a troubleshooter. This time after the successful defense of Mafarkınzade interests, Ahmet demanded that he be taken on as a partner in the cultivation of Seydo. One of the sons of Fazıl, Cemil, who had himself been using the land, refused the request of Kara Ahmet and instead took in another partner. This bitter lesson was not lost on Kara Ahmet. Although he maintained relations with all branches of the family, his personal animosity toward Cemil smoldered through the years, and he tried to get even with him when the opportunities arose.

Although Kara Ahmet lost his foothold in the village of Seydo, he did become a partner for Necip Bey on the lands that he controlled. At the time Necip Bey had not brought in tractors into his village.

Kara Ahmet took the tractors in with his crews and personally faced the consequences. The villagers threatened him and his men, but he prevailed. Later he had yet another brush with Cemil. His partner, Necip Bey, wanted him to work their shares in the village of Seydo. At first the sons of Fazıl Bey agreed to this. But this time Kara Ahmet refused to work the land with them. He knew that the sons of Fazıl would only permit him to work it on an annual basis. Once Kara Ahmet had ousted the villagers, who were working the land of Seydo, and after he had risked his life to plow the land with his crew, he knew that Cemil would say "get out" to him and attempt to cultivate the land on his own account. In Kara Ahmet's colorful words, Cemil wanted him to risk his neck in plowing the land so that they could put in the seed themselves. (The reason, of course, that the sons of Fazıl hesitated to permit Kara Ahmet to work the land at Seydo is because they knew that he would be a partner even more difficult to evict than any others actually on the land.)

Kara Ahmet prospered exceedingly as a partner to Necip Bey. Upon the decease of Necip Bey all the affairs of that branch of the Mafarkınzade family devolved upon him. Particularly since the heirs were men unable to participate in the tough give and take of the Diyarbakır countryside, Kara Ahmet encouraged them to move out of the scene almost entirely. This increased his status, and they became completely dependent on him. When the son, who is a professor, was in Diyarbakır recently, Kara Ahmet offered to accompany him to one of the villages inherited from his father. The professor would not risk his life and declined to go.

Apart from the fifty-fifty partnership of the Mafarkınzade family, Kara Ahmet also branched out on his own. He offered 400,000 TL to buy one of the villages of the Fazıl branch. Even in this matter Cemil would not trust him, and the brothers were getting ready to sell the village to its inhabitants for 300,000 TL. Their price was 150,000 TL as a down payment and 150,000 TL to be paid later. The villagers held out for 80,000 TL as the initial payment and the rest later. Though Kara Ahmet had not yet acquired a foothold in this village, he did get another where the villagers, themselves, claimed to have had some shares. They had threatened the landowner not to sell to anybody but themselves. But Kara Ahmet had bought the landlord's share for a down-payment of 100,000 TL cash and now controlled the entire village. There was no further talk of the shares of the villagers; when I raised the matter with him, he claimed that he intended to compensate them handsomely.

His latest concern was with a village near Çınar where he was again working as a partner with the absentee landlord. The village had about 28,000 *dönüms* of dry land. With the mountains and pasturages included, it could be reckoned as even 36,000 *dönüms.* The village, itself, was a medium-sized one of 132 households. He used for himself about 4-5,000 *dönüms* in the village from which he claimed a revenue of about 200,000 TL. He was, however, again having trouble with the villagers, who demanded the land on which his tractor was working as fallow land for themselves. Note that the village was left with less than 9,000 *dönüms* per year, or about 70 *dönüms* per household, which is felt to be sufficient for subsistence purposes but barely enough for anything else. The villagers as usual did not permit the landlord to enter the precincts of the village and were getting very hostile to Kara Ahmet.

The details of Kara Ahmet's affairs aside, it was clear that this man with burning ambition and considerable intelligence had used the characteristics most valued in the culture of Diyarbakır in the development of his personality. He was outspoken, proud, tough, courageous, authoritative with men, and almost fanatic about his beliefs; and all this had made him a most respected and important Aga in the area. The fact that he had made his way up from the most unpromising background in a poor village had not prevented him from amassing a sizeable personal fortune as well as respect and a large following.

THE DYNAMICS OF AGA POWER IN DIYARBAKIR

It seems clear from the cases discussed above that in Diyarbakır we are faced with an extremely dynamic situation regarding land tenure. It is by no means a fixed picture in which certain powerful families and Agas hold power firmly in their hands. On the contrary, conditions are very unsettled. The law is weak and distant. Only tough men can survive the ruthlessness of the struggle. The landlord who is weak loses all he has and may, indeed, have to write off very considerable and valuable property as a total loss. On the other hand, there are great opportunities for effective and intelligent, albeit ruthless, persons in the shifting land situation. Such a person, like Abdullah Bey, or Kara Ahmet, can turn a basically unlikely condition to great advantage. The mere exile of important Agas or large and powerful families in the region — a method adopted by the government from time to time (the latest in 1960) — will not make material changes in the social system within which the powerful men operate. The total pattern is one which gives opportunities to certain types of men to aggrandize themselves by certain well-tried, one might say "traditional," methods. Unless the vicious circle of lawlessness and insecurity of tenure can be altered, there will always be new Agas rising in place of those that have been deposed.

The reasons which permit the present situation to exist are not simple. To some extent they involve certain special characteristics of Islamic society: the fierce manly pride; the ideas of honor and the blood feud; and patterns of loyalty to leadership which, given the right circumstances such as the Bedouin tribes, the groups in Baluchistan, or the valley of Swat in Pakistan where administration and the law sit lightly in the region, rise to the surface in a violent fashion. The violence of Diyarbakır is in no way surprising when compared with similar desperate conditions among the Pathans. However, though the violence may in part be attributed to a primarily masculine culture which respects manly honor above all else, it is also obvious that the violence only arises where the arm of the law and administration is relatively weak in any case. There are, indeed, very special conditions which have made it difficult to provide effective administration and justice in the Diyarbakır region. Let me turn to these.

The most important single feature is that the region speaks Kurdish and cannot comprehend the language of the administration. The conditions between Turkish-speakers and the speakers of any dialect of Kurdish are of course better than many other imaginable communities. In fact, a Sunni Kurdish-speaker and Sunni Turkish-speaker are much closer to each other in every aspect of their culture and personality than either group is with, for instance, Turkish or Kurdish-speaking Alevi or Bektashi. But still, the immediate effect of the administration using a language other than that of the inhabitants of a province is that a group of intermediaries are developed who can interpret the administration's activities to the population and the wishes of the population to the administration. This intermediate group in southeastern Turkey, is, of course, immense and has deep historic roots. There are large bilingual Turkish-Kurdish speaking communities all over Eastern Turkey. In those places, where the village population is bilingual, such as parts of Malatya, there are no communication barriers between the administration and the village population so far as I can ascertain. There are also fewer Agas. In Diyarbakır, however, the village population in most parts of the province does not speak Turkish and has real difficulty in handling such vital matters as the *kaymakam* (district officer), the law courts and judges, and perhaps most important of all, the gendarmerie. The net effect of this is to produce a need for powerful men who can handle the internal affairs of the community without recourse to the outside administration. We have already underlined that the European type legal codes of the country have not been brought into line with the customary and Islamic legal arrangements in the countryside. Stirling reports the difficulties raised by this hiatus between national codes and local custom in his Kayseri village. If this difficulty is so in Turkish-speaking areas, how much more difficult for the Kurdish-speaking villager to understand what the administration and law courts want of him. And how natural for him to turn to the people whom he knows and respects. Hence, the development of *Seyhs* and *Tarikats* which provide an acceptable local legal system for their followers and effectively insulate the villagers from the European induced singularities of the administration.[13]

[13] Students of the sociology of Turkey are fortunate indeed to have some of the writings of so brilliant an observer as Ziya Gökalp (himself of an old Diyarbakır family) saved by the great efforts of Sevket Beysanoglu. Gökalp writes as follows on the subject of the Aga:

"Once the village Aga has got a member of the administration in his hands through his capacity in the art of surreptitiously gaining the ear of the powerful, he immediately tries to save the men of conscription age in his village from the army, the criminals from the courts, those who owe taxes and labour commutation dues from the tax collector. He lives like an independent prince in the confines of his villages through these services. He collects dues from crimes, marriages, "marriage by capture," and receives various other benefits. The villagers, who in their opinion are now under obligation, pay the sums for animal taxes in the exact amount to the Aga, and in order not to permit any other tax farmer in the village except the Aga, become secretive, commit false accusations, give false evidence, and do all else that is necessary" (my translation) (Beysanoglu, 1956:107-108).

This is the background against which the weakness of law and order must be placed in the southeastern region. The differences between established authority and local custom come out most clearly in a matter such as the blood feud. It is well known that killers in a blood feud often evade the gendarmerie with the full connivance not only of the section of the population on their own side but also with the support of their enemies. In the blood feud context it is of course dishonorable to report your enemy to the gendarmes. Custom demands that you should deal with him yourself. These are deep seated moral imperatives whose effect is often felt in far away Istanbul, or judging from a case of a blood-feud killing on 5th Avenue, even in New York.

These remarks, first on the linguistic barriers between the villagers and the administration and, second, on the distinction between national codes and local custom merely underline some of the reasons for the weakness of the administrative and judicial machinery in the district. To this should be added the well known fact that it is difficult to staff the administration of Eastern Anatolia with sufficient numbers of civil servants and judges, many of whom prefer to be elsewhere in the country. Hence, what administration there is cannot work at top efficiency. The numbers of gendarmes, too, are too small to look after the vast areas with which they are entrusted. The lack of vehicles, jeeps, helicopters, and other communications merely rounds out the somber picture.

Given this situation, is it surprising to find that people turn to forms of self-help to the great extent that is seen in the region?

These observations concerning the relation between local custom and the laws of the nation as applied in the courts, may provide an explanation for the well known fact that there is more reliance on Aga influence and power as we move further away from major centers of administration, such as Diyarbakır, Mardin, or Urfa. There is also correspondingly greater interest in the role of religious or pious personages, such as *Seyhs,* who represent local interests and morality as opposed to the judges or even the *mufti,* who are inevitably (and correctly) identified with the national administration. The use of local personnel with a knowledge of local custom and language goes a long way to bridge the hiatus between the villagers and the administration, but it is also clear that such persons are not very numerous. Nearer the major centers there is clearly much greater interference in the affairs of the local community by the administration, and the landlords do not appear to take over the social control functions of the Aga of the more distant or tribal districts. But unfortunately enough, the situation is probably worst in the regions near such centers as Diyarbakır, where the landlord has fewer traditional responsibilities toward the village community and where, as a result of mechanization, the interests of the two groups have clashed in a manner difficult to reconcile.

This then is the background for landlord village relations in the Diyarbakır region. It should be clear that without much greater improvement in (1) communications (physical and linguistic), (2) schools (to close the gap between national law and local custom), (3) better administration (more, and more effective establishment of, law and order), (4) land settlement (cadastral survey or title insurance), as well as the settlements of rights and obligations between landlord and villagers to provide effective security of title, there can be no end to arbitrary rule, violence, and deep-seated social malaise in the Southeast of Turkey. The social ills inherited from the Ottoman Empire continue unabated in the Republic (Gökalp's own writings are a powerful testimony) and will continue without change unless the responsibility for this state of affairs is placed squarely where it belongs — on inefficient, unimaginative, and uninformed administration.[14]

[14] I would like to record my deep appreciation of the help, hospitality, and great assistance of my many friends in Diyarbakır. One of the great pleasures of working in an intellectual center such as Diyarbakır was the privilege of the intellectual companionship of such remarkable men as Sevket Beysanoglu — who has numerous invaluable volumes to his name on the intellectual and social history and geography of the city — Vefik Pirinccioglu, and Metin Cizreli, both MPs who have a real understanding of the problems of the region; Kenan Koseoglu, then the Judge of Bismil; M. Salih Tanriverdi, the Mufti of Diyarbakir; all of whom gave me their friendship and great hospitality. I had many fascinating discussions with Recai Kutan, the energetic director of the DSI in the Southeast, and with M. Fahreddin Kirzioglu. The great hospitality of Edip and Nejat Pirinccioglu, the generous friendship of Kemal Icmen and Abuzer Bey is recalled with gratitude. The same should be said of many others in the villages who gave me constant hospitality and veritable feasts and made my work in the Southeast a personally memorable event. The work was made possible by the generosity of the Rockefeller Foundation and the University of Chicago. The responsibility for the views expressed and the shortcomings of the paper belong, of course, entirely to the author.

REFERENCES

Barkan, Ömer Lutfi. *XV ve XVI inci Asirlarda Osmanlı Imporatorlugunda Zirai Ekonominin Hukuki ve Mali Esaslari.* Istanbul, 1945.

Barth, Fredrik. *Principles of Social Organization in Southern Kurdistan.* Oslo, 1953.

Beysanoglu, Sevket. *Ziya Gökalp'in Ilk Yazı Hayatı (1894-1909) Talebelik Devrine ait yazıları ile Diyarbekir-Peyman-Dicle Gazetelerinde cıkan yazıları ve Saki Ibrahim Destanı.* Istanbul, 1956.

Beysanoglu, Sevket. *Diyarbakır Cografyası.*

Evans-Pritchard, E. E. *The Sanusi of Cyrenaica.* Oxford, 1949.

"Kara-Amid: Ziya Gökalp Sayısı," *Kara-Amid.* September, 1956. Istanbul.

Karpat, Kemal. *Turkey's Politics: The Transition to a Multi-Party System.* Princeton, 1959.

Leach, E. R. *Social and Political Organization of the Ruwanduz Kurds.* London, 1940.

Lewis, Bernard. *The Emergence of Modern Turkey.* London, O. U. P., 1961.

Lambton, A. K. S. *Landlord and Peasant in Persia.* London, O. U. P., 1953.

Pierce, J. *Life in a Turkish Village.* New York, 1964.

Stirling, P. *Turkish Village.* London, 1963.

Bibliography

G. E. VON GRUNEBAUM

BOOKS AND ARTICLES

1936

1. "Die Jahre 78-177 A. H. in Ibn Katīrs Weltgeschichte al-Bidāya wa'n-Nihāya." ["On the Years A. H. 78-177 in Ibn Katīr's History of the World."] *Wiener Zeitschrift für die Kunde des Morgenlandes,* XLIII (1936): 195-210.

1937

2. *Die Wirklichkeitweite der früharabischen Dichtung. Eine literaturwissenschaftliche Unterschung.* [*Growth of Early Arabic Poetry. A Literary Inquiry.*] Vienna, 1937, 264 pp. (*Beihefte zur Wiener Zeitschrift für die Kunde des Morgenlandes,* Heft 3.)
3. "Von Muhammads Wirkung und Originalität." ["On Muhammad's Influence and Originality."] *WZKM* XLIV (1937): 29-50.
4. "Bemerkungen zum Schlussteil der Hudailitenlieder." ["Some Remarks on the Hudailian Poems."] *WZKM* XLIV (1937): 221-225.
5. "Eine Bemerkung zu den Anfängen neupersischer Dichtung." ["A Note on the Beginnings of Modern Persian Poetry."] *WZKM* XLIV (1937): 226.
6. "Begriff und Aufgaben der arabischen Literaturwissenschaft." ["Theory and Problems of Arabian Literary History."] *Archív Orientální,* Prague, IX (1937): 146-152.

7. "Eine poetische Polemik zwischen Byzanz und Bagdad im 10. Jahrhundert." ["A Poetical Feud between Byzantium and Bagdad in the 10th Century."] *Analecta Orientalia,* Rome, XIV (1937): 41-64.

1939

8. "Bis̲h̲r b. abī K̲h̲āzim: Collection of His Fragments." *Journal of the Royal Asiatic Society,* London (1939): 533-567.
9. "Zur Chronologie der früharabischen Dichtung." ["On the Chronology of Early Arabian Poetry."] *Orientalia,* Rome, n.s., VIII (1939): 328-345.

1940

10. "The Early Development of Islamic Religious Poetry." *Journal of the American Oriental Society* LX (1940): 23-29.
11. "Exodus 23:19 in an Arabic Rhetoric." *Jewish Quarterly Review,* Philadelphia, n.s. XXXI (1940-41): 405-406.

1941

12. "On the Development of the Type of Scholar in Early Islam." In *Corona, Studies in . . . Celebration of . . . S. Singer.* Durham, N. C.: Duke University Press, 1941, pp. 142-247.
13. "Arabic Literary Criticism in the Tenth Century A.D." *JAOS* LXI (1941): 51-57.
14. "Al-Mubarrad's Epistle on Poetry and Prose." (The Oldest Arabic Work on Rhetoric. Edition of the Arabic text.) *Orientalia,* n.s. X (1941): 372-382.

1942

15. "The Present State of Investigation in the Field of Pre-Islamic Poetry." *The Moslem World* XXXII (1942): 147-153.
16. "Greek Form Elements in the Arabian Nights." *JAOS* LXII (1942): 277-292.

1943

17. "A note on Arabic Dream Interpretation." *Psychoanalytic Review* XXX (1943), pp. 146-147.

18. "The Cultural Development of the Arabic Countries, 1918-1939." *World Economics,* Washington, D. C., I (1943): 56-62.

1944

19. "On the Origin and Early Development of Arabic *muzdawij* Poetry." *JNES* III (1944): 9-13.
20. "Observations on City Panegyrics in Arabic Prose." *JAOS* LXIV (1944): 61-65.
21. "Growth and Structure of Arabic Poetry, 500-1000 A.D." In *The Arab Heritage.* Edited by N. A. Faris. Princeton, N.J.: Princeton University Press, 1944, pp. 121-141.
22. "Persian Literature." *Encyclopedia Americana,* 1968.
23. "Persische Wörter in arabischen Gedichten." ["Persian Words in Arabic Poems."] *Le Monde Oriental,* Uppsala, XXXI (1937 — actually published in 1944): 18-22.
24. "The Concept of Plagiarism in Arabic Theory." *JNES* III (1944): 234-253.

1945

25. "The Response to Nature in Arabic Poetry." *JNES* IV (1945): 137-151.
26. "As-Sakkākī on Milieu and Thought." *JAOS* LXV (1945): 62.

1946

27. *Medieval Islam. A Study in Cultural Orientation.* Chicago: University of Chicago Press, 1946, 365 pp.
    a. Second ed., 3rd printing, 1953; 378 pp.
    b. Fourth printing 1954.
    c. Ar. translation: *Hadārat al-islām.* Translated by ᶜAbd al-ᶜAziz Taufīq. Cairo, n.d. (1957), 511 pp. (Collection: *Alf kitāb*).
    d. Ch. 4, 5, and 6 included in *Introduction to Islamic Civilization, Course Syllabus and Selected Readings* by M. G. S. Hodgson. Chicago: University of Chicago Press, 1958, pp. 67-97, 101-140, 394-415 respectively.
28. "The Arab Contribution to Troubadour Poetry." *Bulletin of the*

Iranian Institute, New York, VI-VII (1946): 138-151. (Issued also as a separate booklet.)

29. "A Contribution of a Medieval Scholar to the Problem of Learning." In collaboration with T. M. Abel. *Journal of Personality* XV (1946-47): 59-69.

1947

30. "Attempts at Self-Interpretation in Contemporary Islam." In *Approaches to Group Understanding.* Proceedings of the Sixth Conference on Science, Philosophy and Religion. New York: Harper's 1946 (issued 1947), pp. 785-820.
31. *Az-Zarnūjī: Instruction of the Student — the Method of Learning.* Translated with an Introduction. In collaboration with T. M. Abel. New York: King's Crown Press, 1947, 78 pp.
32. Cooperation on: *Palestine. A Study of Jewish, Arab and British Policies.* New Haven: Yale University Press, 1947, 1237 pp.
33. "Transformation of Culture as Illustrated by the Rise of Islam." In *Conflict of Power in Modern Culture.* Proceedings of the Seventh Conference on Science, Philosophy and Religion. New York: Harper, 1947 (issued 1948), pp. 218-224.

1948

34. "Three Arabic Poets of the Early Abbasid Age. The Collected Fragments of Mutī' b. Iyās, Salm al-Hāsir and Abū 'š-Šamaqmaq. Part I: Mutī' b. Iyās." *Orientalia,* n.s. XVII (1948): 160-204.
35. "The Nature of Arab Literary Effort." *JNES* VII (1948): 116-122.
36. "Nationalist and Internationalist Tendencies in Islam." In *Learning and World Peace.* Proceedings of the Eighth Conference on Science, Philosophy and Religion. New York and London: Harper, 1948, pp. 565-570. Reprinted in *The Moslem World and the West.* Chicago: The University of Chicago Round Table, No. 784, Apr. 19, 1953, pp. 10-15.
37. "Abū Du^{c}ād al-Iyādī: Collection of His Fragments. Part I." *WZKM* LI (1948): 83-105.

1949

38. "Islam in a Humanistic Education." *Journal of General Education* IV (1949): 12-31.

1950

39. "Three Arabic Poets of the Early Abbasid Age. Part II: Salm al-Ḫāsir." *Orientalia*, n.s., XIX (1950): 53-80.
40. *A Tenth-Century Document of Arabic Literary Theory and Criticism.* The sections on poetry of al-Bāqillānī's I'jāz al-Qur'ān translated and annotated. Chicago: University of Chicago Press, 1950, 128 pp.
41. "Attempts at Self-Interpretation in Contemporary Islam." In *Perspectives on a Troubled Decade.* Proceedings of the Tenth Conference on Science, Philosophy and Religion. New York: Harper, 1950, pp. 135-184.
42. "Islam and Hellenism." *Scientia* XLIV (1950): 21-27 (French ed., pp. 11-16).

1951

43. *Muhammadan Festivals.* New York: H. Schuman, 1951, 106 pp. (English ed., 1958, n.p.)
44. "Progress and Prospect in Arabic Studies. Islamic Literature: Arabic." In *Near Eastern Culture and Society.* Edited by T. C. Young. Princeton, N.J.: Princeton University Press, 1951, pp. 48-65.

1952

45. "The Aesthetic Foundation of Arabic Literature." *Comparative Literature* IV (1952): 323-340.
46. "Abū Duᶜād al-Iyādī: Collection of His Fragments. Part II." *WZKM* LI (1952): 249-282.
47. "Avicenna's Risāla fī 'l-ᶜišq and Courtly Love." *JNES* XI (1952): 233-238.

1953

48. "Islamkunde und Kulturwissenschaft." In *Islam und Kultur-*

forschung. Bericht über die Tagung "Islamkunde und Kulturwissenschaft." Mainz, June 28-29, 1952. Wiesbaden, 1953, pp. 2-16. (With *ZDMG,* CIII, no. 1, 1953) Trans. as "Islamic Studies and Cultural Research" in *Islamic Cultural History.* Edited by G. E. von Grunebaum ("Comparative Studies in Cultures and Civilizations," No. 2, American Anthropological Association, Memoir 76), Menasha, Wis., 1954, pp. 1-22.

49. "Government in Islam." In *Freedom and Authority in Our Time.* Proceedings of the Twelfth Conference on Science, Philosophy and Religion. New York: Harper, 1953, pp. 701-716.

50. "Three Arabic Poets of the Early Abbasid Age. Part III. Abū 'š-Šamaqmaq." *Orientalia,* n.s. XXII (1953): 262-283.

51. "Firdausī's Concept of History." In *Mélanges Fuad Köprülü.* Istanbul, 1953, pp. 177-193.

52. "The Spirit of Islam as Shown in Its Literature." *Studia Islamica,* I (1953): 101-119.

1954

53. "The Literary Views of Ibn abī ᶜAun (d. 934)." In *Westösliche Abhandlungen.* Festschrift für R. Tschudi. Wiesbaden, 1954, pp. 225-230.

54. "Persian Literature." *The Encyclopedia Americana.* XXI: 628-629d. New York, Chicago, Washington, D. C., 1954.

1955

55. "Idéologie musulmane et esthétique arabe." *Studia Islamica.* III (1955): 5-23.

56. "Die islamische Stadt." *Saeculum* VI (1955): 138-153.

57. *Islam. Essays in the Nature and Growth of a Cultural Tradition.* Menasha, Wis., and London: Routledge and Kegan Paul, 1955, 260 pp.

   a. Pp. 226-237 "The Intellectual Problem of Contemporary Islam" reprinted in *The University of Chicago Round Table,* No. 887, April 4, 1955, pp. 13-17.

   b. Pp. 85-90 reprinted in *Islamic Literature* VIII, no. 2 (Lahore, 1956): 25-30.

c. Pp. 141-148 "The Structure of the Muslim Town" partially reprinted in *Landscape* VII, no. 3 (Spring, 1958): 1-4.

d. "Du Governement en Islam." Trans. by G. H. Bousquet and Annie Munpère. *Revue Algérienne,* No. 4 (1958): 2-13.

58. "Westernization in Islam and the Theory of Cultural Borrowing." In *Islam: Essays in the Nature and Growth of a Cultural Tradition.* Menasha, Wis., and London: Routledge and Kegan Paul, 1955, pp. 237-246. Arabic trans. *Ta'aṯhṯhur al-umam al-islāmiyyah bi-madaniyyat al-gharb wa nazariyyat al-istimdād al-ṯhaqāfī, in Al-ṯhaqāfa 'l-islāmiyyah wa'l-ḥayāt al-mu^c^āsirah.* Edited by Muhammad Ḵhalaf Allāh. Cairo, n.d. (1956), pp. 184-194, summary on p. 566.

59. *Kritik und Dichtkunst. Studien zur arabischen Literaturgeschichte.* Wiesbaden: Harrassowitz, 1955, 161 pp.

60. Introductory chapter, "The Problem: Unity in Diversity," pp. 17-37, in *Unity and Variety in Muslim Civilization.* Edited by G. E. von Grunebaum. Chicago: University of Chicago Press, 1955, 385 pp.

61. "The Muslim Town and the Hellenistic Town." *Scientia* IL (1955): 1-7. (French ed. pp. 1-7.)

62. "Arabic Poetics." *Indiana University Conference on Oriental-Western Literary Relations.* Edited by H. Frenz & G. L. Anderson. University of North Carolina Studies in Comparative Literature, XIII: 27-46. Chapel Hill, 1955, pp. 27-46.

63. "Muslim World View and Muslim Science." In *Islam: Essays in the Nature and Growth of a Cultural Tradition.* Menasha, Wis., and London: Routledge and Kegan Paul, 1955, pp. 111-126.

64. "Aspects of Arabic Urban Literature Mostly in the 9th and 10th Centuries." *Al-Andalus* XX (1955): 259-281.

1956

65. "The Intellectual Problem of Contemporary Islam." *Islamic Literature, VIII* (Lahore, Feb. 1956): 25-30.

66. "The Problem of Cultural Influence." In *Charisteria orientalia praecipue ad Persiam pertinentia.* Rypka Vol., Prague, 1956,

pp. 86-99. German ed. *Der Islam und das Problem kultureller Beeinflussung.* Wissenschaftliche Zeitschrift der Martin Luther Universität. Halle-Wittenberg, Gesellschafts- und -sprachwissenschaftliche Reihe, VI (1956-57): 19-26.

67. "Fall and Rise of Islam. A Self-View (Nadwī, *Ma dā hasara 'l-ᶜalām bi' nhitāt al-muslimīn?*)." *Studi orientalistici in onore de Giorgio Levi Della Vida* I: 420-433. Rome, 1956.

68. "Lírica románica before the Arab Conquest." *Al-Andalus* XXI (1956): 403-405.

1957

69. "Problems of Muslim Nationalism." In *Islam and the West.* Edited by R. N. Frye. The Hague, 1957, pp. 7-29.

70. Articles: al-ᶜAbbās B. Mirdās, Abu Dhuᶜaib al-Hudhalī, Abū 'š-Šamaqmaq. Abū Dulāma, 'Alkama b. ᶜAbada, Aᶜshà Hamdān, *Encyclopaedia of Islam.* New Edition. Leiden, 1960.

71. "Ralph Marcus (1900-1956)." *JNES* XVI (1957): 143-144.

72. "Le concept de classicisme culturel." In *Classicisme et déclin culturel dans l'histoire de l'Islam.* Actes du Symposium International d'Histoire de la Civilisation Musulmane (Bordeaux, 25-29 juin 1956). Edited by R. Brunschvig and G. E. von Grunebaum. Paris, 1957, pp. 1-27.

1958

73. "Der islamische Kulturkreis in seiner inneren Struktur (750-1550)." *Historia Mundi* (Bern-Francke) VI (1958): 536-556.

74. "Betrachtungen zu einem neuen Buch über den Mittleren Osten." In *The Middle East in Transition.* Edited by W. Z. Laqueur. London, 1958. *NZZ,* 18 Oct. 1958.

75. "Rückblick auf drei internationale islamische Tagungen." *Neue Zürcher Zeitung,* March 8 and 9, 1958, pp. 1-3.
    a. Republished in *Der Islam* XXXIV (1959): 138-149.
    b. English trans, "Three Moslem Conferences in Retrospect," *Swiss Review of World Affairs* VIII, nos. 2-3 (May and June, 1958).

1959

76. "Die politische Rolle der Universität im Nahen Osten, am Beispiel Aegyptens beleuchtet." In *Universität und moderne Gesellschaft*. Edited by Chauncy D. Harris and Max Horkheimer. Frankfurt: Ludwig Oehms, 1959, pp. 88-98.
77. "Bayan." *Encyclopaedia of Islam*. 2nd ed., 1959.
78. "Balāgha." *Encyclopaedia of Islam*. 2nd ed., 1959.
79. *The Comprehensive Dictionary of the Cairene Academy*. Al-Mu^{c}jam al-Kabīr by Murad Kāmil and Ibrāhīm al-Ibyari. *JNES* XVIII, no. 2 (1959): 157-159.
80. "Der Islam in unserer Zeit. Zu einer Internationalen Konferenz in Karachi." *Neue Zürcher Zeitung*, 27 March, 1959.
81. "Ceylon und seine muslimische Minderheit." *Neue Zürcher Zeitung*, 11 April 1959.
82. "Das geistige Problem der Verwestlichung in der arabischen Welt." *Saeculum* X, no.3 (1959): 289-327.
83. "A Statement on the Occasion of the Al-Mas'udi Millenary Celebrations at Aligarh, 18 January 1958." Aligarh Muslim University, Aligarh, India.
84. *Dirāsāt fī 'l-adab al-^{c}arbī*. Beirut, 1959. Trans. under the supervision of M. Y. Najm, 387 pp. (Studies in Arabic Literature.) Translations, in part revised, of nos. 60, 70, 63, 62; 13, 75; 23, 27, 31, 22; 42 and 61.
85. "Aly, Mazahéri, So lebten die Muselmanen in Mittelalter." Stuttgart, 1957. Deutsche Verlagsanstalt, 339 pp. In *Der Islam*, XXXIV, 1959.
86. *Three Abbasid Poets*. Translation and re-edition, *Shu^{c}ara' ^{c}Abbasiyyun*, Beirut, 1959.

1960

87. "Von Begriff und Bedeutung eines Kulturklassizismus." In *Klassizismus und Kulturverfall*. Edited by Gustav von Grunebaum. Klosterman, 1960, pp. 5-43.
88. "Toynbee's Concept of Islamic Civilization." *WZKM* (Festschrift Herbert W. Duda) LVI (1960): 68-77.

89. "Besuch in Alma-Ata." *Neue Zürcher Zeitung,* 3541, 16 Oct. 1960.

90. "Islam: Its Inherent Power of Expansion and Adaptation." In *City Invincible.* Chicago: University of Chicago Press, 1960, pp. 437-448.

91. "Statement" in *al-Masʿūdī Millenary Commemoration Volume.* Edited by S. M. Ahmad and A. Rahman. Aligarh Muslim University, Aligarh, India, 1960, pp. 137-139.

1961

92. "Nationalism and Cultural Trends in the Arab Near East." *Studia Islamica, fasc.* XIV (1961): 121-153.

93. Preface, Arabic translation of *Unity and Variety in Muslim Civilization,* Beirut, 1961.

94. "Kulturwandel in arabischer Sicht." *Die Welt des Islam und die Gegenwart.* Edited by R. Paret. Stuttgart, 1961, pp. 179-192.

95. *Islam. Essays in the Nature and Growth of a Cultural Tradition.* London: Routledge, Kegan Paul, 1961, 266 pp.

96. "Toynbee's Concept of Islamic Civilization." In *The Intent of Toynbee's History.* Edited by E. T. Gargan. Chicago: Loyola University Press, 1961, pp. 97-110.

97. "The Face of the Antagonist." In *Twelfth-Century Europe and the Foundations of Modern Society.* Madison: University of Wisconsin Press, 1961.

98. *Medieval Islam.* Phoenix Books, 1961. Published jointly by University of Chicago Press and University of Toronto Press.

99. Foreword to *The Principles of State and Government in Islam,* by Muhammad Asad. Berkeley and Los Angeles: University of California Press, 1961, pp. v-viii.

1962

100. *L'Islam médiéval.* Paris: Payot, 1962, 380 pp.

101. "The Sacred Character of Islamic Cities," *Mélanges Taha Husain.* Cairo, 1962.

102. "Self-Image and Approach to History." In *Historians of the Middle East.* Edited by B. Lewis and P. M. Holt. New York: Oxford University Press, 1962.

103. "Pluralism in the Islamic World," *Islamic Studies* I, no. 2 (June, 1962): 37-59.

104. "Byzantine Iconoclasm and the Influence of the Islamic Environment." *History of Religions* II, no. 1 (1962): 1-10.

105. *Modern Islam: The Search for Cultural Identity.* Berkeley and Los Angeles: University of California Press, 1962, 303 pp.

106. "Le Problème des échanges culturels." In *Etudes d'Orientalisme dédiées à la mémoire de Lévi-Provencal.* Tome I, Maisonneuve et Larose, 1962, pp. 141-151.

107. "An Analysis of Islamic Civilization and Cultural Anthropology." *Colloque sur la Sociologie Musulmane,* 11-14 Septembre 1961 (Correspondance d'Orient No. 5). Publications du Centre pour l'Etude des Problèmes du Monde Musulman Contemporain, pp. 1-53.

108. "Acculturation as a Theme in Contemporary Arab Literature." *Diogenes* 39 (1962): 84-118. Also French translation, *Diogène* 39 (1962): 97-137; Spanish trans., pp. 95-129.

109. "Concept and Function of Reason in Islamic Ethics." *Oriens* XV (1962): 1-17.

1963

110. "Der Islam: seine Expansion im Nahen und Mittleren Osten, Afrika und Spanien." *Propyläen-Weltgeschichte* V (1963): 21-179.

111. *Der Islam im Mittelalter* (revised and enlarged German edition of *Medieval Islam*). Zurich-Stuttgart, 1963, 652 pp. (Bibliothek des Morgenlandes.)

112. "Reflections on the Community Aspect of the Muslim Identification." *International Islamic Colloquium, December 29, 1957 — January 8, 1958.* Lahore, 1960, pp. 39-42. (Actually published in 1963.)

113. "Der Einfluss des Islam auf die Entwicklung der Medizin." *Bustan* 3 (1963): 19-22.

114. "The Arabian Nights." In *Midway,* No. 14, Chicago, 1963, pp. 40-63. (Taken from Chapter IX, "Creative Borrowing: Greece in the Arabian Nights" in *Medieval Islam,* 2nd edition, pp. 294-319.)

115. *Unity and Variety in Muslim Civilization* (Persian trans. by Abbass Aryanpour: Waḥdet wa-tanawwu[c] dar tamaddun-i Islāmī), Tabriz, Iran, 1963.

116. Introduction to *The Principles of State and Government in Islam* by Muhammad Asad (Urdu trans.). Lahore, 1963, pp. 1-5.

117. "The Nature of Arab Unity before Islam." *Arabica* X, no. 1 (Leiden, 1963): 5-23.

1964

118. Bengali translation of *A Tenth Century Document of Arabic Literary Theory and Criticism.* East Pakistan, Bengali Academy, 1964.

119. Preface *Muslim Communities in Gujarat* by S. C. Misra. Bombay: Asia Publishing House, 1964.

120. "Hellenistic and Muslim Views on Cities." In *Economic Development and Cultural Change* III, no. 1 (Oct. 1954). Bobbs-Merrill Reprint Series in Social Science, S-484.

121. Article on fasāha in the *Encyclopaedia of Islam.* New Ed., Vol. II, fasc. 35, Leiden-London, 1964, pp. 824-827.

122. "La Letteratura Franco-Africana e la sua Inserzione nella Cultura Occidentale." *Oriente Moderno* LXIV, no. 34 (Mar.-Apr. 1964): 280-299.

123. Introduction to *Principles of State and Government* by Muhammad Asad. Translated into Indonesian. Djakarta, 1964.

124. "L'Expérience du sacré et la conception de l'homme dans l'Islam." *Diogène* 48 (Oct.-Déc. 1964): 82-101.

125. *French African Literature. Some Cultural Implications.* The Hague: Mouton & Co., 1964, 41 pp.

126. *Modern Islam. The Search for Cultural Identity.* New York: Vintage Books, 1964.

127. "Parallelism, Convergence, and Influence in the Relations of

Arab and Byzantine Philosophy, Literature, and Piety." *Dumbarton Oaks Papers,* No. 18, Washington, D. C., 1964, 91-111.

128. "The Inherent Adaptive Potentialities of Islam." In *Islam in the Modern World.* Dacca and Karachi, 1964, pp. 42-57.

129. Introduction to *Los sueños y las sociedades humanas.* Editorial Sudamericana Sociedad Anonima. Buenos Aires, 1964, pp. 7-32.

1965

130. "Acculturation and Self-Realization." In *The Contemporary Middle East.* Edited by Benjamin Rivlin and Joseph S. Szyliowicz. New York: Random House, 1965, pp. 141-148.

131. "The Body Politic: Law and the State." In *Readings in World Civilization,* Vol. 3. Prepared and edited by Young Hum Kim and Woodrow C. Whitten. Division of Basic Studies, California Western University, 1965, pp. 267-283.

132. "Islam: Religion, Power, Civilization." In *Bucknell Review* XIII, no. 3 (1965): 32-38.

133. "Specialization." In *Arabic and Islamic Studies in Honor of Hamilton A. R. Gibb.* Edited by G. Makdisi. Leiden, 1965, pp. 285-292.

134. "L'Espansione dell'Islam: La Struttura della nuova Fede." In *Settimane di studio del Centro italiano di studi sull'alto medioevo, L'Occidente e l'Islam nell'alto medioevo.* Spoleto, 2-8 aprile 1964. Spoleto, 1965, pp. 65-91, discussione: pp. 337-348.

135. *Islam. Experience of the Holy and Concept of Man.* Berkeley and Los Angeles: University of California Press, 1965, 39 pp.

1966

136. "Muslim Civilisation in the Abbasid Period." In *Cambridge Medieval History,* Ch. XVI, Vol. IV, Pt. 1, pp. 662-695; also Bibliography, pp. 1014-1027. Cambridge: Cambridge University Press, 1966.

137. *Unity and Variety in Muslim Civilization.* In Arabic, translated by Sidqī Hamdī. Dar Al Mutanabbi, Baghdad, 1966, 552 pp.

138. "The First Expansion of Islam: Factors of Thrust and Containment." *Diogenes* 53 (1966): 64-72.

139. "The Place of Parapsychological Phenomena in Islam." *International Journal of Parapsychology* VIII, no. 2 (Spring, 1966): 264-280.

140. "Problems of Muslim Nationalism (1954)." In *Social Change: The Colonial Situation.* Edited by Immanuel Wallerstein. Wiley: New York, London, Sydney, 1966, pp. 658-674. Reprinted from *Islam and the West.* Edited by R. N. Frye. The Hague: Mouton & Co., 1959, pp. 7-29.

141. *Der Islam in seiner klassischen Epoche, 622-1258.* Zurich-Stuttgart: Artemis, 1966, 318 pp. (Bibliothek des Morgenlandes.)

142. "Islam: The Problem of Changing Perspective." In *The Transformation of the Roman World.* Edited by Lynn White, Jr. Berkeley and Los Angeles: University of California Press, 1966, pp. 147-178.

143. *The Dream and Human Societies.* Edited by G. E. von Grunebaum and Roger Caillois. Berkeley and Los Angeles: University of California Press, 1966. Foreword, pp. v-vi; Introduction, "The Cultural Function of the Dream as Illustrated by Classical Islam," pp. 3-21.

144. "The World of Islam: The Face of the Antagonist." In *Twelfth-Century Europe and the Foundations of Modern Society.* Edited by M. Clagett. Madison: University of Wisconsin Press, 1966, pp. 189-211.

145. *Il sogno e le civiltà umane.* Edited by G. E. von Grunebaum and Roger Caillois. Bari, Editori Laterza, 1966. Il sogno e le civiltà umane, pp. 3-25.

145a. "Islam in a Humanistic Education." In *The Traditional Near East.* Edited by J. Stewart-Robinson. Englewood Cliffs, N.J.: Prentice-Hall, 1966, pp. 36-68.

145b. Foreword to *The Principles of State and Government in Islam* by M. Asad. Bengali translation "Islam-E-Rashtro-O-Sharkar Parichalonar Mulniti," 1966.

1967

146. "The First Expansion of Islam: Factors of Thrust and Containment." *Nord-Sud,* Colloque tenu les 16 et 17 septembre 1965

à Copenhague à l'occasion de la VIIIe Assemblée Générale du C.I.P.S.H. Copenhagen, 1967, pp. 47-55.

147. "The First Expansion of Islam: Factors of Thrust and Containment." *Islamic Literature* XIII, pt. 6 (Lahore, June 1967): 49-58.

148. "Randbemerkungen zum Internationalen Orientalistenkongress." In *Neue Zürcher Zeitung,* Monday, Sept. 18, 1967.

149. *Unity and Variety in Muslim Civilization* (editor and contributor). Chicago: University of Chicago Press, 1967 (4th impression).

150. *Le Rêve et les sociétés humaines.* Edited by G. E. von Grunebaum and Roger Caillois. Paris: Editions Gallimard, 1967. Introduction: "La Fonction culturelle du rêve dans l'Islam classique," pp. 7-20.

151. "Islam: Religion, Power, Civilization. A Note." In *Der Orient* in der Forschung, Festschrift für Otto Spies zum 5. April 1966. Edited by Wilhelm Hoenerbach. Wiesbaden, 1967, pp. 233-239.

1968

152. "Presentation" in *Arabic Writing Today. The Short Story,* Cairo, 1968, pp. 13-14.

153. "L'Islam. Traduzione di Maria Attardo Magrini in I. Propilei, Grande Storia Universale Mondadori a cura di Golo Mann e August Nitschke." Vol. quinto *L'Islam: La Nascita dell'Europa,* Mondadori, 1968, p. 13-203.

154. Preface to *Arabische Literaturgeschichte* by Gibb and Landau. Zurich and Stuttgart: Artemis, 1968, pp. 5-9.

155. "Philosophie der Einzelsprache." *Festschrift Werner Caskel zum siebzigsten Geburtstag 5. März 1966.* Edited by Erwin Gräf. Leiden: Brill, 1968, pp. 145-149.

156. "Die Kulturfunktion des Traumes im klassischen Islam." *Bustan* 3-4 (Vienna, 1968): 50-58.

1969

157. "The Source of Islamic Civilization." *Der Islam* XLVI (1969): 1-53.

158. "Some Recent Constructions and Reconstructions of Islam." In *The Conflict of Traditionalism and Modernism in the Muslim Middle East*. Edited by Carl Leiden. Austin, Texas: University of Texas Humanities Research, 1969, pp. 141-160.

159. "Literature in the Context of Islamic Civilization." *Oriens* XX (1967 —, published 1969), pp. 1-14.

160. *Studien zum Kulturbild und Selbstverständnis des Islams.* Zurich: Artemis, 1969, 481 pp.

161. Islam, *Das Fortwirken der Antike in unsere Gegenwart* (Artemis-Symposion). Zurich-Stuttgart: Artemis, 1969, pp. 69-86.

162. Aspects of Arabic Urban Literature Mostly in Ninth and Tenth Centuries, *Islamic Studies* (Journal of the Islamic Research Institute of Pakistan) VIII, No. 4 (Dec. 1969): 281-300.

163. Article on I^cd̲jāz in *The Encyclopaedia of Islam.* New Ed., Vol. III, fasc. 55-56, Leiden-London, 1969, 1018-1020.

1970

164. *Classical Islam.* London: Allen and Unwin; Chicago: Aldine, 1970, 244 pp.

165. *Muslim Self-Statement in India and Pakistan, 1857-1968.* Edited by Aziz Ahmad and G. E. von Grunebaum. Wiesbaden: Harrassowitz, 1970, 240 pp.

166. The Sources of Islamic Civilization, *Der Islam* XLVI, 1-2 (1970): 1-54.

167. Approaching Islam: A Digression, *Middle East Studies,* London (1970) VI, 2: 127-149.

168. In Memoriam. Joseph Schacht (15 March 1902-1 August 1969), *International Journal of Middle East Studies* 1, No. 2 (April 1970): 190-191.

169. Editor and contributor (Presentation, pp. 1-4; Introduction, pp. 5-7) *Logic in Classical Islamic Culture,* First Giorgio Levi Della Vida Biennial Conference. Wiesbaden: Harrassowitz, 1970.

170. The Sources of Islamic Civilization in *The Cambridge History of Islam,* Vol. 2, Cambridge University Press, 1970, pp. 469-510.

171. Preface to Gibb and Landau, *Arabische Literaturgeschichte,* Hebrew Edition, Tel-Aviv, 1970, pp. 9-11.

172. Observations on the Muslim Concept of Evil, *Studia Islamica* XXXI (1970): 117-134.

REVIEWS

1936

1. W. Ivanow. *Kalami Pir. A Treatise on Ismaili Doctrine.* Bombay, Islamic Research Association Series, No. 4, 1935. *Wiener Zeitschrift für die Kunde des Morgenlandes* XLIV (1936): 142-143.
2. Sir E. Denison Ross. *The Journal of Robert Stodart.* London: Luzac and Co., 1935. *WZKM* XLIV (1936): 143.
3. M.-S. Meïssa. *Le Message du pardon d'Abou 'l^c^Ala de Maarra.* Paris: Librairie Orientaliste Paul Geuthner, 1932. *WZKM* XLIV (1936): 143-144.
4. A. R. Nykl and Ibrāhim Ṭūqān, eds. *Kitāb al-Zahrah by al-Iṣfahānī.* Studies in Ancient Oriental Civilization, No. 6. Chicago: University of Chicago Press, 1932. *WZKM* XLIV (1936): 144-145.
5. Miguel Asin Palacios. *La Espiritualidad de Algazel y su sentido cristiano.* Publicaciones de las escuelas de estudios arabes de Madrid y Granada, Serie A, No. 2. Madrid: Estanislao Maestre, 1934-35. *WZKM* XLIV (1936): 145-146.

1937

6. Abraham S. Halkin, trans. *Moslem Schisms and Sects by al-Baghdādī.* Tel Aviv: Luzac and Co., 1935. *WZKM* XLIV (1937): 305-306.
7. Régis Blachère, trans. *Livre des Catégories des Nations by Sā^c^id al-Andalusī.* Publications de l'Institut des Hautes Etudes Marocaines, No. 28. Paris: Larose, 1935. *WZKM* XLIV (1937): 306-307.
8. Salomon Pines. *Beiträge zur islamischen Atomenlehre.* Berlin: Harrassowitz, 1936. *WZKM* XLIV (1937): 307.
9. Walther Hinz. *Irans Aufstieg zum Nationalstaat im 15. Jahr-*

hundert. Berlin u. Leipzig: De Gruyter, 1936. *WZKM* XLIV (1937): 308.

10. Edward Edwards, ed. *The Collected Poems of Ẕu 'l-Faḳār Shirwānī*. London: British Museum, 1934. *WZKM* XLIV (1937): 308.

1938

11. Al-Mutanabbi. *Recueil publié à l'occasion de son millénaire*. Mémoires de l'Institut Français de Damas. Beyrouth: Institut Français de Damas, 1936. *WZKM* XLV (1938): 146-147.
12. J. Heyworth-Dunne, ed. *Kitāb el-Awrāk by Abu Bakr Muḥammad b. Yaḥya aṣ Ṣūlī*. London: Luzac and Co., 1934 (section on contemporary poets). *WZKM* XLV (1938): 147-148.
13. J. H. Sanders, trans. *Tamerlane or Timur the Great Amir by Ahmad ibn ᶜArabsāh*. London: Luzac and Co., 1936. *WZKM* XLV (1938): 148-149.
14. Helmut Wangelin. *Das arabische Volksbuch vom König aẓ-Ẓāhir Baibars*. Bonner orientalistische Studien Nr. 17. Stuttgart: W. Kohlhammer, 1936. *WZKM* XLV (1938): 150-151.
15. Omar A. Farrukh. *Das Bild des Frühislam in der arabischen Dichtung von der Higra bis zum Tode ᶜUmars*. Leipzig, 1937. *WZKM* XLV (1938): 292-295.
16. Paul Krüger. *Das syrisch-monophysitische Mönchtum im Tur-Ab(h)din von seinen Anfängen bis zur Mitte des 12. Jahrhunderts*. Münster, 1937. *WZKM* XLV (1938):295.
17. J. Heyworth-Dunne, ed. *Ashᶜār awlād al-khulafā' wa akhbānuhum, from the Kitāb al-Awrāk* by Abū Bakr Muḥammad b. Yaḥyā aṣ-Ṣūlī. E. W. J. Gibb Memorial Trust. London: Luzac and Co., 1936. *WZKM* XLV (1938): 295-296.
18. Oskar Löfgren. *Arabische Texte zur Kenntnis der Stadt Aden im Mittelalter*. Uppsala: Almquist and Wiksell, 1936; Leiden: E. J. Brill. *WZKM* XLV (1938):296-297.
19. I. A. Edham. *Abushādy the Poet; a Critical Study*. Edham's Essay No. 6. Berlin: Gustav Fischer, 1937. *WZKM* XLV (1938): 297.
20. Paul Sbath. *Traités religieux, philosophiques et moraux, ex-*

traits des oeuvres d'Isaac de Ninive (VIIe siècle) par Ibn as-Salt (IXe siècle). Le Caire, 1936. *WZKM* XLV (1938): 297-298.

21. *Massime d'Elia Metropolitano di Nisibi (975-1056). Testo arabo curato e pubblicato per la prima volta, con traduzione italiana e francese.* Cairo, 1936. *WZKM* XLV (1938): 297-298.
22. Werner Caskel. *Arabic Inscriptions in the Collection of the Hispanic Society of America.* New York: Hispanic Society, 1936. *WZKM* XLV (1938): 298-299.

1940

23. Muḥammad Rahatullah Khan. *Vom Einfluss des Qur'āns auf die arabische Dichtung. Eine Untersuchung über die dichetrischen Werke von Hassān b. Ṯābit, Ka^c^b b. Mālik und ^c^Abdallāh b. Rawāha.* Leipzig: Harrassowitz, 1938. *Orientalia,* IX, Nova Series, Fasc. 1/2, 1940, pp. 179-182.

1941

24. Haidar Bammate (Georges Revoire). *Visages de l'Islam.* Lausanne: Payot, 1936, 587 pp. *Middle East Journal* I, no. 3 (1941): 337.

1943

25. Faïez J. Aoun. *Fawzi Ma^c^lūf et son oeuvre.* Paris: G.-P. Maisonneuve, 1939, 199 pp. *Orientalia,* XII, Nova Series, Fasc. 1/2, 1943, pp. 178-179.
26. Mohammad E. Moghadam and Yahya Armajani. *Descriptive Catalog of the Garrett Collection of Persian, Turkish and Indic Manuscripts, Including Some Miniatures, in the Princeton University Library.* Princeton Oriental Texts, Vol. VI. Princeton, N.J.: Princeton University Press, 1939, 94 pp. *Orientalia,* XII, Nova Series, Fasc. 1/2, 1943, pp. 179-180.
27. Moshe Brill, D. Neustadt and P. Schusser. *The Basic Word List of the Arabic Daily Newspaper.* Jerusalem: Hebrew University Press Association, 1940, 22+iv pp. *Journal of the American Oriental Society* LXIII, no. 1 (March 1943): 80-81.

28. Philip W. Ireland, ed. *The Near East Problem and Prospects. Lectures on the Harris Foundation.* Chicago: University of Chicago Press, 1942, 266 pp. *The Jewish Social Studies* II, no. 2 (1943): 391-392.

1945

29. A. J. Arberry. *Modern Persian Reader.* Cambridge: Cambridge University Press, 1944, 158 pp. *Journal of Near Eastern Studies* IV, no. 2 (1945): 134.

1946

30. R. Walzer. *Galen, On Medical Experience.* Edition of Arabic version with English translation and notes. Oxford: Oxford University Press, 1944, 164 pp. *Classical Philology* XLI, no.3 (1946): 186-187.

1948

31. M. Gaudefroy-Demombynes, trans. *Ibn Qotaiba's Introduction au livre de la poésie et des poètes. Texte arabe d'après l'édition De Goeje.* Paris: Les Belles Lettres, 1947, 108 pp. *Journal of the American Oriental Society* LXVIII, no. 4 (Oct.-Dec. 1948): 194.
32. Alfred Bloch. *Vers und Sprache im Altarabischen.* Basel: Verlag für Recht und Gesellschaft, 1946, 160 pp. *Muslim World* XXXVIII, no. 2 (1948): 160.
33. A. Yellin and L. Billig. *An Arabic Reader.* Jerusalem: Government of Palestine, Dept. of Educ., 1948, 132 pp. *JNES* VII, no. 4 (1948): 275.
34. Joseph A. Dagher. Manuel pratique de bibliographie et de bibliothéconomie à l'usage des pays du Proche-Orient. Beirut: Joseph A. Dagher, 1944, 634 pp. (Arabic). *JNES* VII, no. 4 (1948): 276.
35. Abū Firās al-Hamdānī. *Le Diwan.* Edited by Sami Dahan. 3 vols. Collection de textes orientaux XI. Beyrouth: Institut Français de Damas, 1944. *JNES* VII, no. 4 (1948): 275-276.
36. Franz Rosenthal. *The Technique and Approach of Muslim Scholarship.* Analecta Orientalia 24. Rome: Pontificum Insti-

tutum Biblicum, 1947, 74 pp. *Speculum* XXIII, no. 3 (1948): 726-727.

1950

37. Phillip K. Hitti. *History of the Arabs,* 4th rev. ed. New York: Macmillan Co., 1949, 767 pp. *JNES* IX, no. 2 (1950): 115.

38. Norman H. Baynes and H. St. L. B. Moss, eds. *Byzantium: An Introduction to East Roman Civilization.* Oxford: Clarendon Press, 1948, 436 pp. *JNES* IX, no. 2 (1950): 116-117.

39. Herbert W. Duda. *Vom Kalifat zur Republik; Die Türkei im 19. und 20. Jahrhundert.* Vienna: Verlag für Jugend und Volk, 1948, 183 pp. *JNES* IX, no. 3 (1950): 186.

40. H. Hickmann. Terminologie Arabe des Instruments de Musique. Cairo, 1947, 37 pp. *JNES* IX, no. 4 (1950): 265.

41. Earl Edgar Elder, ed, and tr. *A Commentary on the Creed of Islam: Sa^c^d al-Din al Taftazani on the Creed of Najm al-Din al-Nasafi.* New York: Columbia University Press, 1950, 187 pp. *Speculum* XXV, no. 4 (1950): 565-566.

1951

42. A. J. Arberry. *Modern Arabic Poetry: An Anthology with English Verse Translations.* Cambridge Oriental Series, No. 1. London: Taylor's Foreign Press, 1950, 70 pp. *Journal of the American Oriental Society* LXXI, no. 2 (Apr.-June): 1951, 1955.

1952

43. Daniel C. Dennett, Jr. *Conversion and the Poll Tax in Early Islam.* Harvard Historical Monograph No. 22. Cambridge, Mass.: Harvard University Press, 1950, 136 pp. *JNES* XI, no. 1 (1952): 87.

44. C. G. Campbell. *Tales from Arab Tribes: A Collection of the Stories Told by the Arab Tribes of the Lower Euphrates.* Illus. by J. Buckland-Wright. New York: Macmillan Co., 1950, 252 pp. *JNES* XI, no. 2 (1952): 146.

45. Charles D. Matthews. *Palestine — Mohammedan Holy Land.* Foreword by Julian Obermann. Yale Oriental Series Vol. 24.

New Haven: Yale University Press, 1949, 176 pp. *JNES* XI, no. 3 (1952): 230-232.

1953

46. N. A. Faris, trans. *The Book of Idols: Being a translation from the Arabic of the Kitāb al-Aṣnām by Hishām ibn al-Kalbi.* Princeton, N.J.: Princeton University Press, 1952, 59 pp. *Journal of the American Oriental Society* LXXIII, no. 1 (Jan.-Mar., 1953): 44-46.

47. Johann Fück. *Arabiya: Untersuchungen zur arabischen Sprache- und Stilgeschichte.* Abhandlungen der sächsischen Akademie der Wissenschaften in Leipzig, Philolog.-hist. Klasse, Bd. XLV, Hft. 1. Berlin: Akademie Verlag, 1950, 148 pp. *JNES* XII, no. 1 (1953): 71-72.

48. Cyril Elgood. *A Medieval History of Persia and the Eastern Caliphate from Earliest Times to the Year A.D. 1932.* Cambridge: Cambridge University Press, 1951, 616 pp. *JNES* XII, no. 2 (1953): 142-143.

49. Chaim Rabin. *Ancient West-Arabian.* London: Taylor's Foreign Press, 1951, 616 pp. *JNES* XII, no. 4 (1953): 298.

50. Reuben Levy, ed. *Kai-ká-ūs b. Iskandar b. Qābūs b. Washmgir, the Nasihat-Nāma known as Qābūs-Nama.* London: Luzac and Co., 1951, 155 pp. *JNES* XII, no. 4 (1953): 293.

1954

51. Max Freiherr von Oppenheim. *Die Beduinen. Bd. III, Teile 1 u. 2, bearbeitet und herausgegeben von Werner Caskel, "Die Beduinenstämme in Nord- und Mittelarabien und im Irak."* Wiesbaden: Otto Harrassowitz, 1952, 495 pp. *JNES* XIII, no. 3 (1954): 195.

52. L. A. Mayer. *Mamluk Costume.* Geneva: Albert Kundig, 1952, 119 pp. *JNES* XIII, no. 3 (1954): 196.

53. Bertold Spuler. *Geschichte der islamischen Länder. Erster Abschnitt: Die Chalifenzeit, Entstehung und Zerfall des islamischen Weltreichs.* Handbuch der Orientalistik, Bd. 6, Abs. 1. Leiden: E. J. Brill, 1952, 135 pp. *JNES* XIII, no. 3 (1954): 207.

54. L. P. Elwell-Sutton. *A Guide to Iranian Area Study.* Published for American Council of Learned Societies. Ann Arbor: J. W. Edwards, 1952, 235 pp. *JNES* XIII, no. 3 (1954): 207.

55. Hans Wehr. *Arabisches Wörterbuch für die Schriftsprache der Gegenwart.* 2 vols. Leipzig: Otto Harrassowitz, 1952, 986 pp. *JNES* XIII, no. 3 (1954): 208.

56. Hans Wehr. *Der Arabische Elativ. Akademie der Wissenschaften und der Literatur, Mainz, "Abhandlungen der geistes- und sozialwissen-schaftlichen Klasse,"* Jahrgang, 1952, Nr. 7. Wiesbaden, 1952, 57 pp. *JNES* XIII, no. 3 (1954): 208.

1955

57. Ḥamd b. Muḥammad al-Xaṭṭābī. *Al-Bayān fī i^{c}jāz al-Qur'ān.* Edited by ^{c}Abd-al ^{c}Alīm. Aligarh, 1372/1953. *Oriens* VIII, Nr. 2, 1955, p. 370.

58. Rolla Foley. *Song of the Arab.* New York: Macmillan, 1953, 170 pp. *JNES* XIV, no. 2 (1955): 136.

59. Muhammad al-Ghazzāli. *Our Beginning in Wisdom.* Trans. by Isma^{c}il R. el Faruqi. ACLS, Near Eastern Translation Program, No. 5. Washington, 1953, 144 pp. *JNES* XIV, no. 3 (1955): 200-202.

60. Merrit Boutros Ghali. *Policy of Tomorrow.* Trans. by Isma^{c}il R. el Faruqi. ACLS, Near Eastern Translation Program, No. 2. Washington, 1953, 128 pp. *JNES* XIV, no. 3 (1955): 200-202.

61. Khalid M. Khalid. *From Here We Start.* Trans. by Isma^{c}il R. el Faruqi. ACLS, Near Eastern Translation Program, No. 3. Washington, 1953, 165 pp. *JNES* XIV, no. 3 (1955): 200-202.

62. Osman Amin. *Muhammad Abduh.* Trans. by Charles Wendell. ACLS, Near Eastern Translation Program, No. 4. Washington, 1953, 103 pp. *JNES* XIV, no. 3 (1955): 200-202.

63. Bertold Spuler. *Geschichte der islamischen Länder. Zweiter Abschnitt: Die Mongolenzeit. Handbuch der Orientalistik, Vol. VI.* Leiden: E. J. Brill, 1953, 124 pp. *JNES* XIV, no. 3 (1955): 202.

64. T. F. Mitchell. *Writing Arabic: a Practical Introduction to Ruq^{c}ah Script.* Oxford: Oxford University Press, 1953, 163 pp. *JNES* XIV, no. 3 (1955): 203.

65. Sayed Kotb. *Social Justice in Islam.* Trans. by John B. Hardie. ACLS, Near Eastern Translation Program, No. 1. Washington, 1953, 298 pp. *JNES* XIV, no. 3 (1955): 187.
66. Helen Miller Davis. *Constitutions, Electoral Laws, Treaties of the States in the Near and Middle East.* Durham, N.C.: Duke University Press, 1953, 541 pp. *JNES* XIV, no. 3 (1955): 187.
67. Paul Humbert. *Observations sur le vocabulaire arabe du Chāh-nāmeh. "Mémoires de l'Université de Neuchatel,"* Vol. 22. Neuchatel: Secrétariat de l'Université, 1953, 74 pp. *JNES* XIV, no. 3 (1955): 186.
68. K. S. Twitchell. *Saudi Arabia with an Account of the Development of Its Natural Resources.* With the collaboration of Edward J. Jurji. Princeton, N.J.: Princeton University Press, 1953, 231 pp. *JNES* XIV, no. 3 (1955): 185-186.
69. César Dubler. *Abū Hāmīd, el granadiño y su relación de viaje por tierras eurasíaticas.* Madrid, Imprenta y Editorial Maestre, 1953, 425 pp. *JNES* XIV, no. 4 (1955): 276-277.

1956

70. Majid Khadduri. *War and Peace in the Law of Islam.* The Johns Hopkins Press, 1955, 321 pp. *Bulletin of the Research Exchange on the Prevention of War,* University of Michigan IV, no. 1, 1956.
71. Abū ᶜAbd ar-Rahmān as-Sulamī. *Kitāb ādāb as-suhba.* Edited by M. J. Kester. Oriental Notes and Studies, No. 6. Jerusalem: Israel Oriental Society, 1954, 92 pp. *JNES* XV, no. 3 (1956): 199.
72. Mazheruddin Siddiqi. *Marxism or Islam?* 2nd ed. Lahore: Orientalia, 1954, 168 pp. *JNES* XV, no. 3 (1956): 199.
73. H. H. Bilgrami. *Glimpses of Iqbal's Mind and Thought.* Lahore: Orientalia, 1954, 124 pp. *JNES* XV, no. 4 (1956): 260.
74. Irène Melikoff-Sayar. *Le Destin d'Umūr Pacha* (*Düstūrnāme-i Enverī*). Bibliothèque Byzantine, Documents, No. 2. Paris: Presses Universitaires de France, 1954. *JNES* XV, no. 4 (1956): 260-261.

75. ᶜOmar A. Farrukh. *The Arab Genius in Science and Philosophy.* Washington, D.C.: American Council of Learned Societies, 1954. (English trans. by J. B. Hardie of ᶜAbqariyyat al-ᶜArab fī 'l-ᶜilm wa'l-falsafa, 2nd ed., Beirut, 1952). *Middle Eastern Affairs* VII (1956): 116-119.

1957

76. Jörg Kraemer. *Theodor Noeldekes Belegwörterbuch zur klassischen arabischen Sprache.* Berlin: Walter de Gruyter, 1954, 24 pp. (Part I) and 25-59 (Part II). *JNES* XVI, no. 1 (1957): 65-66.

77. Reuben Levy. *The Social Structure of Islam.* Cambridge: Cambridge University Press, 1957, 536 pp. *American Journal of Sociology* LXIII, no. 2 (1957): 221.

78. Helmer Ringgren. *Studies in Arabian Fatalism.* Wiesbaden: Uppsala, 1955, 224 pp. *Oriens* X, no. 2 (1957): 347-348.

1958

79. Walther Hinz. *Persisch. I. Leitfaden der Umgangssprache.* ("Anastatie" reprint of the first ed. of 1942) Berlin: Walter de Gruyter, 1955, 278 pp. *JNES* XVII, no. 1 (1958): 95.

80. René Dussaud. *La Pénétration des Arabes en Syrie avant l'Islam.* Institut Français d'Archéologie de Beyrouth, "Bibliothèque Archéologique et historique," Tome LIX. Paris: P. Geuthner, 1955, 234 pp. *JNES* XVII, no. 1 (1958): 94.

81. Majid Khadduri and Herbert J. Liebesny, eds. *Law in the Middle East.* Vol. I, *Origin and Development of Islamic Law.* Washington, D.C.: Middle East Institute, 1955, 395 pp. *JNES* XVII, no. 1 (1958): 94.

82. W. C. Smith. *Islam in Modern History.* Princeton, N.J.: Princeton University Press, 1957, 317 pp. *Journal of Religion* XXXVIII, no. 2 (1958): 135.

83. Philip K. Hitti. *Lebanon in History from the Earliest Times to the Present.* New York: Macmillan and Co., 1957, 548 pp. *Middle East Journal* XII, no. 3 (1958): 339-340.

1959

84. A. von Bulmerincq. *Das Buch der Wunderbaren Erzählungen und Seltsamen Geschichten.* Herausgegeben von Hans Wehr. "Bibliotheca Islamica," No. 18. Wiesbaden: Franz Steiner Verlag, 1956, 516 pp. *JNES* XVIII, no. 1 (1959): 103-104.
85. Kenneth W. Morgan, ed. *Islam — The Straight Path. Islam Interpreted by Muslims.* New York: Ronald Press, 1958. *Commentary* XXVII, no. 4 (1959): 358-360.
86. Hans Wehr. *Supplement zum arabischen Wörterbuch für die Schriftsprache der Gegenwart. JNES* XVIII, no. 1 (1959): 103-104.
87. Tor Andrae. *Mohammed: the Man and His Faith.* Trans. by Theophil Menzel. New York: Barnes and Noble, 1957, 196 pp. *JNES* XVIII, no. 3 (1959): 232.
88. Walter Z. Laqueur. *The Soviet Union and the Middle East.* New York: Praeger, 366 pp. *Commentary* XXVIII, no. 5 (1959): 449-451.
89. A. S. Tritton. *Materials on Muslim Education in the Middle Ages.* London: Luzac, 1957, 208 pp. *Zeitschrift der deutschen morgenländischen Gesellschaft,* CIX, no. 1 (1959): 217.
90. I. Mahmud. *Muslim Law of Succession and Administration.* Karachi, Pakistan Law House, 1958, 237 pp. *Muslim World* XLIX (1959): 153-154.
91. Murad Kāmil and Ibrāhim al-Ibyārī. *Al-Mu*[c]*jam al-Kabīr.* (The Comprehensive Dictionary of the Cairene Academy, Vol. I, Pt. 1.) Cairo, 1956, 519 pp. *JNES* XVIII, no. 2 (1959): 159-160.
92. A. Ben Shemesh, ed. and tr. *Taxation in Islam,* Vol. I, *Yahya Ben Adam's Kitāb al-Kharāj.* Leiden: E. J. Brill, 1958. *Muslim World* XLIX, no. 3 (1959): 253.
93. Franz Rosenthal, trans. *Ibn Khaldun: the Muqaddimah, an Introduction to World History,* 3 vols. Bollingen Series XLIII. Pantheon: New York. *American Anthropologist* LXI, no. 1 (1959): 128-129.

1960

94. Herbert W. Duda. *Die Seltsckukengeschichte des Ibn Bībī:*

Kitāb al-awāmir al-ᶜalāᶜiyya fī 'l-umūr al-ᶜalāᶜiyya. Copenhagen: Munksgaard, 1959, 366 pp. *Speculum* XXXV (1960): 451-453.

95. Ulrich Thilo. *Die Ortsnamen in der altarabischen Poesie: ein Beitrag zur vor- und fruhislamischen Dictung und zur historischen Topographie Nordarabiens.* Schriften der Max-Freiherr v. Oppenheim-Stiftung, 3. Wiesbaden: Harrassowitz, 1958, 117 pp. *WZKM* LVI (1960): 317-318.

96. Clifford Geertz. *The Religion of Java.* Glencoe, Ill.: The Free Press, 1960, 392 pp. *American Journal of Sociology* 67, no. 2 (Sept., 1961), pp. 211-212.

1961

97. Jorg Kraemer. *Das Problem der islamischen Kulturgeschichte.* Tübingen: Max Niemeyer Verlag, 1960, 69 pp. *JAOS* LXXXI (1961): 132-133.

1962

98. Walther Braune. *Der islamische Orient zw. Vergangenheit und Zukunft.* Bern-Munich: Francke Verlag, 1960, 223 pp. *BSOAS,* 1962.

99. J. Sauvaget. *Introduction à l'histoire de l'Orient* (*Initiation à l'Islam*). Paris, 1961. *ZDMG* CXIII, no. 2 (1962): 286-287.

100. Uriel Heyd, ed. *Studies in Islamic History and Civilization.* Scripta Hierosolymitana, IX. Jerusalem: Magnes Press, 1961, 228 pp. *The Middle East Journal* XVI, no. 1 (1962): 106-108.

101. Syed Abdul Latif. *Bases of Islamic Culture.* Hyderabad: Institute of Indo-Middle East Cultural Studies, 1959. *JAOS* LXXXII, no. 1 (1962): 82-83.

102. John Alden Williams, ed. *Islam.* New York: Braziller, 1961, 256 pp. *JAOS* LXXXII, no. 1 (1962): 83.

103. Ettore Rossi and Alessio Bambaci. *Elenco di Drammi Religiosi Persiani* (*Fondo Mss. Vaticani Cerulli*). Studi et Testi 209. Città del Vaticano, Biblioteca Apostolica Vaticana, 1961, 416 pp. *JAOS* LXXXII, no. 1 (1962): 84.

104. Heinrich Simon. *Ibn Khaldūns Wissenschaft von der men-*

schlichen Kultur. Der Islam XXXVIII, nos. 1 & 2 (Berlin, Oct. 1962): 185-187.

105. James Robson, ed. *Mishkat-ul-Masabih.* Lahore: Sh. Muhammad Ashraf, 1960, 72 pp. *JAOS* LXXXII (1962): 563.

106. H. A. R. Gibb. *Studies on the Civilization of Islam.* Edited by Stanford J. Shaw and William R. Polk. Boston: Beacon Press, 1962, 369 pp. *Middle East Journal* XVI, no. 4 (1962): 547-548.

107. Claude Cahen, ed. *L'Elaboration de l'Islam.* Colloque de Strasbourg, 12-14 juin 1959. Paris: Presses Universitaires de France, 1961. *Der Islam* XXXVIII, nos. 1 & 2 (Berlin, Oct. 1962).

1963

108. Helmut Ritter, trans. *Die Geheimnisse der Wortkunst* (*Asrār al-Balāga*) *des* [c]*Abdalqāhir al-Curcānī.* Wiesbaden: Franz Steiner Verlag, 1959, 478 pp. *Oriens* XVI (1963): 338-339.

109. H. A. R. Gibb, ed. *The Travels of Ibn Battuta, A. D. 1325-1354.* Vol. II. The Hakluyt Society. Second Series, No. CXVII, Cambridge, 1962. *Isis* LIV, pt. 3, No. 177, 1963, p. 421.

110. Mansour Shaki. *Modernì perskà frazeologie a converzace* [A Modern Persian Phrase-Book]. Praha: Statni pedagogicke nakladatelstvi, 1963, 991 pp. *JAOS* LXXXIII, no. 3 (1963): 373.

111. *Muslim World View and Muslim Science. Dialectica* XVII, no. 4 (1963): 353-368.

1964

112. W. Montgomery Watt. *Muslim Intellectual: a Study of al-Ghazali.* Edinburgh and Chicago: Aldine, 1963. *Speculum* (April 1964), pp. 357-359.

113. Roger Mercier. *L'Afrique noire dans la littérature.* Dakar: Université de Dakar, Faculté des Lettres et Sciences Humaines, 1962, 242 pp. *Revue de Littérature Comparée* XXXVIII (Paris, March 1964): 458-461.

114. Mia I. Gerhardt. *The Art of Story-Telling: Literary Study of*

the Thousand and One Nights. Leiden: E. J. Brill, 1963, 500 pp. *JAOS* LXXXIV, no. 1 (1964): 85-86.

115. Salāma Mūsā. *The Education of Salāma Mūsā.* Trans. by L. O. Schuman. Leiden: E. J. Brill, 1961, 267 pp. *Der Islam* XL, no. 1 (Berlin, Mai 1964): 78-81.

1966

116. Karl Jahn. *Rashid al-Din's History of India: Collected Essays with Facsimiles and Indices.* The Hague: Mouton & Co., 1965. *Studies in Islam,* Quarterly Journal of Indian Institute of Islamic Studies III, no. 1 (New Delhi, January 1966): 47-49.

117. J. J. Saunders. *A History of Medieval Islam.* New York: Barnes and Noble, 1965. *Speculum* (January, 1966).

118. E. I. J. Rosenthal. *Islam in the Modern National State.* Cambridge: Cambridge University Press, 1965. *Political Science Quarterly* LXXXI, no. 3 (Sept. 1966): 489-491.

119. W. Montgomery Watt. *A History of Islamic Spain.* With additional sections by P. Cachia. Edinburgh: Edinburgh University Press, 1965, 210 pp. *Studies in Islam,* Quarterly Journal of Indian Institute of Islamic Studies III, no. 4 (New Delhi, Oct. 1966): 242-243.

120. Christina Phelps Harris. *Nationalism and Revolution in Egypt: the Role of the Muslim Brotherhood.* The Hague, London, and Paris: Mouton & Co., 1964. *Der Islam* XLII, nos. 2 & 3 (Berlin, Sept. 1966).

1967

121. Muhammad ᶜAbduh. *The Theology of Unity.* Trans. from the Arabic by Isḥāq Musaᶜad and Kenneth Cragg. London, 1966. *Der Islam* XLIII, nos. 1 & 2 (1967): 180-181.

122. *The Islamic Law of Nations: Shaybānī's Siyar.* Trans. with an introduction, notes and appendices by Majid Khadduri. Baltimore: Johns Hopkins Press, 1966, 311 pp. *American Historical Review,* Jan. 1967, pp. 650-651.

123. *Anthologie de la littérature arabe contemporaine: Les Essais.* Edited by Anouar Abdel-Malik. Paris: Editions de Seuil, 1965, 464 pp. *JOAS* LXXXVII, no. 1 (Jan.-Mar., 1967): 75-76.

124. S. D. Goitein. *Studies in Islamic History and Institutions.* Leiden: E. J. Brill, 1966, 391 pp. *Speculum* XLII, no. 3 (July 1967): 529-532.

1968

125. Albert Hourani. *Arabic Thought in the Liberal Age.* London: Oxford University Press, 1962, 403 pp. *Oriens* XVIII-XIX (1965-1966 — published 1968): 377-379.
126. Manfred Ullmann. *Untersuchungen zur Ragazpoesie. Ein Betrag zur arabischen Sprach- und Literaturwissenschaft.* Wiesbaden: Harrassowitz, 1966, 254 pp. *Der Islam* XLIV (June 1968): 292-293.
127. Sulaiman Mousa. *T. E. Lawrence. An Arab View.* Trans. by Albert Boutros. London, New York and Toronto: Oxford University Press, 1966. *Der Islam* XLIV (June 1968): 278-280.
128. *Francesco Gabrieli, L'Islam nella storia.* Bari: Dedalo Libri, 1966, 271 pp. *Der Islam* XLIV (June 1968): p. 254.
129. Ira M. Lapidus. *Muslim Cities in the Later Middle Ages.* Cambridge, Mass.: Harvard University Press, 1967, 307 pp. *Canadian Journal of History* (University of Saskatchewan) III, no. 2 (Sept. 1968): 70-71.

1969

130. Denys Johnson-Davies, *Modern Arabic Short Stories,* selected and translated. London: Oxford University Press, 1967, 194 pp. *Der Islam* XLV, nos. 1 & 2 (February 1969): p. 156.
131. Gernot Rotter. *Die Stellung des Negers in der islamisch-arabischen Gesellschaft bis zum XVI. Jahrhundert.* Diss. (Bonn) Bonn, 1967, 192 pp. *Der Islam* XLV, nos. 1 & 2 (February 1969): 147-148.

INDEX

Abᶜad min Moskū wa Washington (Nuᶜaima), 60
al-Ābā wa'l-banūn (Nuᶜaima), 55, 56
ᶜAbduh: exile of, 77; as Director of the Press, 81; and constitution, 85; defends participation in the Revolt, 86, 87; and literary reforms, 92
ᶜAbdullāh (King of Jordan), 27; and negotiations with Israel, 27, 28, 31; and Col. ᶜAbdullāh al-Tall, 33; decision on peace negotiations, 34; and Arab League Council meeting, 47
Afghānī, al-: teachings of, 79, 81, 87
Afrasiyab (character in *Shah-nama*), 4, 5
Aga system in Turkey, 181, 189-191
Ahmad, Jalal Al-i, 167, 176; political ideas of, 168; *Dīd u Bāzdīd,* 171, 172, 173; social criticisms of, 175, 177; *Mudīr-i Madrasa,* 175, 176
Ākhund: character of, 171, 175, 176
Al-Ahrām: role in 1950 Israeli-Jordanian peace negotiations, 35, 36, 43
Alevi (religious community), 183
Ali, the Prophet, 104, 106
Alides: beliefs of, 104
Amina: and *Dāniyāl-nāme,* 148, 149; *Eḥterāz-nāme,* 149
Anglo-Egyptian Treaty of 1936, 39, 45
ᶜAqqād, al-: and al-Bārūdī, 93
Arabic, classical: phonemic inventory of, 114; graphemes of, 115, 116; and use of by other languages, 139-141
Arabic orthography: description of, 113; phonemic equivalents for graphemes, 114; use of diacritics, 114, 115; used by other languages, 117
Arab League, 33; and Israeli-Jordanian peace negotiations, 34
Arab League Council: meeting of, 39, 46, 47
Arab League Permanent Committee on Palestine, 28
Arab nationalism, 27
Arab press: and reports on Israeli-Jordanian peace negotiations, 35, 36
Ardashir-nāme (Shahin), 146
ᶜArīḍa, Nasīb, 58
as-Sā'iḥ (periodical of *Rābiṭa*), 55
Averroes: as commentator on Aristotle, 10; and Aristotle's *Poetics,* 10, 11; misunderstanding of his writings, 10, 11; and translations of Aristotle, 11, 13; terms used by, 11, 13, 14, 15, 16, 18, 19, 20, 21, 22, 23, 25, 26; and ideas about poetic art, 12; and differences with Aristotelian theory, 12, 13; use of inductive method, 14; and poetic mimesis, 14, 15, 16, 17, 18, 19, 23; de-intellectualizing poetic art, 17; and subject matter of poetic art, 18; and difference between Poetry and Rhetoric, 20, 21; and rhythm in poetry, 21, 22, 23, 24, 25; and categories in examining poetry, 24; and definition of poetic discourse, 26
Avesta: scripture of the Parsis, 66
Avesta characters: used in Parsi literature, 68, 69, 71, 72
Ayātkār i Žāmāspīk, 69
Ayyām (Husein), 52
Azerbaijani language: use of Arabic orthography, 125-126

NOTES ON CONTRIBUTORS

AMIN BANANI, Ph.D. (Stanford, 1959), Professor of Persian and History at the University of California, Los Angeles, also taught at Stanford and at Reed College and served as a consultant to the Peace Corps. He is editor of *The Epic of Kings* (University of Chicago, 1967), and author of *Quest for Tajik Identity* (1965) and *Modernization of Iran* (Stanford University, 1961).

VICENTE CANTARINO, Ph.D. (Munich, 1962), Professor of Hispana-Arabic studies at the University of Texas, Austin (1969——), also taught at Indiana University, Bloomington, and the University of North Carolina, Chapel Hill. His publications include *Der Neuaramaeische Dialekt von Gubb Adin* (1962); *Dante and Islam: History and Analysis of a Controversy* (1965); "Ibn Gabirol's Metaphysics of Light" in *Studia Islamica*, 1967; "Ibn Arabi, Poet of Love: An Ode to Nizam" in *Literature of East and West*, 1967.

CLARENCE ERNEST DAWN, Ph.D. (Princeton, 1948), is Professor of History, University of Illinois, Urbana. He is author of "Amir of Mecca al-Husayn ibn Ali and the Origin of the Arab Revolt" in *Proceedings* of the American Philosophical Society, 1960; "From Ottomanism to Arabism" in *Rev. Polit.*, 1961; "Rise of Arabism in Syria" in *Middle East Journal*, 1962.

FRANCESCO GABRIELI is Professor of Arabic Language and Literature in the University of Rome, member of the Accademia Nazionale dei Lincei, corresponding member of the Arab Academies of Cairo and Damascus, and President of the Istituto per l'Oriente. Several of his books, for example *Risorgimento arabo* and *Storici arabi delle Crociate*, have been translated into English (*Arab Revival*, Random House, New York, and *Arab Historians of the Crusades*, Routledge and Kegan Paul, London). Other major works are *Storia della letteratura araba, Dal mondo dell'Islam*, and *L'Islam della storia*.

SVEN S. HARTMAN, Ph.D. (Uppsala, 1953), is Professor of Religion at the University of Lund, Sweden. He has also taught at the Swedish University of Åbo (Åbo Akademi), Finland, and was lecturer at the University of Uppsala, Sweden. His publications include "Gayōmart. Etudes sur le syncrétisme dans l'ancien Iran" (dissertation, Uppsala, 1953); "Aspects de l'histoire religieuse selon la conception de l'Avesta non-gàthique" in *Orientalia Suecana* XIV-XV, 1965-1966; "Der grosse Zarathustra" in *Orientalia Suecana* XIV-XV, 1965-1966. He has also been editor of "Syncretism" (Scripta instituti Donneriani aboensis III, 1969).

MOUNAH A. KHOURI, Ph.D. (Harvard, 1964), is Professor of Arabic Literature, University of California, Berkeley, and Director, Center for Arabic Study Abroad. He is author of *Arabic Poetry and the Making of Modern Egypt, 1882-1922* (Brill, Leiden, 1970), and co-author of *Elementary Modern Standard Arabic and Advanced Arabic Readers I* and *II.*

FRITZ MEIER, Ph.D. (Basle, 1941), Professor of Oriental Philology, University of Basle, also taught at the Faruk I University in Alexandria. His books include *Vom Wesen der Islamischen Mystik* (Basle, 1943); *Die Vita des Scheich Abu Ishaq al-Kazaruni* (Leipzig, 1948); *Westostliche Abhandlungen* (Wiesbaden, 1954); *Die Fawa'ih al-gamal wa-fawatih al-galal des Nagm ad-din al-Kubra* (Wiesbaden, 1957); *Die Schone Mahasati* (Wiesbaden, 1963).

C. MOHAMMED NAIM is Assistant Professor of Urdu at the University of Chicago. He is co-editor of *Mahfil,* a quarterly of South Asian literature.

AMNON NETZER, Ph.D. (Columbia, 1969), is Assistant Professor of Persian, University of Illinois, Urbana. He is author of "Education in Syria and Lebanon" in *Setareh Shargh* (1966); "Hafiz the Persian Poet" in *Hebrew Encyclopedia,* Vol. 17; *Judeo-Persian Poetry in Iran and Bokhara* (forthcoming).

GIRDHARI LAL TIKKU, Ph.D. (Teheran, 1961), Professor of Persian and Associate Director of the Center for Asian Studies, University of Illinois, Urbana, also taught at Indiana University, Bloomington, and the University of California, Los Angeles and Berkeley. His publications include *Sarūdhā-i jāvadānī* (Teheran, 1961, trans.); *Pārsīsarāyān-i-Kashmīr* (Teheran, 1963, collector and ed.); *Dīvāni-i-Fānī* (1963, ed.); *Persian Poetry in Kashmir* (University of California, 1971); *Modern Persian Prose Fiction* (UNESCO, forthcoming).

NUR O. YALMAN, Ph.D. (Cambridge, 1958), is Professor of Anthropology and Director, Center for Middle Eastern Studies, University of Chicago. He has been Visiting Professor at Clare Hall, Cambridge, England, and Fellow at the Center for Advanced Study in the Behavioral Sciences, Stanford University. His publications include *Under the Bo Tree; Studies in Caste, Kinship and Marriage in the Interior of Ceylon* (California, 1967); "On the Purity of Women in the Castes of Ceylon and Malabar" in *Journal of the Royal Anthropological Institute,* Vol. 93, Part I, 1963 – Curle Prize; "Islamic Reform and the Mystic Tradition in Eastern Turkey" in *Archiv. Europ. Sociol.,* X, 1969.

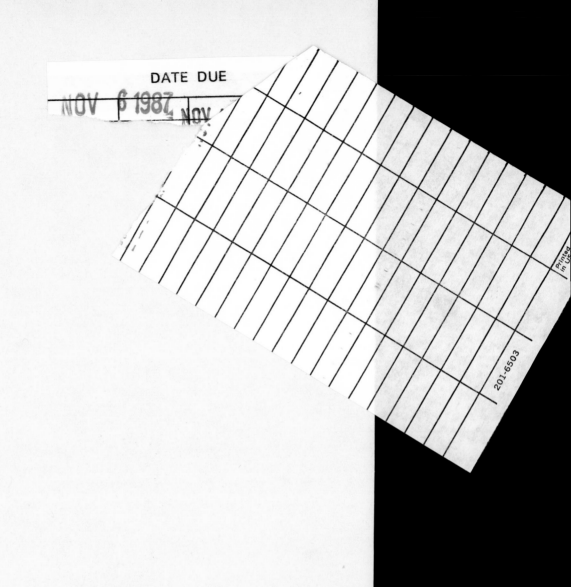